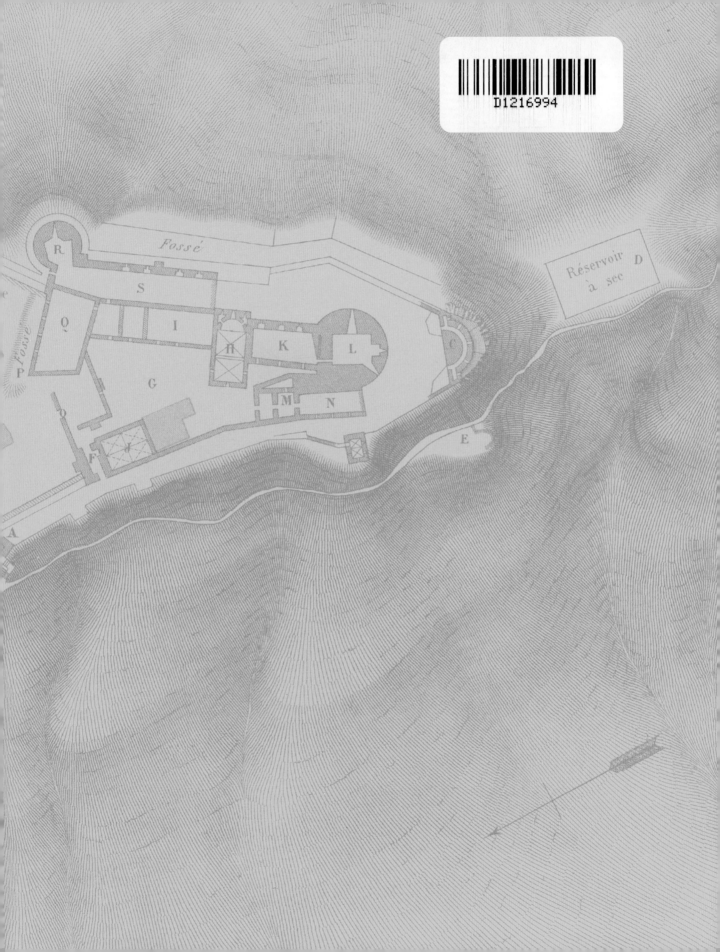

Fossé

Fossé

Réservoir à sec D

R

S

Q

I

P

G

H

K

L

O

M

N

F

J

A

E

C

D1216994

Castles

Castles

A history of fortified structures

ANCIENT, MEDIEVAL & MODERN

CONSULTANT EDITOR
Charles Stephenson

ST. MARTIN'S GRIFFIN

NEW YORK

CASTLES. Copyright © 2011 by The Ivy Press
Limited. All rights reserved. Printed in China.
For information, address St. Martin's Press,
175 Fifth Avenue, New York, N.Y. 10010.

www.stmartins.com

Library of Congress Cataloging-in-Publication Data
Available Upon Request

ISBN 978-0-312-54140-8

First U.S. Edition: September 2011

10 9 8 7 6 5 4 3 2 1

Cover image: © Topfoto/Granger Collection
Title page image: Mont St. Michel, Normandy, France

Color origination by Ivy Press Reprographics
Typeset in Bembo and Helvetica Neue

For my son, James D. Stephenson

This book was conceived,
designed, and produced by

Ivy Press
210 High Street, Lewes
East Sussex BN7 2NS
United Kingdom

Creative Director: PETER BRIDGEWATER
Publisher: JASON HOOK
Editorial Director: CAROLINE EARLE
Senior Editor: STEPHANIE EVANS
Art Director: MICHAEL WHITEHEAD
Design: JC LANAWAY
Assistant Editor: JAMIE PUMFREY
Picture Manager: KATIE GREENWOOD
Illustrators: ADAM HOOK, CORAL MULA,
 PETER SCHOLEFIELD
Map Artwork: LYNDSEY GODDEN

Contents

Introduction

There is a cliché to the effect that armies equip and arm their troops, but navies man their armaments. Although generally unarguable there is one singular exception, and that is with respect to fortification. Armies—or at least bodies of fighters—man fortifications and have done so ever since members of the human race began to have something worth defending. Fortification, a word derived from the Latin *fortis*, "strong," and *facere*, "to make," is the military art, or science, dependent upon how one views it, of strengthening positions against attack.

The rationale for this is obvious; strengthened positions—fortifications—are force multipliers. Put simply they allow a smaller number to defy a greater, with a superior prospect of success than if fighting on open ground. Conversely, mounting attacks on fortifications is costly in every sense and always has been. According to "the oldest military treatise in the world," generally considered to have been written in the sixth century BCE, the "worst policy of all is to besiege walled cities." The skillful leader, Sun Tzu tells us, captures his enemy's cities without laying siege to them. Unfortunately for practical exponents of the art of war, he is silent on how this may be achieved.

Fortification, of whatever size and nature, has a double tactical object which Sir George Sydenham Clarke conveniently summarized in 1890: "The only scientific fortification is that which enables the defender to use his weapons to the best advantage, while minimizing the potency of the weapons of the attacker." Achieving these desiderata requires two elements: protection for defenders and obstruction of attackers. The protection shielded the defender from the attackers' weapons, whilst the obstacle prevented the attacker from coming to close quarters, and delayed him under fire. These principles are enduring, though the means by which they were achieved vary greatly according to time and place and were subject to evolution and occasional revolution.

Iron Age hill forts, Ireland
Grianen of Aileach in County Donegal is a group of ancient monuments, principal of which is an Iron Age stone fortress. The ruins of the fortress, or *cashel*, were surveyed by George Petrie in the 1830s, who described it as a circular wall enclosing an area of nearly 80 ft (24 m) in diameter. Flights of steps lead to terraces on the inside of the perimeter wall. Originally, this was a dry-stone wall believed to have been built in about the eighth century CE, but it was restored at the end of the 19th century. The use of the hilltop site as a settlement may be much older: a nearby tumulus is Neolithic. The fortress is thought to have been destroyed by the King of Munster in 1101, by which time the Kingdom of Aileach had been invaded by the Normans.

Introduction

When viewing the plans of military fortifications, which in their later manifestations can appear hideously complex, it is worth bearing in mind the fundamental considerations that dictated their design; the need to prevent attackers from getting over the top, through, or indeed under them. In the days of pre-industrial warfare there was, essentially, only one method of getting attacking troops into a fortress; they had to run or creep toward, or tunnel under, the defenses and then physically occupy them. If they were undamaged this might be achieved by climbing up and over them, a process known as escalade. However, if a portion of them had been damaged, perhaps by undermining (mining), then an attempt might be made to attack, or storm, through the resultant breach. All fortification systems, no matter how apparently complex, had as their object the obstruction or prevention of these operations.

The first attempts at strengthening a position probably involved the use of thorny vegetation and similar materials. The next step utilized wooden palisades, ditches, and earth banks, or a combination of all three. There is evidence of such techniques being utilized in the Neolithic period, ca. 5400–4900 BCE, in farming communities along the Rhine and Neckar valleys.

The walls at Antioch
Founded in 300 BCE by Seleucus I, the King of Syria, the city of Antioch stood on the Orontes River at the meeting point of the Lebanon and the Taurus Mountains. Once rival to Alexandria as the chief city of the Near East, repeated Mongol conquests caused the trade routes between east and west to be changed, leaving Antioch to fend for itself.

However, the use of timber had shortcomings, both from the defensive and the archaeological perspective. In terms of the latter it decays, leaving only fragmentary evidence. Thucydides relates the other major problem; during the sieges of Plataea (429 BCE) and Delium (424 BCE) attempts were made to destroy the defenses, which in the latter case were "principally constructed of vines and other wood" by setting fire to them. The attempt at Plataea was thwarted by a rainstorm, but at Delium it succeeded in driving the defenders from their posts.

Earthworks are largely immune from combustible weapons, and although largely superseded in permanent works by masonry and similar materials they regained and retained their usefulness. It was with the introduction of the wall, whether of masonry, sun-dried brick, or mud, that permanent fortification came into being and as Colonel Edward Henry Kelly stated it in the 14th edition of the *Encyclopaedia Britannica* in 1929: "The history of the development of the wall and of the methods of attacking it is the history of fortification for several thousand years."

Introduction

This was no exaggeration; excavations have revealed that the cities of Harappa and Mohenjo Daro, dating from ca. 2600 BCE and sited along the Indus river valley, had substantial mudbrick citadels built on stone mounds. The one at Harappa has been calculated as being about 50 feet (15 meters) high and constructed in the form of a parallelogram measuring about 460 yards (420 meters) north–south by 220 yards (200 meters) east–west. These appear to have been surrounded by crenelated walls. Sir Mortimer Wheeler, under whose directorship the Archaeological Survey of India excavated the area in the 1940s, noted that "beneath the Harappan citadel are the remains of an earlier fortified area."

Though different cultures and societies devised their own ways of doing things, essentially no major refinements were needed to the science until the advent of gunpowder-fired weapons, which began to make the high wall and its associated features vulnerable. This led to the development of bastioned fortifications, in which the wall was lowered and sunk in a ditch to protect it. The development of bastions and other elements of fortification also allowed defensive artillery to be mounted. Evolution, in terms of increasing complexity, was then relatively constant until the development of long range, shell-firing rifled artillery began to render bastioned works obsolete in turn. Thus the polygonal system of smaller, detached, works began to evolve. These were usually built in the context of a larger defensive scheme, designed to keep the

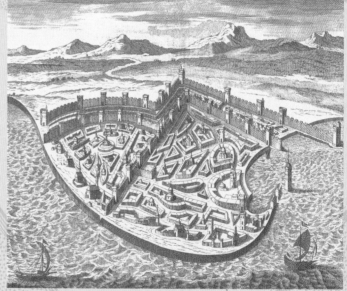

City of Acre, Israel
Medieval Acre, as the richest port in the Levant, was clearly worth defending. Fortified by a double ring of walls, it effectively became the capital of the Crusader States in the Holy Land.

Kalemegdan Fortress, Belgrade, Serbia
Situated at the confluence of the Sava and the Danube rivers, Belgrade occupies a position of great strategic importance and has been the focus of repeated Ottoman military attention since the 12th century.

Plan of San Fernando de Figueres, Catalonia, Spain
This bastioned fort was built in 1753 to defend Catalonia against French invasion (*see pages 252–3*). At the time it was one of the largest in Europe, able to accommodate some 20,000 men and 500 horses, and 262 artillery pieces of various calibers and types were mounted on the parapet.

attackers' artillery well away from the area being defended and in their later form were often constructed from reinforced concrete.

This process of evolution, whereby defensive architecture changed in response to increases in the efficiency of offensive weapons (or perhaps, to turn it around, offensive weapons evolved in order to deal with improvements in defensive technology and techniques) was encapsulated by another Chinese military leader, Mao Zedong, in 1938: "To the present-day, all weapons are still an extension of the spear and the shield. The bomber, the machine-gun, the long-range gun, and poison gas are developments of the spear, while the air-raid shelter, the steel helmet, the concrete fortification, and the gas mask are developments of the shield."

It is then the purpose of this book to chart the evolution of "the shield" of defensive architecture, from antiquity through to the beginning of the 20th century via the examination of selected examples. Each author has chosen the sites to illustrate this progress and has, inevitably, had to be selective. We can only hope that these selections will meet with general approval.

Purists, however, will no doubt find cause for complaint in the main title. Castles, strictly speaking, are a particular kind of fortification, and the subtitle more accurately reflects the content. In forsaking accuracy for snappiness we can only crave their forgiveness.

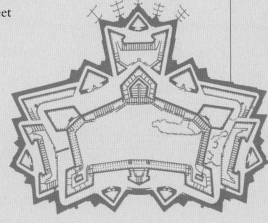

The Ancient World

Introduction

The emergence of sedentary, agricultural societies from around the fifth millennium BCE on the banks of great rivers such as the Euphrates, the Nile, and the Indus produced a degree of social organization that was unknown to earlier pastoral cultures. The settlement of relatively large numbers of people in one place led to the development of institutional structures to administer the work of planting and irrigation, and to store and distribute agricultural surpluses. All this had to be protected both from rival polities and from pastoralist tribes that would periodically threaten the city granaries. It is likely, then, that the art of fortification is as old as civilization itself.

At a time when the options available to attacking forces were limited to hand tools, the walled city was an imposing symbol of power. As siege weaponry developed, so did the scale of defenses and, according to Herodotus, the city of Babylon as rebuilt by Nebuchadnezzar in ca. 600 BCE had walls thick enough for a four-horse chariot to be driven along its top walkway. It is likely that as many cities were taken by treachery or famine as by direct assault, and at the very least the defenses might hold an enemy at bay long enough for reinforcements to arrive, or for a truce to be agreed.

The military powers of the ancient world also developed offensive structures. The Egyptians, the Assyrians, and the Romans all built garrison forts and watchtowers to protect the frontiers of their territories, symbols in brick and stone of their imperial power. Ironically, the city of Rome itself was not fortified until the third century CE, when its walls were not a symbol of power but of terminal decline.

Timeline

ca. 5000 BCE

First evidence of fortified urban settlements in Sumeria and the Indus river valley

ca. 1850 BCE

Senusret III builds a series of fortresses to protect Egypt's southern frontier

ca. 1600 BCE

The Mycenaeans develop cyclopean masonry to build fortresses at Mycenae and Tiryns

Cyclopean Masonry

ca. 1500 BCE

The Hittite king Hantili I fortifies his capital Hattusha with a double curtain wall

Siege Engine

ca. 900 BCE

Assyrian bas-reliefs offer first evidence of siege engines being used

612 BCE

The Medes overthrow the Assyrian Empire and sack the city of Nineveh

539 BCE

The first Achaemenid emperor, Cyrus the Great, diverts the Euphrates so as to enter Babylon through culverts in the city walls

4th century BCE

First reference made to portcullises in a treatise on war by Aeneas Tacticus

305 BCE

Demetrius I of Macedon unsuccessfully besieges the city of Rhodes for an entire year, with equipment including a siege tower over 100 ft (33 m) tall

Wood and Earth Rampart

ca. 300 BCE

Maiden Castle, occupied since around 2000 BCE, is fortified with earth ramparts and ditches

251 BCE

The defensive machinery of Archimedes successfully repels the Roman siege of Syracuse

250 BCE

The Romans, their siege engines destroyed by fire, decide to starve out the citizens of Lilybaeum in Sicily. Their walled encampment becomes the model for the later legionary *castra*

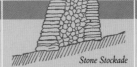

Stone Stockade

ca. 220 BCE

China's first emperor, Qin Shinghuandi, reconstructs and extends the Great Wall

190 BCE

At the siege of Ambracia (a Corinthian colony), Roman engineers trying to undermine the walls are repulsed by the besieged citizens pumping pungent smoke from burning feathers into the mine

169 BCE

First known use of the "tortoise" by Roman troops at the siege of Heracleum, whereby they advanced up to the city walls under a roof made from their interlocking shields

37 BCE

Herod the Great fortifies Jerusalem and builds the three-towered Citadel

1st century CE

Augustus begins to establish permanent garrison forts across the Roman Empire

68 CE

Vespasian uses a force of 160 siege engines, transported by mules in sections, to besiege Jotapha

70 CE

Titus sacks Jerusalem, and the Roman siege of the fortress at Masada ends in the mass suicide of the Jewish defenders

79 CE

Pompeii is destroyed by the eruption of Mount Vesuvius, with the result that its fortifications are preserved almost unaltered

Roman Watchtower

122 CE

Hadrian begins construction of a defensive wall on the northern frontier of the province of Britannia

ca. 200 CE

Completion of the *Limes germanicus*, a line of fortifications from the Rhine to the Danube built to protect the Roman Empire's northern frontier

271 CE

Aurelian begins construction of defensive walls around Rome

270–290 CE

The Romans build a series of forts on the south and east coast of Britannia to repel the raids of the Saxons

410 CE

The Visigoths under Alaric sack Rome

413 CE

A wall is built by the Roman emperor Theodosius II to defend Constantinople from the west, with a second wall and moat added in 447

CASTLES LOCATER MAP

Ancient World

The great civilizations of the ancient world developed through settlement, often on the vast floodplains of rivers such as the Nile, the Indus, and the Euphrates. Settlement meant permanent structures and ownership. Land and property had to be defined and the territory staunchly defended, and, frequently, expanded. This map pinpoints the locations of some of the remarkable examples of the earliest fortified structures in rammed earth, mud, brick, and stone, including the fortresses, citadels, and walled cities of Egypt, Mesopotamia, Greece, Canaan, and Rome.

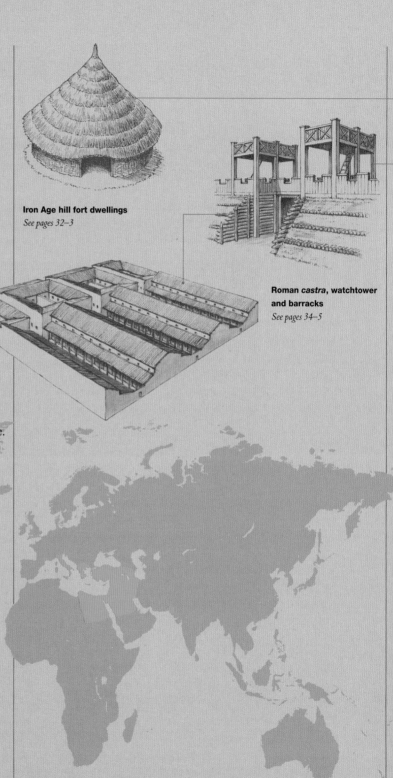

Iron Age hill fort dwellings
See pages 32–3

Roman *castra*, watchtower and barracks
See pages 34–5

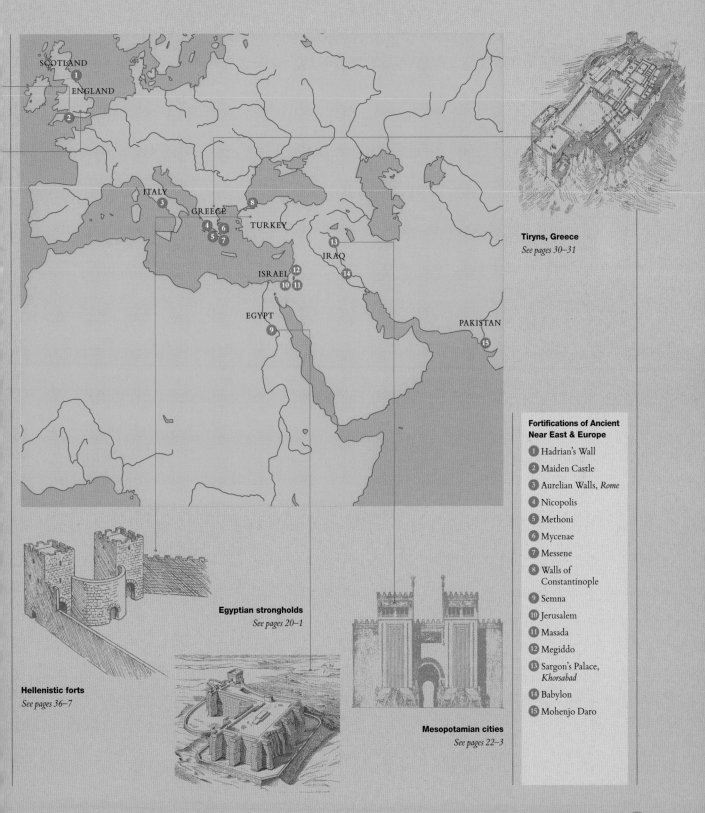

Tiryns, Greece
See pages 30–31

SCOTLAND
ENGLAND
ITALY
GREECE
TURKEY
IRAQ
ISRAEL
EGYPT
PAKISTAN

**Fortifications of Ancient
Near East & Europe**

1 Hadrian's Wall
2 Maiden Castle
3 Aurelian Walls, *Rome*
4 Nicopolis
5 Methoni
6 Mycenae
7 Messene
8 Walls of
Constantinople
9 Semna
10 Jerusalem
11 Masada
12 Megiddo
13 Sargon's Palace,
Khorsabad
14 Babylon
15 Mohenjo Daro

Hellenistic forts
See pages 36–7

Egyptian strongholds
See pages 20–1

Mesopotamian cities
See pages 22–3

T HE REGION KNOWN AS THE FERTILE CRESCENT, an arc extending north from the Arabian Gulf to southern Anatolia and then west to the Levant and the River Jordan, was arguably where the fundamentals of western civilization developed from the fifth millennium BCE. Intensive agriculture, industrial production, urbanism, and national government all started here—as did fortification.

CHAPTER I

Ancient Near East

The fortifications of the Ancient Near East shared a number of common features. At first city walls were built from mudbrick, the raw materials for which were cheap and readily available. To overcome the relative friability of this material, the walls were immensely thick, as much as 25 feet (7.5 meters). Later military engineers began to use a base, or socle, made from rubble or stone up to a height of about 7 feet (2 meters), with a mudbrick wall on top of that. This pattern of stone base and mudbrick superstructure was common across the region, although the Egyptians retained a preference for using mudbrick alone. Gateways and weak points were protected with towers, which projected beyond the walls to allow flanking fire against besiegers. Sometimes the walls themselves were built with offsets, so as to limit the amount of "dead" space at the foot of the wall where an attacker could begin the process of undermining. Posterns or sally ports were often incorporated into the walls to allow an aggressive defense, enabling defenders to emerge briefly to engage the besieging army on the ground. Beyond the walls, one or more ditches fronted by sloping ramparts further slowed the advance of attackers. The entire arrangement was designed to sap the morale and resources of the besiegers before they were able to make a breach in the defenses.

Babylon, modern-day Iraq
Early settled peoples protected themselves and their property within fortified cities, a clear demarcation between civilized society and the nomadic barbarians outside. The defenses of Babylon, built by King Nebuchadnezzar (604–562 BCE) consisted of canals, earthworks, and huge walls to protect the citizens within.

Egyptian Strongholds

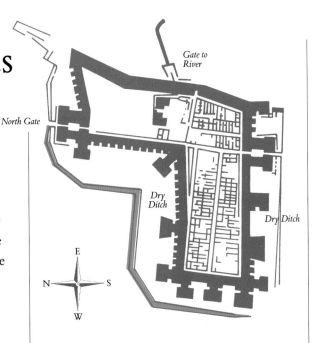

Middle Kingdom fortresses

The Middle Kingdom period of Ancient Egypt (ca. 2055–ca. 1650 BCE) saw the development of fortifications that, according to many scholars, were unequaled in engineering terms by anything built in Western Europe before the 16th century. The primary impetus for the group of fortresses that sprang up in the area around the second cataract of the Nile was to secure the region known as lower Nubia, which was rich in resources including gold. The pharaoh Senusret III (1882–1872 BCE) was primarily responsible for these fortifications, which included Askut, Shalfak, Uronarti, and a complex of three forts, Semna-south, Semna-west, and Kumma. The rise of the Kingdom of Kerma to the south coincided with the Egyptian Middle Kingdom period, and was another reason for this extensive regime of fortresses, which effectively policed a buffer zone between the second cataract and the traditional border of Egypt about two hundred miles farther north, at present-day Aswan. The completion of the Aswan High Dam in 1970 led to the flooding of much of this area, and although some of the buildings were salvaged by a UNESCO salvage campaign during the 1960s, many of the fortresses are now underwater.

Plan of the Semna-west fortress
The unique L-shape of the fortress was dictated by the rocky outcrop on which it was built. The main gates were to the north and south, and projected from the outer wall. They had two wooden doors with the space between open to the ramparts above so that intruders would be exposed to attack. Another gate to the east gave access to the river, and the path was protected by a drystone wall.

Stelae
A stele located at a boundary asserts the pharaoh's control over the region and encourages his troops to defend the frontier. Numerous rock inscriptions from the site of Semna-west indicate that the garrison monitored trade across the border, as well as recording information, such as the height of the river level.

Semna-west

Built on a promontory on the west bank of the Nile, the Semna-west fortress was protected on the landward side by a dry ditch and a stone wall about 25 ft (8 m) wide. The main walls were built of mudbrick and were between 16 and 20 ft (5 and 6 m) wide, and about 45 ft (14 m) high. On the opposite bank of the Nile stood the fortress of Kumma (Kumneh).

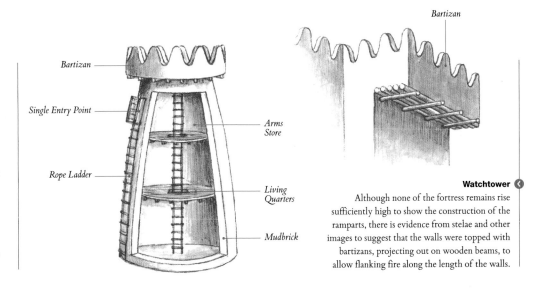

Bartizan

Single Entry Point

Rope Ladder

Arms Store

Living Quarters

Mudbrick

Bartizan

Watchtower

Although none of the fortress remains rise sufficiently high to show the construction of the ramparts, there is evidence from stelae and other images to suggest that the walls were topped with bartizans, projecting out on wooden beams, to allow flanking fire along the length of the walls.

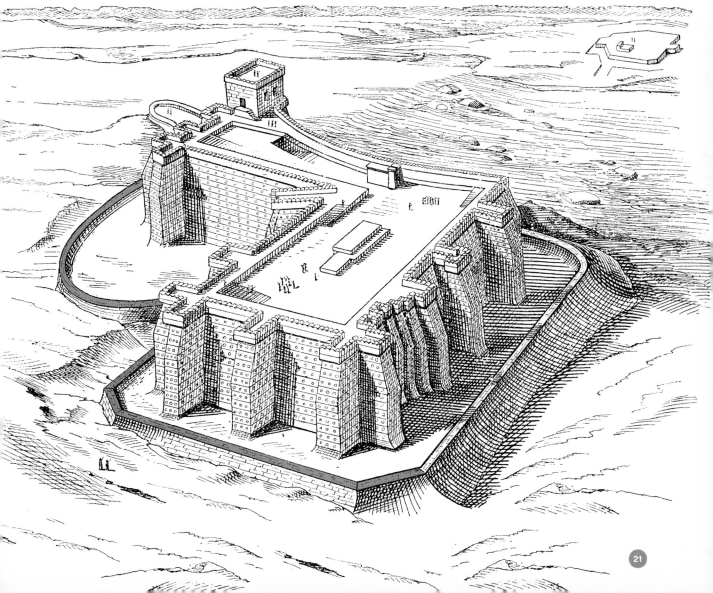

Ancient Mesopotamia

Fortified cities of Assyria

The earliest Mesopotamian city for which archaeological evidence exists, Uruk, had a population of about 50,000 people by 2900 BCE with a city wall enclosing some 1,240 acres (500 hectares). Uruk was one of about a dozen city-states at this period. These early Sumerian city-states were strongly independent, and jealously guarded their autonomy from any kind of central control—a characteristic that marked Mesopotamian history well into the second millennium BCE. On the flat Mesopotamian plains the walls of a city would dominate the landscape for several miles as the clearest marker of the boundary between the "civilized" world and the "primitive," as well as offering protection to the inhabitants. By the middle of the first millennium BCE the region was more clearly divided into Assyria in the north and Babylonia in the south, and the Assyrians in particular had a reputation as an effective and accomplished military nation, controlling an empire that extended to the Mediterranean and southern Asia Minor (Anatolia). The fortified cities of Nineveh, Dur Sharrukin, and Nimrud were intended as a clear expression of the power of the Assyrian king.

Gateway of Dur Sharrukin
The remains of one of the seven gateways of the ancient fortified city of Dur Sharrukin show a double entrance with two further chambers behind. The entrances would have been closed with wooden doors faced with bronze. The walls themselves were about 60 ft (20 m) thick. The stone projections show the position of towers, of which there were 150 or more.

Gateway to Sargon's Palace, Dur Sharrukin
The gateway to the palace had two crenelated towers flanking a narrow arch. On either side of the gateway are the characteristic portal guardians, the man-bulls or *lamassu*, each carved from a single piece of stone and set into the door jambs. These colossi were sculpted in low relief with five legs so that when seen head-on, the two front legs were visible, while from the side four legs were shown. This gave the impression of a four-legged creature from whichever angle the sculpture was viewed.

Plan of Sargon II's Palace, Dur Sharrukin

The palace at Dur Sharrukin, present-day Khorsabad, was built in 720 BCE. This plan and the artist's reconstruction are based on what is known from the excavations. The palace was built into the city wall—a common feature of Assyrian cities that gave prominence to the rule—and was raised on a huge mound that was faced with stone.

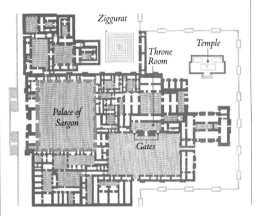

Masonry of Town Wall

Masonry of city wall

Although sources of limestone and sandstone were relatively close at hand, the Assyrians used mudbrick as their principal building material. These could be made easily and cheaply in large quantities and either dried in the sun or baked. The outer walls at Dur Sharrukin were brickwork built on a stone substructure.

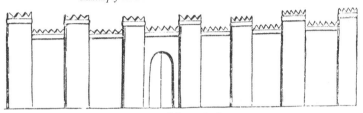

Assyrian Wall showing Battlements

Fortified Cities of Canaan

Megiddo, Israel

Jericho is widely recognized as the oldest fortified settlement in the world, with some of its defenses dating back to the eighth millennium BCE. However, the first systematic use of defensive walls in ancient Palestine dates from the early Bronze Age, around 3000 BCE, for which there is evidence of settlements protected by walls with semicircular towers. Walls were made from mudbrick on a stone base, and buttressed on the outside with a glacis or ramp of stone and packed earth. The later Bronze Age, up to ca. 1600 BCE, saw the establishment of fortified Canaanite city-states, protected by walls built on packed earth ramparts up to 50 feet (15 meters) high. Within the walls of one of these—Megiddo—are Bronze and Iron Age temples, a palace, and a sophisticated water system.

This period also saw the first appearance of fortresses and watchtowers, probably as a result of Egyptian rule over the region from the 14th century BCE. Two centuries on, Egypt's control over Palestine was at an end and the establishment of the Kingdom of Israel saw increasing sophistication in town planning and architecture, including defensive architecture.

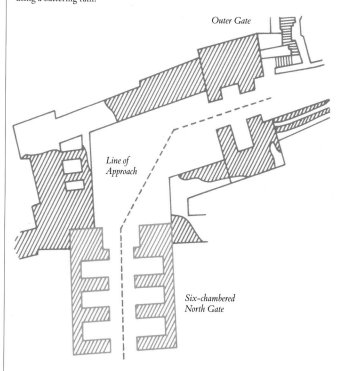

Plan of the north gate at Megiddo
The layout of Megiddo's main city gate shows a number of defensive features. The approach road has a separate entrance with towers either side, and runs parallel to the line of the city wall, so that anyone entering the city has to pass though a narrow passage with their flank exposed to defenders on the walls above. The right-angled approach also acts against any frontal attack using a battering ram.

Outer Gate

Line of Approach

Six-chambered North Gate

Water system at Megiddo
In the long period before gunpowder, the chief method of overcoming a fortified city was by siege, which in turn required the defenders to protect their supplies. The water system at Megiddo shows the sophistication of the Iron Age planners. A spring beyond the walls to the southwest served the city, and in order to secure it a shaft was dug down nearly 120 ft (36 m) through the rock within the city walls and then a tunnel cut through to the spring. The external opening to the spring was then blocked by a massive wall.

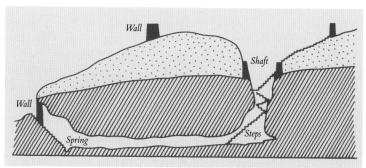

Wall

Shaft

Wall

Spring

Steps

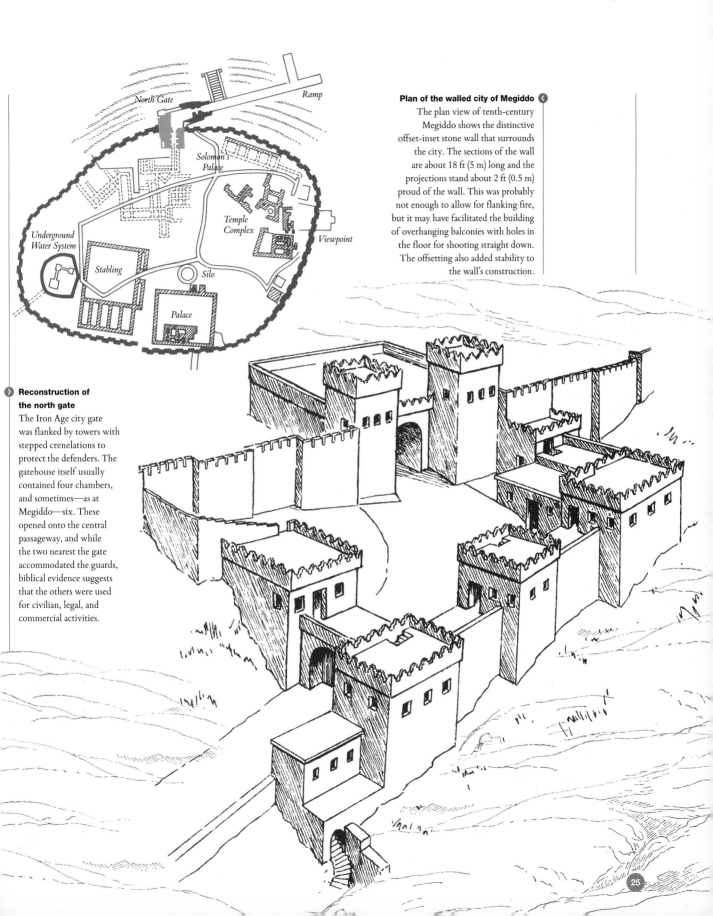

Plan of the walled city of Megiddo
The plan view of tenth-century Megiddo shows the distinctive offset-inset stone wall that surrounds the city. The sections of the wall are about 18 ft (5 m) long and the projections stand about 2 ft (0.5 m) proud of the wall. This was probably not enough to allow for flanking fire, but it may have facilitated the building of overhanging balconies with holes in the floor for shooting straight down. The offsetting also added stability to the wall's construction.

North Gate

Ramp

Solomon's Palace

Temple Complex

Viewpoint

Underground Water System

Stabling

Silo

Palace

Reconstruction of the north gate
The Iron Age city gate was flanked by towers with stepped crenelations to protect the defenders. The gatehouse itself usually contained four chambers, and sometimes—as at Megiddo—six. These opened onto the central passageway, and while the two nearest the gate accommodated the guards, biblical evidence suggests that the others were used for civilian, legal, and commercial activities.

THEN & NOW
Walls of Jerusalem

Jerusalem is one of the oldest and one of the most fought-over cities in the world. Its situation on a rocky outcrop offered a readily defensible position, and the earliest known archaeological evidence of walls around the city dates from around 1700 BCE.

King David is credited in the Bible with fortifying the city around 1000 BCE when he made it his capital. Jerusalem was destroyed by Babylonian forces in 587 BCE, rebuilt by Nehemiah in the fifth century BCE, destroyed again by the Seleucid Empire in the second century BCE, and extensively rebuilt by the Roman emperor Hadrian during the second century CE. Jerusalem's religious significance to Jews, Christians, and Muslims ensured that the city continued to be a focus for conflict, particularly during the period of the Crusades. Between 1219 and 1244 the walls were razed and rebuilt three times. Even the current walls, which date from the 16th century, show the marks of recent conflict, with bullet holes visible around the Zion Gate and the Jaffa Gate dating from the War of Independence in 1948.

Sixth-century Medeba map
The adoption of Christianity as the religion of the Roman Empire during the reign of Theodosius in the fourth century CE gave Jerusalem real prestige, and it grew into an important and wealthy city. The Medeba map, a mosaic of the Holy Land discovered in the 19th century during the construction of St. George's Church in Medeba, Jordan, includes an image of Jerusalem that shows the city walls as they were in the Byzantine period. Several of the gates are identifiable— the Damascus Gate, the Golden Gate, and the Lions' Gate—and the Citadel or Tower of David can also be seen. This was originally a fortified palace built by Herod the Great, with three huge towers, and was one of the few sections of the city's fortifications to survive the destruction of the city by the Roman emperor Titus in 70 CE. The construction of the present fortress dates chiefly from the 14th century.

The city walls today

The walls of Jerusalem as they appear now are the work of the Ottoman Turks, who took control of the city in 1517. Suleiman the Magnificent began reconstruction of the defenses in 1538. The walls extend for about 3 mi (5 km), and vary in height between 16 and 50 ft (5 and 15 m), with a thickness of about 10 ft (3 m). The Ottoman walls follow the foundations of the earlier Byzantine walls, and the circuit includes seven gates, the finest of which is the Damascus Gate, formerly the main northern entrance to the city. This was originally part of Hadrian's fortifications, and there are still remains of the Roman gate, with a Latin inscription above the arch. Suleiman's gate is flanked by two projecting towers with machicolations and distinctive stepped merlons.

B Y THE SECOND CENTURY BCE military architecture was a specialized science, best exemplified by the engineers of the Roman Empire. Treatises such as those written by Philo of Alexandria and Vitruvius offered prescriptions for building walls and other defensive structures, with recommended designs and measurements. As siege engines and battering rams became ever larger and more sophisticated, so defensive measures had to keep pace.

CHAPTER 2

Ancient Europe

The Greeks and the Hittites of Asia Minor took advantage of the topography of their territories, building defensive structures on rocky outcrops that commanded the surrounding area. Cities such as Mycenae, Athens, and Hattusha were built around an acropolis, an elevated citadel to which the citizens could withdraw if threatened. Access to the citadel was usually via a ramp that was overlooked by the walls, with a tower at its head. Particular attention was given to the gateways, as potentially the weakest point, and there would frequently be more than one set of gates with enclosed courts in between where attackers would be exposed to defensive fire from all sides. Around the city itself would be one or more curtain walls, punctuated with towers. The Greeks and Hittites both used stone, dressing immense blocks so as to fit them tightly together without mortar to build walls that could be as much as 25 feet (7.5 meters) thick and 60 feet (18 meters) high.

The preeminent European military power during this period was Rome, and Roman military engineers developed a standardized system of fortification that could be applied across the vast territory of the empire. The fortified Roman camp was of uniform design, and so could be built by the legionaries with a minimum of technical expertise. The Romans also protected the frontiers of their empire, building a defensive wall about 300 miles (480 kilometers) long between the Rhine and the Danube, and a similar wall across the northernmost frontier of Britain. Toward the end of their dominance they produced perhaps their finest works—the walls of Rome itself that still stand today.

Housesteads, Northumberland, England
Built around 124 CE as part of Hadrian's Wall, the 73-mi (117-km) frontier defense built by order of the emperor Hadrian, Housesteads Fort covers an area of 5 acres (2 ha). Known to the Romans as Vercovicium, Housesteads housed a garrison of about 1,000 legionaries and follows the standard rectangular layout of the Roman castra that guarded the frontier provinces of the Empire.

Eastern Mediterranean Citadels

Mycenaean Greece

The Mycenaeans dominated much of the eastern Mediterranean during the late Bronze Age, advancing their power through military conquest. Famously featuring in the epics of Homer, the civilization declined in the 12th century BCE, possibly as a result of invasion by the enigmatic Sea People who are also linked to the collapse of the Hittite Empire.

Ancient Greek architecture before the Classical period was rough and massive in character, as exemplified by the heavily fortified citadels at Mycenae itself and at Tiryns. The thick walls were built using huge boulders, which the later Greeks believed could only have been moved by the giant one-eyed Cyclops, hence the name cyclopean masonry. An inner and an outer wall were built from stone, and the space between filled with earth and rubble. Walls varied in construction: without recourse to mortar, the Mycenaeans often cut their wall blocks so as to fit more closely together.

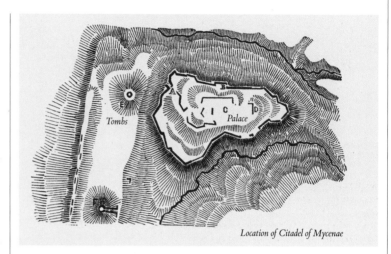

Location of Citadel of Mycenae

Citadel of Mycenae

The city of Mycenae was made up of a number of small settlements overlooked by the citadel, which was set on the highest of the several hills that mark the site. In times of danger the population who lived below the citadel would withdraw behind its walls, which in some places are 20 ft (6 m) thick. The citadel was supplied with water from an underground reservoir, which was dug out of the rock outside the city, and accessed via a stepped passageway built through the north wall.

Lion Gate, Mycenae

The Lion Gate that gave access to the citadel (marked A on the plan) is built from huge rectangular blocks of conglomerate stone that form an entrance 20 ft (6 m) wide and 40 ft (12 m) long. The triangular relief from which the gate takes its name is carved from a block of limestone, and fills the space beneath the corbeled arch that lessens the weight on the lintel below it. The relief shows two lions flanking a column that tapers from capital to base (unlike the classical column, where the base is thicker), a feature of both Minoan and Mycenaean architecture.

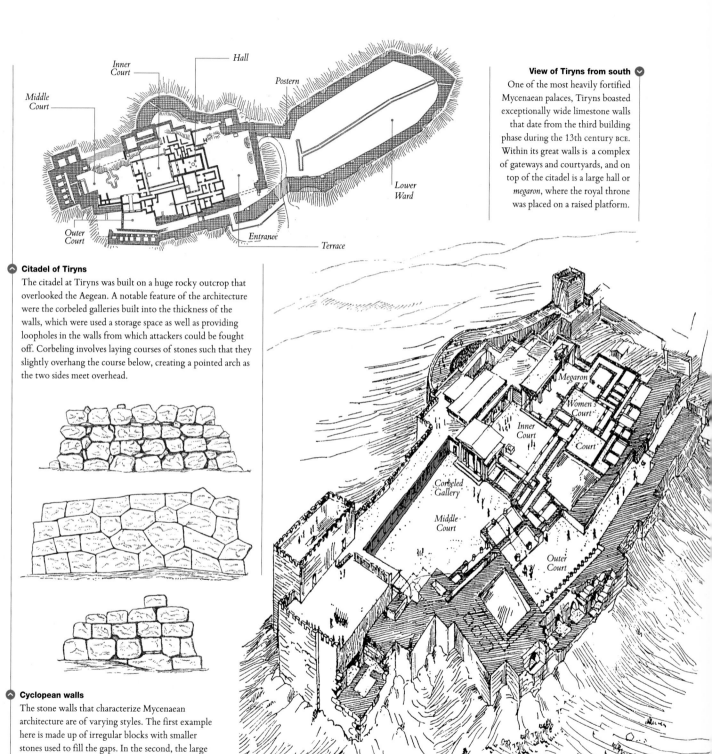

Inner
Court
Hall
Middle
Court
Postern
Lower
Ward
Outer
Court
Entrance
Terrace

View of Tiryns from south ⌄
One of the most heavily fortified
Mycenaean palaces, Tiryns boasted
exceptionally wide limestone walls
that date from the third building
phase during the 13th century BCE.
Within its great walls is a complex
of gateways and courtyards, and on
top of the citadel is a large hall or
megaron, where the royal throne
was placed on a raised platform.

⌃ **Citadel of Tiryns**
The citadel at Tiryns was built on a huge rocky outcrop that
overlooked the Aegean. A notable feature of the architecture
were the corbeled galleries built into the thickness of the
walls, which were used a storage space as well as providing
loopholes in the walls from which attackers could be fought
off. Corbeling involves laying courses of stones such that they
slightly overhang the course below, creating a pointed arch as
the two sides meet overhead.

Megaron
Women's
Court
Inner
Court
Court
Corbeled
Gallery
Middle
Court
Outer
Court

⌃ **Cyclopean walls**
The stone walls that characterize Mycenaean
architecture are of varying styles. The first example
here is made up of irregular blocks with smaller
stones used to fill the gaps. In the second, the large
blocks are cut such that the adjacent faces lie close
together, and the third example shows blocks cut
to near-rectangular shape and laid in courses. The
different styles overlapped chronologically, so they
are not always a reliable way of dating a building.

Iron Age Defenses in Britain

Celtic hill forts

The hill forts scattered widely across Wales and southwestern England are highly distinctive features of the landscape. Dating from the period when the Celtic peoples of northern France and the Low Countries began to colonize the British Isles in large numbers, forts of this kind are found in most parts of western and central Europe. They all share a basic structure —a combination of ditches and ramparts enclosing a central area, although there are numerous variations, and not all are sited on hills. More than half of the forts in England and Wales cover less than 3 acres (1 hectare), and very few are larger than 30 acres (12 hectares). They were essentially defensive structures, designed to protect the homes and herds of an individual settlement, and even in areas in which there is a high concentration of forts there is no evidence of interdependence or any overall strategic planning. Thus it was that when the Romans arrived in 43 CE, they were able to add Britain to their empire without encountering much in the way of organized resistance from the Celtic tribes responsible for the construction of the forts.

Stockades and Palisades

Simple stockade of stone and earth retained by wooden stakes

Stone stockade with inner core of masonry

Wooden palisade of tree trunks, strengthened with earth

Stockade of stone and rubble, with palisade of wood

Badbury Rings, Dorset
As with all types of fortifications, the entranceways of hill forts were the weakest points, and builders adopted numerous methods to reinforce them from attack. The near-circular fort of Badbury Rings originally had three offset entrances on the western side (the openings in the outer rings in line with that in the inner are modern). The second entrance led into a substantial bastion that would have exposed an attacking force to the defensive fire of those within the fort.

Stockades and palisades
Ramparts were built using various combinations of earth, stone, and timber. The outer face of timber or coursed stonework fronted a heap of packed earth or rubble, which sloped back to buttress the front wall Sometimes a rear wall was also built, so that two stone walls enclosed a core of rubble. The rampart would be topped with a stone stockade or timber palisade, reinforced with earth.

West Entrance

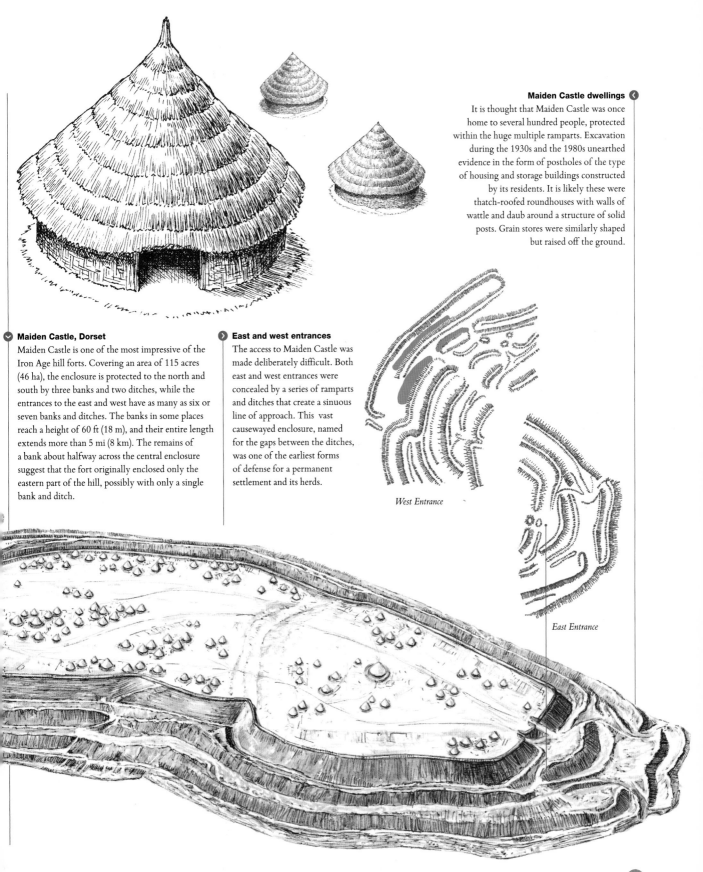

Maiden Castle dwellings

It is thought that Maiden Castle was once home to several hundred people, protected within the huge multiple ramparts. Excavation during the 1930s and the 1980s unearthed evidence in the form of postholes of the type of housing and storage buildings constructed by its residents. It is likely these were thatch-roofed roundhouses with walls of wattle and daub around a structure of solid posts. Grain stores were similarly shaped but raised off the ground.

Maiden Castle, Dorset

Maiden Castle is one of the most impressive of the Iron Age hill forts. Covering an area of 115 acres (46 ha), the enclosure is protected to the north and south by three banks and two ditches, while the entrances to the east and west have as many as six or seven banks and ditches. The banks in some places reach a height of 60 ft (18 m), and their entire length extends more than 5 mi (8 km). The remains of a bank about halfway across the central enclosure suggest that the fort originally enclosed only the eastern part of the hill, possibly with only a single bank and ditch.

East and west entrances

The access to Maiden Castle was made deliberately difficult. Both east and west entrances were concealed by a series of ramparts and ditches that create a sinuous line of approach. This vast causewayed enclosure, named for the gaps between the ditches, was one of the earliest forms of defense for a permanent settlement and its herds.

West Entrance

East Entrance

A Roman *Castrum*

The legionary fortress

Emperor Augustus (27 BCE–14 CE) was the first emperor to establish a standing Roman army. Comprising 27 legions, the army was based in permanent quarters around the Roman Empire. Previously armies had been raised for particular campaigns and disbanded thereafter. The fortresses, or *castra*, in which the legions were housed were modeled closely on the arrangements of the temporary camps. These had tents arranged in orderly ranks around the commander's tent, with two main roads running across the encampment.

Usually housing one legion each, the fortresses were built by the soldiers themselves, under the direction of the prefect of the camp and various technical specialists such as stonemasons and surveyors. A ditch about 10 feet (3 meters) deep and 15 feet (4.5 meters) wide backed onto earth banks topped by a timber palisade, creating a rampart about 10–12 feet (3–3.5 meters) high with a walkway about 7 feet (2 meters) wide. From the middle of the first century CE the earth rampart was faced with stone, and gradually the earth and timber fortresses were replaced with more durable stone structures.

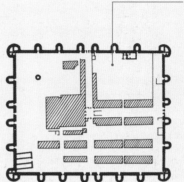

Typical layout of Roman *castra*
After the restructuring of the legions into smaller units from the time of Diocletian (284–305 BCE) onward, fortresses were smaller than their imperial predecessors, though they kept the same layout. The fortress at Betthorus, present-day El-Lejjun in Jordan, for example, had accommodation for about 1000 men. The limestone ramparts were about 8 ft (2.5 m) thick, with 24 semicircular towers and four three-portaled gateways.

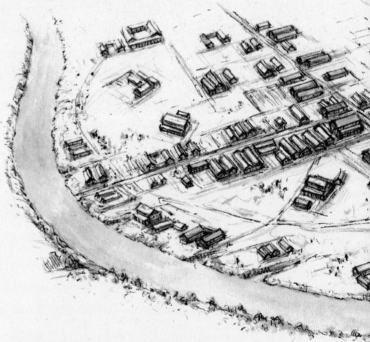

Servicing the *castrum*
Each fortress contained everything the legion required, including baths, a granary, a hospital, and workshops. Fortresses were often situated near rivers to ensure a reliable supply of water—it has been estimated that an average fortress would have used 70,000 gallons (320,000 liters) of water each day. Beyond the fort itself there was often a civilian settlement which developed to service the fort by providing a market, an amphitheater, and so forth.

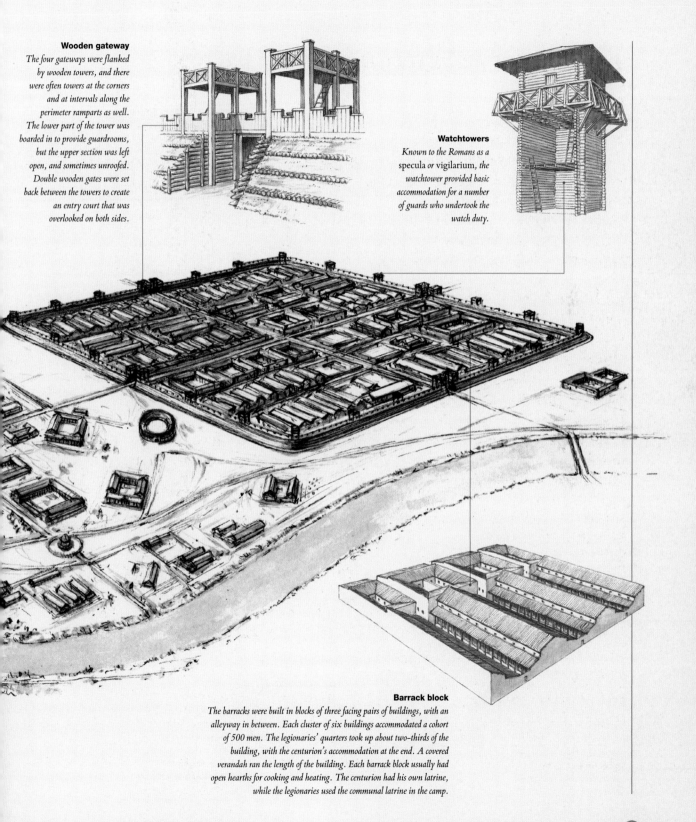

Wooden gateway
The four gateways were flanked by wooden towers, and there were often towers at the corners and at intervals along the perimeter ramparts as well. The lower part of the tower was boarded in to provide guardrooms, but the upper section was left open, and sometimes unroofed. Double wooden gates were set back between the towers to create an entry court that was overlooked on both sides.

Watchtowers
Known to the Romans as a specula or vigilarium, the watchtower provided basic accommodation for a number of guards who undertook the watch duty.

Barrack block
The barracks were built in blocks of three facing pairs of buildings, with an alleyway in between. Each cluster of six buildings accommodated a cohort of 500 men. The legionaries' quarters took up about two-thirds of the building, with the centurion's accommodation at the end. A covered verandah ran the length of the building. Each barrack block usually had open hearths for cooking and heating. The centurion had his own latrine, while the legionaries used the communal latrine in the camp.

Hellenistic Forts, Asia Minor

Greek city colonies

The western part of Asia Minor was one of the most fought-over regions of the ancient world. Immigrants from Greece had settled in the region from the beginning of the first millennium BCE, and by the sixth century BCE there were a number of Greek cities on the western coast of what is now Turkey. These were conquered successively by the Lydians and then the Persians, before Alexander the Great restored their independence in 334 BCE. Thereafter the Seleucid Empire and then the Pergamonic Kingdom held sway, until Rome added Asia Minor to its empire in the mid-second century BCE. Throughout this period the Greek city colonies such as Perge, Side, Halicarnassus, and Miletus found themselves in a buffer zone between rival power blocs, and they were frequently subject to siege and attack. Accordingly, the defensive structures that they developed to withstand these assaults were among the most sophisticated in the ancient world.

Priene, East Gate,
View from Exterior

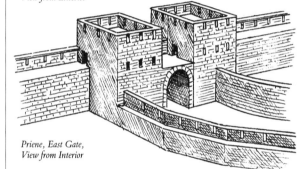

Priene, East Gate,
View from Interior

Sillyon, Main Gate

❯ Fortified entrances

As potentially the most vulnerable point in the walls, the gateways received particular attention. They were flanked by towers that were usually rectangular, although those at Perge were circular. The towers had windows on the upper floors for the archers and stone-throwing catapults, and small gates or posterns at ground level so that the defenders could sally forth to make surprise attacks on the besiegers. An enclosed courtyard was frequently built behind the gateway to trap any attackers who managed to break through.

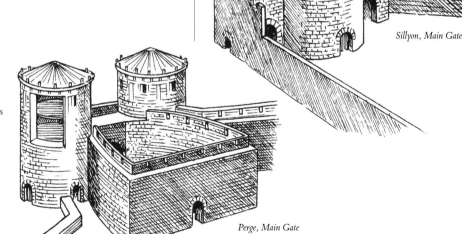

Perge, Main Gate

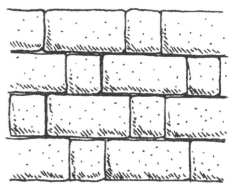

Watchtower

Watchtowers were situated near Greek cities to give advance warning of attack, so as to allow the citizens to retreat to the fortified acropolis. They were also built along essential trade routes and other important sites, offering shelter to the surrounding populace. This tower at Andros guarded the nearby iron mines.

Isodomic ashlar

The walls of the fifth-century BCE Greek cities of Asia Minor were almost invariably built from stone rather than mudbrick, which was more prevalent in the warmer and drier climate of Egypt and Mesopotamia. Various masonry types have been identified, and offer some guidance as to the age of a particular structure. During this period the preference was for walls built from regular rectangular blocks laid in courses, a type known as isodomic ashlar.

Curtain walls

City walls were usually 4–6 ft (1.2–1.8 m) thick and up to 25 ft (7.5 m) high. They were surmounted by a walkway wide enough to accommodate stone-throwing engines, which was protected by a parapet. Sometimes there was more than one defensive story—the curtain walls of Perge, built in the third century BCE, had arched buttresses behind them which supported a gallery for archers beneath the upper walkway.

Aurelian Walls of Rome

By the middle of the third century CE, the Roman Empire was hard pressed on several fronts, and a succession of weak emperors had jeopardized the smooth running of imperial affairs. In the east the empire was under threat from the Persian Sassanid Empire, and in the west the Gothic tribes along the Danube had begun to act in concert against Rome. Almost the first challenge facing the soldier-emperor Aurelian in 270 CE was an invasion by the Iuthungi into northern Italy. The attack was repulsed at the battle of Ticinum, but so alarmed was Aurelian that he immediately set in train a program of fortifications for the city.

The walls that Aurelian started to construct in 271 CE eventually extended for nearly 12 miles (19 kilometers) and enclosed an area of more than 6,000 acres (2,400 hectares). Built using a core of tufa rubble bound together with a lime-based cement, and faced with baked brick, the walls rose to about 20 feet (6 meters) and were almost 12 feet

Painting by Vittore Carpaccio c. 1465–1525
From the 13th century, the fortress at Rome was used as a papal castle, and an elevated covered passageway was built by Pope Nicholas III to connect it with the Vatican. Known now as Castel Sant' Angelo, the fortress served as a refuge for popes during times of siege or civil unrest. This painting from around 1490 of the legendary Pope Cyriac receiving pilgrims to the city clearly shows the imposing fortifications, and much of the medieval fortress remains.

(3.5 meters) thick. The design of the walls and the towers that were placed at intervals of about 90 feet (27 meters) was relatively simple, reflecting the fact that they were built quickly by civilians rather than by military engineers, who would have been conversant with the latest methods of defensive fortification. The towers projected outward from the face of the wall, and at the top of each was a chamber with forward- and side-facing windows to permit the firing of ballistae.

The Aurelian walls and the Castel Sant' Angelo today

The need for swift construction meant that a number of existing buildings were incorporated into the walls, notably the pyramidal tomb of Caius Cestius, dating from around 18 BCE, and the Claudia-Anio Novus aqueduct, part of which was converted into the Praenestina-Labicana Gate. It is highly likely that the walls also incorporated the huge cylindrical drum of Hadrian's mausoleum near the Pons Aelius. Although there is no direct evidence of this, it would have been strategically advantageous for Aurelian to bring the fortified mausoleum into the general wall system to protect the bridge. Certainly by the time Procopius was writing his *Wars of Justinian* in the sixth century CE, the fortress was an important element of the city's defenses, and was besieged by the invading Ostrogoths in 537 CE. The Aurelian walls were strengthened and restored on numerous occasions, particularly by Maxentius in the early fourth century CE and Honorius in the fifth, but much of the circuit that is visible today is the original work.

GALLERY OF
Fortifications of the Ancient World

Permanent fortifications came into being with the
introduction of the wall—whether of hewn stone,
baked brick, or sun-dried mud—and some of the
most remarkable defenses ever constructed are as
old as civilization itself.

**Methoni, Greece,
seventh century BCE**
No strategic site is too
small to be defended.
This Peleponnese islet
later became a Byzantine
fortress from 395 to 1204.

Masada, Israel, first century BCE
The rock fortress first fortified by Herod in ca. 35–31 BCE

Nicopolis, Greece ca. 31 BCE
The fortified capital of Epirus in northwest Greece, built by Augustus

Citadel at Mohenjo Daro, Sindh, Pakistan, ca. 2500 BCE
Representing one of the largest centers of the Harappan civilization,
Mohenjo Daro was built entirely in kiln-fired brick

Walls of Babylon, Iraq, sixth century BCE
The defenses built by Nebuchadnezzar during his reign (604–562 BCE)

Walls of Constantinople (Istanbul), Turkey, 413 CE
Built by Theodosius II to defend the new capital of the Roman Empire

SECTION

2

Western Castles
of the
Middle Ages

Introduction

During the early Middle Ages, serious fortification in Western Europe had been the preserve of emperors, kings, and princes. Only they had the power to muster the huge labor forces needed in order to create walled towns and cities, and the ability to raise the armies with which such strongholds could be taken.

But in the ninth and tenth centuries, public authority exercised on this scale began to collapse. The extensive empire forged by the famous Charlemagne ceased to expand and, under pressure from attacks by Vikings and Saracens, began to fragment. Around the turn of the first millennium CE, against this background of chaos and confusion, a new order of lesser lords emerged, and a new breed of fortification: the castle.

If these new fortresses offered any advantage to the local population, it was coincidental. Castles were not public defenses, but private ones, and their owners aimed not to protect their surroundings but to dominate them. They could, accordingly, be built on a much smaller scale than the public defenses of old. No need for stone walls to shield thousands of people—a castle owner needed only to protect himself and his armed retainers, or knights. No need, for that matter, to build in stone. In their race to dominate and outdo their rivals, the new lords threw up fortresses made from earth and timber. What they did crave was height: castle-builders sought out hills or created artificial ones, on top of which they constructed tall towers. Castles, in a nutshell, were small and tall.

In time of course, many of these early castles were rebuilt in stone, and grew into the forms we are more familiar with today. Yet they never lost the essential characteristic of being private fortresses. Only when the states of Western Europe grew strong enough to regain the monopoly of fortification did the Middle Ages, and the age of the castle, draw to a close.

Timeline

950
The first standing castle is built in France

Tower of London

987
The first mention of Château de Foix, Ariège, Midi-Pyrenées

1066
Castles introduced to England by William the Conqueror

1070s
Construction of the Tower of London begins

1123
The building of Château de Falaise, Calvados, Normandy

1139
The Pope bans the use of crossbows in warfare

1160
Round keeps are introduced

1161
Château Gisors, Eure, Normandy, is rebuilt in stone

1196–98
Château Gaillard, Eure, Normandy, is built

Château Gaillard

1200
About 400 castles exist in England and Wales

Château Gisors

1204
Château Gaillard is taken through an unguarded window

1211–12
Château de Foix is under siege during the Albigensian Crusade

1220
The building of Carcassonne, Aude, Languedoc, commences

Carcassonne

1220
The building of Coucy-le-Château, Aisne, Picardy, commences

1224
The siege of Bedford Castle, Bedfordshire

1266
The siege of Kenilworth Castle, Warwickshire

1270
The birth of the concentric castle design

1277
Edward I's castle-building program begins in Wales

Conwy Castle

1295
Beaumaris, the last of Edward I's castles is built but never completed

1314
Robert the Bruce captures Edinburgh Castle by scaling the rock

ca. 1320
Gunpowder is introduced into Europe

1327
The earliest picture of a cannon

ca. 1365
The introduction of pistols

1385
Bodiam Castle, Sussex, is built with round and square towers

Bodiam Castle

1403
Tiny force of archers defends Caernarfon Castle, Wales, against two assaults

ca. 1450
The introduction of the musket

ca. 1500
The first development—in Italy—of an artillery platform

CASTLES LOCATER MAP
Western Medieval

The evocative stone ruins that still dot the cities, towns, and fields of Europe punctuate the chronology of an age of kingmakers, conquerors, and countries at war but an age also defined by great dynasties with vast wealth and a desire to display. A history of the needs—defensive and domestic—of castle builders in Britain and France can be mapped in stone, while tales of siege and crusade weave through the castles of Spain, Italy, and beyond.

Tower of London
See pages 62–3

Carcasson
See pages 1

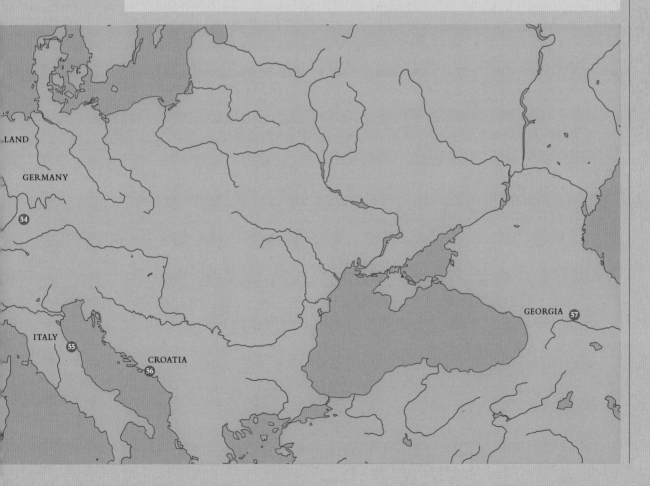

British Castles

1. Edinburgh
2. Borthwick
3. Threave
4. Caerlaverock
5. Dromore
6. Skipton
7. Clifford's Tower/York
8. Conisbrough
9. Goltho
10. Tattershall
11. Castle Rising
12. Kenilworth
13. Warwick
14. Stafford
15. Hen Domen
16. Conwy
17. Beaumaris
18. Caernarfon
19. Harlech
20. Kidwelly
21. Goodrich
22. Restormel
23. Windsor
24. Tower of London
25. Hedingham
26. Colchester
27. Rochester
28. Lewes
29. Bodiam
30. Dover

French and other European Castles

31. Arques la Bataille
32. Mont St. Michel
33. Falaise
34. Gaillard
35. Gisors
36. Louvre
37. Coucy
38. Vincennes
39. Pierrefonds
40. Metz
41. Vez
42. Roche-Guyon
43. Etampes
44. Provins
45. Angers
46. Langeais
46. Loches
46. Montbazon
47. Mehun-sur-Yèvre
48. Bonaguil
49. Carcassonne
50. Narbonne
51. Aigues-Mortes
52. Castillo de la Mota
53. Muiderslot
54. Hohenzollern
55. San Marino
56. Dubrovnik
57. Ananuri

LAND

GERMANY

54

ITALY

55

CROATIA

56

GEORGIA 57

C ASTLES WERE INTRODUCED TO ENGLAND (and later to the rest of the British Isles) by the Normans. Uniquely, England around the turn of the first millennium had not experienced the collapse of public authority of the kind seen on the Continent—far from it. In the tenth and early eleventh centuries the English state had become stronger, richer, more centralized, and better organized. As such it had avoided Europe's plague of castles.

CHAPTER 3

Early British Medieval Castles, 1066–1200

Hence the surprise of the Anglo-Saxon Chronicle when, in 1051, some Norman friends of King Edward the Confessor (r. 1042–66) "built a castle in Herefordshire … and inflicted all the injuries and insults they could upon the men in the region." Not only was this the first castle in England; it is the first recorded use of the word "castle" in English. Yet within 50 years, thanks to the William the Conqueror and his followers, England would be full of these newfangled fortifications: about 500 by the year 1100 is the conservative modern estimate.

Most of these early castles, like their continental counterparts, were constructed from earth and timber, thrown up quickly by the conquerors in order to secure their territorial gains and to keep down the reluctant natives. At the same time, the richest Normans—the king and his greatest barons—were already erecting buildings in stone. Typically these took the form of giant towers, today called keeps, but known to contemporaries as *donjons*. The fact that this medieval term gives us the modern word "dungeon" can be dangerously misleading. From the outside, by design, these great towers were looming presences: proud, menacing, impregnable. Yet on the inside, they were palaces: residences suitable for the most important people in medieval society, equipped with all the creature comforts that the age could devise. The fusion of the fortress and palace, the military and the domestic, is there from the very beginning, and the problem of how to fuse them effectively is what makes medieval castles so endlessly fascinating.

Dromore, County Down, Northern Ireland
A motte-and-bailey castle was built at Dromore in County Down by Sir John de Courcy, following the Norman conquest of Ireland in the 13th century. The distinctive, 40-ft (12-m) mound, set in a loop of the River Lagan, provides an excellent example of an Anglo-Norman fortification. Below the motte itself a rectangular bailey would have been surrounded by a wooden palisade. Its location would have provided clear views of the valley and it is thought that the mound was topped by an archery tower. Today it remains an imposing and distinctive landmark.

ANATOMY OF

An Anglo-Saxon *Burh*

The first fortified towns

Since the late eighth century, the British Isles, like the rest of Western Europe, had been repeatedly raided by Vikings. In the last decades of the ninth century these pirates had started to settle, and large parts of northern and eastern England had come under their control. At this time "England" was not one kingdom but several, and, as the Vikings had advanced, so these kingdoms had fallen.

Wessex, ruled by Alfred the Great (r. 871– 99), was the exception. Alfred, and his tenth-century successors, halted and reserved the Viking advance. In doing so, they established a single, united Kingdom of England, similar in shape to the England of today, and to consolidate their hold on this reconquered territory, they constructed a series of fortified towns, known as *burhs*. Many are the basis for modern English counties and cities: Oxford, for example, began life as a *burh*. Crucially *burhs* were great public defenses, built by royal authority, to protect whole communities. In this respect, they differed fundamentally from the fortifications introduced by the Normans after 1066.

Walkway
The raised earthworks, often turfed, served as an elevated walkway as well as an effective means of patrol. They were fronted by a deep ditch and a palisade in wood or stone.

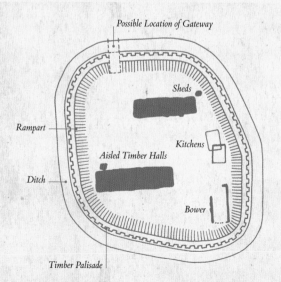

Establishing the *burh*
There were three main types of burh: *those based on existing Roman fortifications, those established on the sites of Iron Age forts, and those on newly established sites where the burh was protected by an earthen rampart. In time, a network of burhs was developed to serve the rural area and become urban centers—the boroughs.*

Goltho, Late Saxon settlement, Lincolnshire

We know from documentary evidence that some Anglo-Saxon lords built their own fortified homes—*burgheats*—sometimes (confusingly) also called *burhs*. Some historians are inclined to regard these as castles in all but name, and thus see little difference between the defenses of Anglo-Saxon England and those being built on the continent. Excavations carried out in the 1960s at Goltho, a small Norman castle in Lincolnshire, revealed that it was built on top of an earlier, late Anglo-Saxon fortified dwelling.

But if Goltho is representative of a lost species of Anglo-Saxon fortified dwelling, they must have been comparatively rare (precious few other examples have been found) and, to judge from Goltho itself, comparatively puny. Most experts would accept that castles in England begin with the Normans. As the contemporary chronicler Orderic Vitalis famously put it, "the fortifications called castles by the Normans were scarcely known in the English provinces, and so the English—in spite of their courage and love of fighting—could put up only a weak resistance to their enemies."

Possible Location of Gateway

Sheds

Rampart

Kitchens

Aisled Timber Halls

Ditch

Bower

Timber Palisade

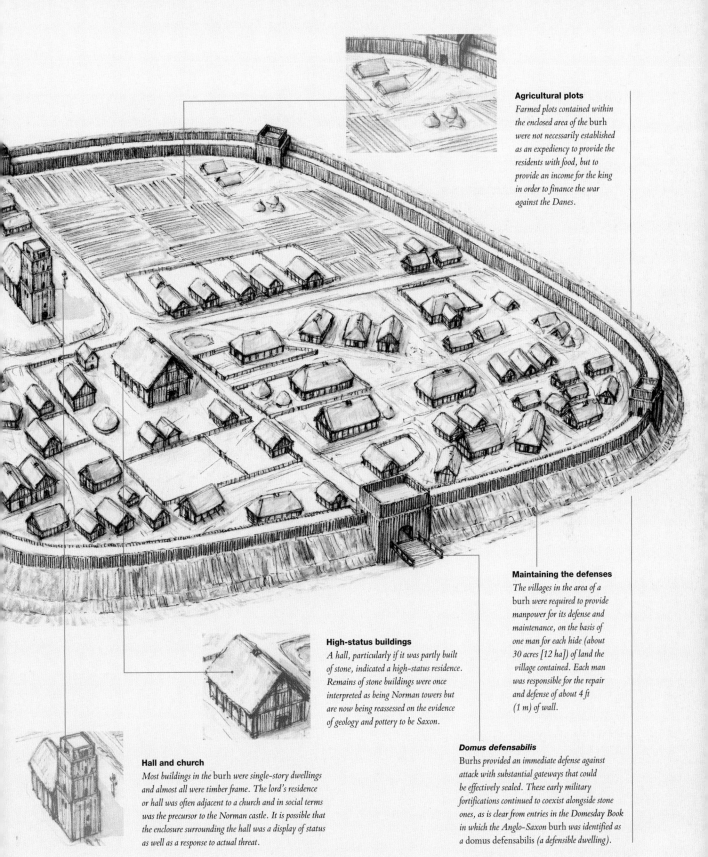

Agricultural plots
Farmed plots contained within the enclosed area of the burh were not necessarily established as an expediency to provide the residents with food, but to provide an income for the king in order to finance the war against the Danes.

High-status buildings
A hall, particularly if it was partly built of stone, indicated a high-status residence. Remains of stone buildings were once interpreted as being Norman towers but are now being reassessed on the evidence of geology and pottery to be Saxon.

Hall and church
Most buildings in the burh were single-story dwellings and almost all were timber frame. The lord's residence or hall was often adjacent to a church and in social terms was the precursor to the Norman castle. It is possible that the enclosure surrounding the hall was a display of status as well as a response to actual threat.

Maintaining the defenses
The villages in the area of a burh were required to provide manpower for its defense and maintenance, on the basis of one man for each hide (about 30 acres [12 ha]) of land the village contained. Each man was responsible for the repair and defense of about 4 ft (1 m) of wall.

Domus defensabilis
Burhs provided an immediate defense against attack with substantial gateways that could be effectively sealed. These early military fortifications continued to coexist alongside stone ones, as is clear from entries in the Domesday Book in which the Anglo-Saxon burh was identified as a domus defensabilis (a defensible dwelling).

ANATOMY OF

A Motte-&-Bailey Castle

The Norman model

The majority of castles built by the Normans in the decades after 1066 (roughly three-quarters of all known sites) conform to a common type, known as the motte-and-bailey. The bailey is simply an enclosure formed by a ditch and embankment, topped with a wooden palisade, and intended to contain the majority of the castle's buildings: the hall, chapel, houses, stables, and so on. The motte, by contrast, is a far more substantial fortification, an artificial hill or mound, which serves several purposes (*see opposite*). Since mounds of earth are difficult to date, the precise origin of mottes remains uncertain, but the Normans and their neighbors certainly had them before the Conquest.

Buildings

The bailey would typically contain the barracks for the garrison, stables and stalls for horses and livestock, a blacksmith's forge and armory, a large hall, and a chapel. Vital also was a well or cistern to supply water. Timber was in plentiful supply from local forests and woods.

Kit Castles

The Norman invasion fleet consisted of almost 700 ships. Alongside the soldiers, their horses, and the supplies was a contingent of carpenters and builders with all the materials needed to quickly construct a timber fortress. They are pictured in the Bayeux Tapestry, with their axes, planes, and adzes. The timbers were precut to size and were then simply bolted together. The first kit castle was erected on the site of an old Roman fort, situated on high ground overlooking Pevensey Bay. A Norman chronicler described it as follows:

"They took counsel together, and looked for a good spot to build a castle on. They had brought with them in the fleet, three pre-built wooden castles from Normandy, all in pieces, ready for fitting together, and they took the materials of one of these out of the ships, all shaped and pierced to receive the pins which they had brought cut and ready in large barrels; and before evening had set in they had finished a good Castle on English ground, and placed their stores there. All then ate and drank, and were glad to be ashore."

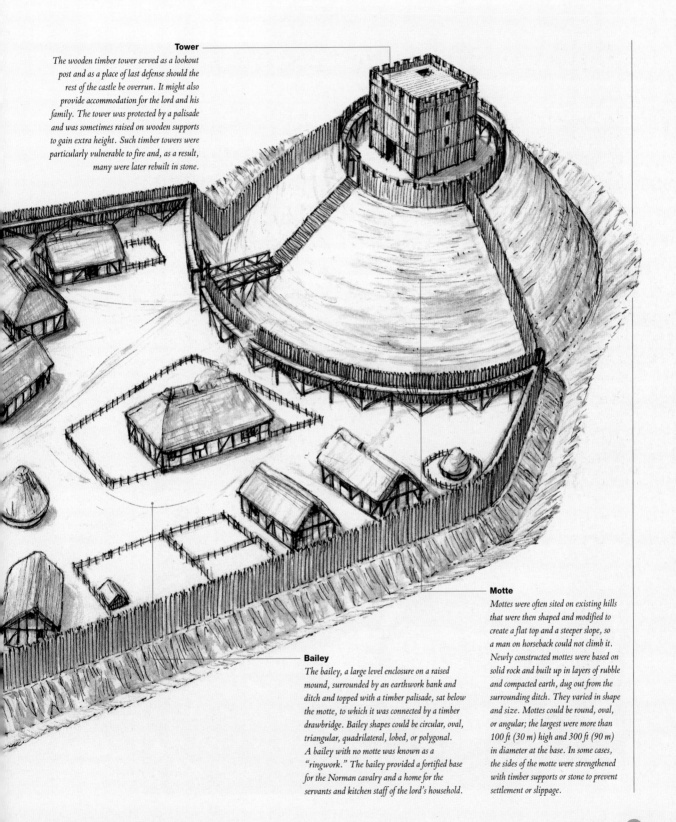

Tower

The wooden timber tower served as a lookout post and as a place of last defense should the rest of the castle be overrun. It might also provide accommodation for the lord and his family. The tower was protected by a palisade and was sometimes raised on wooden supports to gain extra height. Such timber towers were particularly vulnerable to fire and, as a result, many were later rebuilt in stone.

Bailey

The bailey, a large level enclosure on a raised mound, surrounded by an earthwork bank and ditch and topped with a timber palisade, sat below the motte, to which it was connected by a timber drawbridge. Bailey shapes could be circular, oval, triangular, quadrilateral, lobed, or polygonal. A bailey with no motte was known as a "ringwork." The bailey provided a fortified base for the Norman cavalry and a home for the servants and kitchen staff of the lord's household.

Motte

Mottes were often sited on existing hills that were then shaped and modified to create a flat top and a steeper slope, so a man on horseback could not climb it. Newly constructed mottes were based on solid rock and built up in layers of rubble and compacted earth, dug out from the surrounding ditch. They varied in shape and size. Mottes could be round, oval, or angular; the largest were more than 100 ft (30 m) high and 300 ft (90 m) in diameter at the base. In some cases, the sides of the motte were strengthened with timber supports or stone to prevent settlement or slippage.

Defense of the Western Frontier

Hen Domen, Powys

Hen Domen is situated just west of Offa's Dyke, the border between England and Wales, on a strategic site overlooking a shallow crossing of the River Severn. Here the Normans built a timber and earth castle in the 1070s, which went on to be occupied for 200 years.

The site's importance and distinction rests on the fact that extensive archaeological excavations were carried out here over three decades, beginning in 1960. Robert Higham and Philip Barker led the excavations that made this the most fully explored site of its kind in Europe. "The earthworks which are now the only surface remains of such sites," they write, "conceal a history of development which only detailed excavation can illuminate."

The original castle was a forward military outpost built by Roger de Montgomery, a close friend of William the Conqueror, who was created Earl of Shrewsbury in 1068. He named his castle Montgomery after his home town in Normandy, and in time the surrounding area became known as Montgomeryshire.

The earl held Hen Domen (the Welsh name for the castle) down to his death in 1094, using it as a base for further conquest. By 1086, as the famous Domesday Survey shows, the earl controlled large areas that had once been part of the Welsh Kingdom of Powys. In addition, he also held most of Shropshire and lands in Sussex, making him one of the richest land-owners in England after the king himself.

The Old Mound
Hen Domen is a Welsh name meaning "old mound." Its motte, 26 ft (8 m) high and 130 ft (40 m) in diameter at its base, dominates the site. The bailey was ringed with double ramparts and ditches.

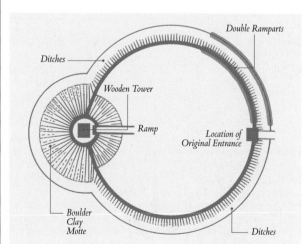

Ditches —
Double Ramparts
Wooden Tower
Ramp
Location of Original Entrance
Boulder Clay Motte
Ditches

Clay ramparts
Hen Domen is one of the most fully explored early medieval sites of its kind and has provided much of the evidence for what is now known about timber castles. The extensive excavations provided no evidence that any part of its construction was of stone. The boulder and clay ridge on which the castle was built was separated out into its main constituents, with the clay being used to build up the ramparts and clad walls, and the small boulders serving to pack out post holes for the wooden buildings and the surrounding palisades.

Reconstruction of Hen Domen

During the 30-year excavation at Hen Domen, archaeological evidence revealed that timber castles could be permanent, substantial fortifications with impressive accommodation. According to Higham and Barker (2004), timber castles were not "temporary, second-rate erections, easily overcome and replaced in stone as soon as possible." As they observe, this castle dominated its landscape for two centuries and was rebuilt, always in timber (and clay), several times. "The earthworks of these monuments are only a pale reflection of their true character." In 1223, after Henry III ordered the construction of a new Montgomery Castle—in stone—Hen Domen became a purely military outpost for the next 50 years.

Hen Domen during the 11th century

Hen Domen was held by Montgomery's sons until a failed revolt against Henry I, after which it came into the hands of a family of lesser lords, the de Boulers, who held it until 1207. During their century-long tenure, Hen Domen became an important domestic and administrative center. Excavations have produced evidence of its defenses and its bailey, crowded with domestic buildings.

The Wooden Giant

Stafford Castle, Staffordshire

Stafford Castle is not actually in the town of Stafford, but lies a mile and half to the west on a natural clay ridge. It is, therefore, unlikely to be the castle that William the Conqueror is reported to have built in the town in 1070 as he returned from the north of England, having completed a ruthless campaign to extinguish native resistance to his rule (his notorious "Harrying of the North").

The likeliest builder of Stafford Castle is Robert de Tosny (or Toeni), a Norman knight in the service of the Conqueror. He had demonstrably obtained land in Staffordshire before 1072 and, by the time of the Domesday Survey of 1086, he had become the single greatest landowner in the county (and also probably its sheriff). Unlike Roger de Montgomery, who named his principal seat in England after himself, Tosny adopted the identity of his new home, and henceforth styled himself Robert of Stafford. A second interesting contrast is that of size: compared with Montgomery's fairly humble castle at Hen Domen, Stafford Castle is massive. Recent extensive excavations have suggested that its earthworks must once have been covered in substantial timber buildings, reminding us that there was nothing low status or impermanent about castles made of wood.

The first garrison
A wooden fort was erected at Stafford as a garrison from which Robert and some of his knights could consolidate control over the Normans' newly acquired territory. Thereafter Robert also completed a residence and an extensive range of buildings befitting the size and ranking of his household. His success and loyalty were further recognized by William who granted him further holdings in seven counties. As Robert I of Stafford he was listed in the Domesday Book (1086) as a major landholder.

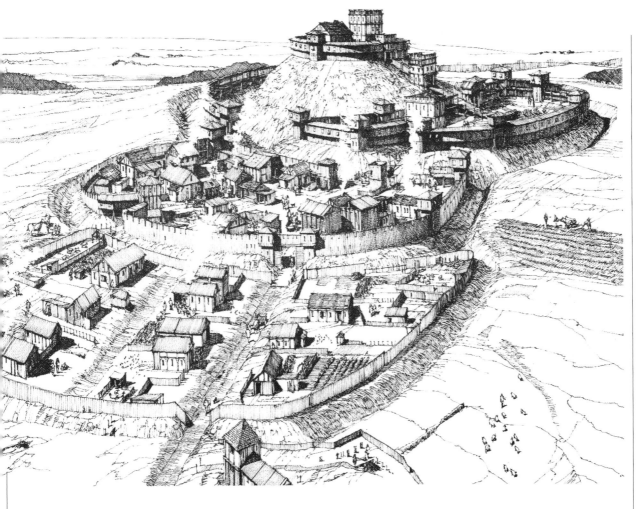

◄

English origins

The site of Stafford castle may have been a Saxon *burh*, established by Aethelfleda, the daughter of Alfred the Great. "Staethford," from which Stafford is derived, is a Saxon name meaning "fortified town at a place where a water course can be forded or crossed." It is likely that the extensive earthworks at Stafford were built using the Saxons as slave labor. Many of these massive earthworks are still visible and cover an area of more than 10 acres (4 ha).

Reconstruction of Stafford in ca. 1100

This reconstruction shows Stafford to be of significant size, a clear indication of the nature and importance of its site. It had several key defenses: first, the wooden tower that once topped a large, oval motte. Below it was a heavily defended inner bailey, beyond which was a less-fortified outer bailey. A third enclosure, roughly rectilinear, contained a fortified settlement.

The Wooden Giant

The inner bailey
Based on evidence from other excavations it is believed that the formidable earthworks at Stafford supported equally massive timber defenses and that, over time, the original site developed into a small, walled town with a sizeable population.

Outer bailey approach
The approach from the village to the outer bailey was via a further ring of timber walls.

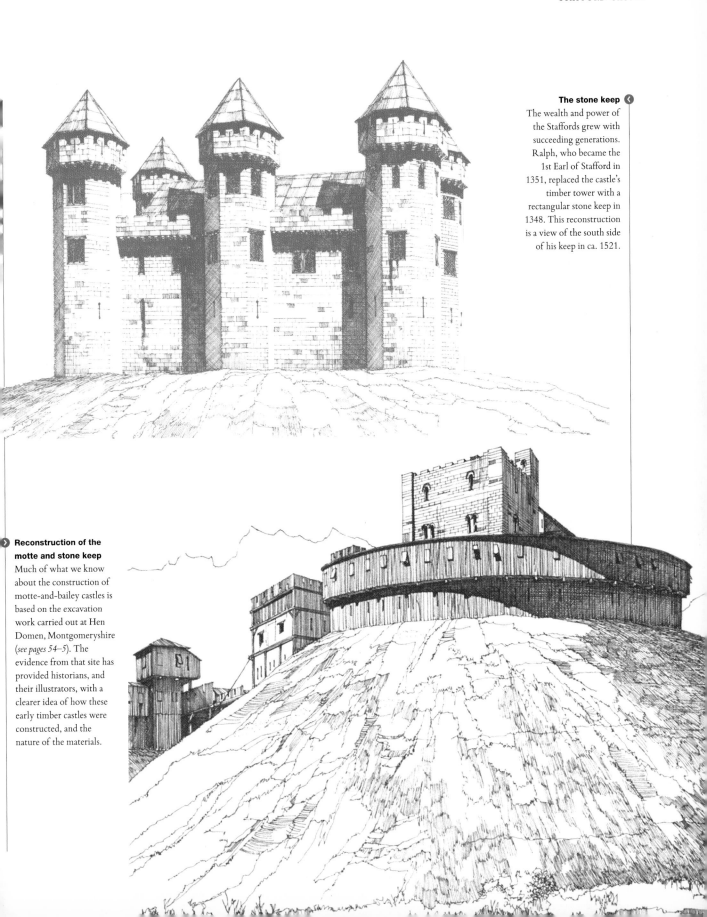

The stone keep
The wealth and power of
the Staffords grew with
succeeding generations.
Ralph, who became the
1st Earl of Stafford in
1351, replaced the castle's
timber tower with a
rectangular stone keep in
1348. This reconstruction
is a view of the south side
of his keep in ca. 1521.

**Reconstruction of the
motte and stone keep**
Much of what we know
about the construction of
motte-and-bailey castles is
based on the excavation
work carried out at Hen
Domen, Montgomeryshire
(*see pages 54–5*). The
evidence from that site has
provided historians, and
their illustrators, with a
clearer idea of how these
early timber castles were
constructed, and the
nature of the materials.

Rebuilding in Stone

Lewes Castle, Sussex

Perhaps the most striking thing about Lewes Castle is that it has not one motte, but two (a distinction it shares with only one other English castle, Lincoln). The larger motte at Lewes, composed mainly of chalk blocks, is believed to have been raised on an existing mound that dates back to prehistoric times.

Lewes also serves as a fine example of a motte-and-bailey castle that was rebuilt in stone at an early date. The surviving walls around the bailey self-evidently follow lines established by the original wooden palisades. This is also true of the walls on the top of the mottes, which give rise to a building dubbed by modern historians as "the shell keep."

The castle was established very soon after 1066 by William de Warenne, one of the Conqueror's closest companions, and hence first in line when it came to rewards. Warenne also obtained lands in many other English counties, and built castles at Reigate (Surrey), Castle Acre (Norfolk), Conisbrough and Sandal (both Yorkshire). Lewes was rebuilt in stone by his descendants in either the late 11th or early 12th century, and adapted and improved down to the death of the last of his family in the 14th century.

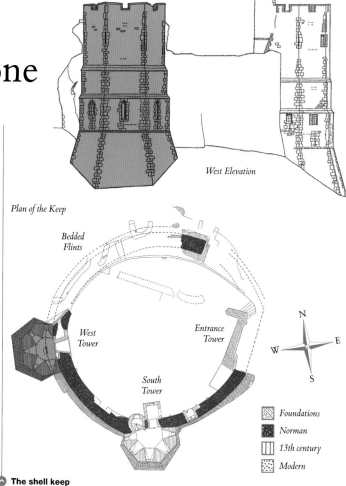

West Elevation

Plan of the Keep

Bedded Flints

West Tower

Entrance Tower

South Tower

Foundations

Norman

13th century

Modern

The shell keep
A plan and view (above) and cross-section (top) of the remains of the elliptical shell keep at Lewes, which stills sits atop the western mound of the castle. According to the architect Walter H. Godfrey, the originator of these drawings, the projecting towers were added in the 13th century when such features were in fashion. He says: "There is no evidence of a third tower to the north, but there was probably an entrance tower of some sort to protect the stairway on the east."

Plan view of the castle layout
No trace remains of the shell keep on the right, though the mound, now named Brack Mount, is extant. Portions of the curtain wall also remain. The central space in the bailey, once used for jousting and archery, was later turned, in the 18th century, into a bowling green, which is still in use. No evidence exists of the domestic buildings of the castle.

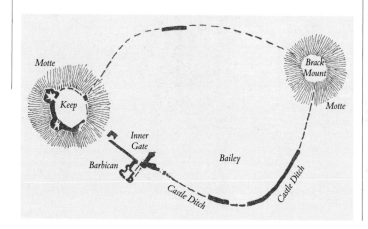

Motte

Brack Mount

Keep

Motte

Inner Gate

Bailey

Barbican

Castle Ditch

Castle Ditch

Prospect from the southwest

This 18th-century view shows the main mound of Lewes castle, topped by the remains of the shell keep with towers. The nature of the building in ruins in the foreground is unknown and was demolished in ca. 1780.

The double-motte castle

This artist's reconstruction of Lewes Castle must date to around the 14th century as the barbican stands proud as an impressive entrance to the castle proper. The unusual and immediately distinctive appearance of the castle's twin mottes is apparent and striking.

William's Stronghold

The Tower of London

In December 1066, two months after the Battle of Hastings, the citizens of London finally submitted to the superior might of William the Conqueror. In advance of his coronation on Christmas Day, the king-to-be sent a force of Normans into the city with instructions to build a fortress. This was the beginning of the Tower of London.

The key reason for constructing a castle in London was, of course, security—"a defense against the inconstancy of the numerous and hostile inhabitants," as William's contemporary biographer puts it. But London, then as now, was England's principal city, and therefore also demanded a grand statement about the permanence of Norman power. Accordingly, in the 1070s, building work began on a giant stone tower. William never lived to see it finished—work was ongoing during the reigns of his sons, William II and Henry I—but the result was astounding: the largest secular building in Britain since the days of the Romans. Its later history as a Tudor prison should not detract from the fact that the Tower was, in the words of one 12th-century writer, "a fortress-palace" (*arx palatina*).

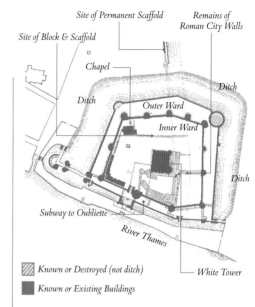

Site of Permanent Scaffold
Remains of Roman City Walls
Site of Block & Scaffold
Chapel
Ditch
Outer Ward
Ditch
Inner Ward
Ditch
Subway to Oubliette
River Thames
White Tower

▨ *Known or Destroyed (not ditch)*
■ *Known or Existing Buildings*

Norman castle, Roman walls
The entire site of the Tower of London encloses an area of almost 12 acres (5 ha). The initial phase of the building would have been some form of timber structure, enclosed by a ditch and defended by a timber palisade. However, there was no motte inside the bailey. Instead, William's Norman builders adapted their usual design to take advantage of their chosen site. The castle was built onto the southeast corner of the existing Roman town walls, which are indicated in this plan, dated 1907. These defenses, along with the River Thames, provided excellent protection.

The castle layout in the 14th century
The site of the Tower of London underwent several phases of expansion and, by the 14th century, had evolved into a complex of buildings set within two concentric rings of fortification, surrounded by a moat. Kentish ragstone and local mudstone provided the main building material with the details in the facing of the Tower being picked out in limestone, imported from Caen in Normandy. Little of the French limestone survives; it was replaced by Portland stone in the 17th and 18th centuries.

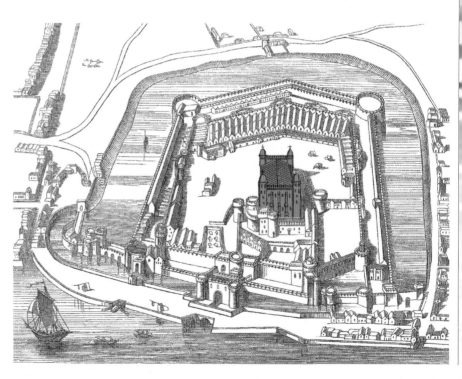

The Keep

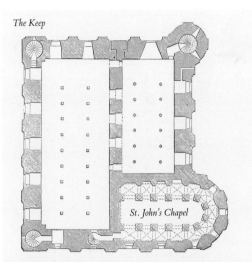

St. John's Chapel

The Keep, Upper Stage

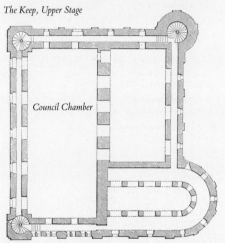

Council Chamber

Floor plans of the keep

Originally the keep had three stories, comprising a basement (or undercroft) used for storage, an entrance level, and an upper floor. Each story was divided into three chambers, the largest in the west, a smaller one in the northeast, and the chapel taking up the entrance and upper floors of the southeast.

The two western corners of the building have square towers, while to the northeast a round tower contains a spiral staircase. The semicircular projection at the southeast corner accommodates the apse of the chapel.

Norman London's tallest tower

The White Tower is a massive construction, 90 ft (27 m) high and 118 ft (36 m) by 107 ft (33 m) across. The thickness of the walls varies from 15 ft (4.5 m) at the base to almost 11 ft (3 m) in the upper parts. The entrance, as is usual in Norman keeps, was at second-floor level, in this case on the south face, and accessed via a wooden staircase that could be removed in the event of an attack. Above the battlements rise four turrets; three of them are square, but the one on the northeast is circular. This fourth turret once contained the first Royal observatory.

Prisoners in the Tower

It was in the White Tower that the young Princes in the Tower, Edward V and Richard, Duke of York, were held during the late 15th century. Over the next 200 years many disgraced figures were also held here, including Elizabeth I before she became queen. The phrase "sent to the Tower" entered the language and it developed a black reputation as a place of death and execution.

In fact, the Tower of London never had a permanent torture chamber and up until the 20th century only seven people were actually executed at the Tower; most met their end on nearby Tower Hill (where 112 executions were carried out over a 400-year period). During the two World Wars, the Tower served again as a prison and 12 men found guilty of espionage were executed within its walls.

Imperial Grandeur

Colchester Castle, Essex

The only castle built by William the Conqueror that can compete with the Tower of London is Colchester, in Essex. Begun around the same time as the Tower, possibly by the same builder, and taking a similarly long time to construct, Colchester is in some respects the greater of the two, measuring at base one and a half times the size of its London cousin.

The reason for the impressive scale is that, a thousand years earlier, Colchester had been the capital of Roman Britain, and William's castle is constructed over the vaulted remains of the Roman Temple of Claudius. It also, like the Tower of London, incorporated salvaged Roman stones in its construction, which was obviously economical, but at the same time ideological: the Normans were consciously associating themselves with the imperial grandeur of the past, and proclaiming themselves the Romans' worthy successors.

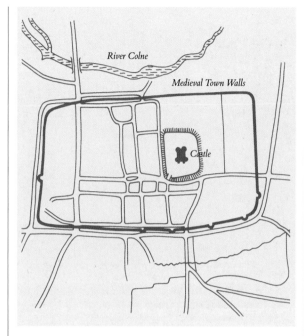

Castle keep

Colchester Castle's 11th-century keep, built on the vaults of a Roman temple, was the dominant landmark in the medieval city. Clearly, the Normans were determined to make their mark on a location of great significance to the English. Part of the medieval town walls and the ruins of one of its gates are still evident.

Reconstruction

Much of the upper part of the original castle was pulled down to sell off as building material in the town. In 1726, the building was bought by Charles Gray (then Member of Parliament for Colchester) who restored it and added an Italianate façade and tower, believing (erroneously) that he was restoring a Roman building. The round cupola, another feature that dates from the time of Gray's ownership, has replaced one of the original square towers.

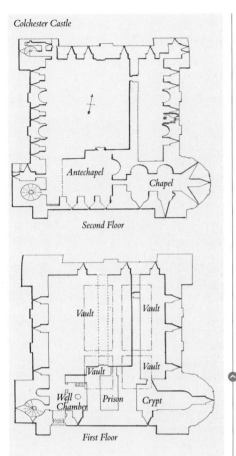

Colchester Castle

Antechapel

Chapel

Second Floor

Vault

Vault

Vault

Vault

Well Chamber

Prison

Crypt

First Floor

Architectural clues

Impressive outer bailey walls surround the great keep. It is thought that the entire castle was built using materials from the earlier Roman temple on the site, which was destroyed by Queen Boudica in ca. 60 CE. The county of Essex has little natural stone and the castle builders would have reused whatever was available to them. The arched windows in the square tower were not part of the original, Norman design, which would have taken the form of narrow slits as shown on the flanking wall.

Clockwise staircase

With a diameter of 16 ft (4.5 m), the spiral stone staircase of Colchester's keep is the largest of any castle in Britain. Its ascending stairs spiral clockwise, a defensive design feature that ensured that would-be attackers mounting the stairs had no space to swing their swords, giving the advantage to those defending the stairs.

A question of height

A lively and continuing archaeological debate concerns the original height of Colchester Castle. According to Philip Crummy of the Colchester Archaeological Trust: "Opinion is divided about how much has been removed from the top of the castle. Broadly, there are three different views: that it had another two stories, one story, or very little apart from towers and battlements. Each view can be justified, and none can claim proof."

The Norman Skyscraper

Rochester Castle, Kent

Rochester in Kent was yet another Roman town in which the Normans planted a castle. Probably established soon after the Conquest, it is first mentioned by the Anglo-Saxon Chronicle under the year 1088, where it is identified as the property of William the Conqueror's notorious half-brother, Odo of Bayeux. At this time it had neither motte nor keep, but its original wooden walls were rebuilt in stone by Gundulf, Bishop of Rochester (*see box*).

Forty years on, however, Rochester acquired a truly superlative great tower. Soaring to 125 feet (38 meters), it remains the tallest building of its type in Western Europe. Begun around 1127 by William of Corbeil, Archbishop of Canterbury (1123-36), it must have taken at least a decade to complete. The construction of a tower was a condition imposed on the archbishop by King Henry I when he had granted him the castle.

This unusual arrangement became crucially important when King John famously fell out with his barons in 1215 (*see pages 72–3*, "The Siege of Hedingham"), for the archbishop was on the side of the rebels and allowed them to seize the castle. The siege that followed was one of the most bitter England had ever seen, concluding only when the king undermined and partially collapsed the keep. Repaired in the reign of John's son, Henry III, the castle today still bears the visible scars of this spectacular struggle.

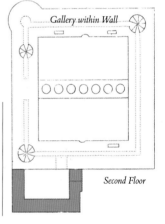

Southeast tower

Staircase

Keep

Staircase

Staircase

Staircase

Forebuilding

First Floor

> **Evolving design**
> Following King John's death in October 1216 the southeast corner tower was rebuilt in the latest defensive style, as a cylindrical tower. This offered better protection than the square design of the original towers. The walls of the keep were of sufficient thickness for several spiral staircases and passageways or galleries to be built within. These passages are still accessible today.

Gallery within Wall

Second Floor

> **Roman remains**
> Rochester's keep, built of Kentish ragstone, took some 10–15 years to build. It stands adjacent to Rochester Cathedral. The Roman city wall was reused as a foundation for the south wall of the new building.

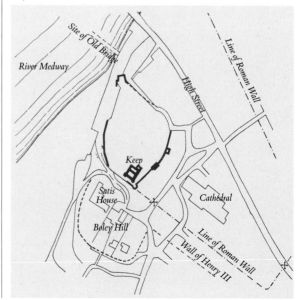

Site of Old Bridge

River Medway

Line of Roman Wall

High Street

Keep

Satis House

Cathedral

Boley Hill

Line of Roman Wall

Wall of Henry III

Gundulf of Rochester

Gundulf was a Norman monk who came to England in 1070. He was appointed Bishop of Rochester in 1077, where he soon began reconstructing the derelict church. William I, having identified his architectural and building skills, paid Gundulf to act as principal overseer and surveyor on the construction of the White Tower. Gundulf is also believed to be responsible for the construction of Colchester Castle due to its similarity in plan and design to the White Tower. He was responsible for the construction of the stone curtain walls at Rochester in the late 11th century around the original castle and later built the town's cathedral and priory. Gundulf died in 1108 and his statue adorns the cathedral's west door.

Strategic location

Guarding a key crossing point on the River Medway and affording its incumbents an uninterrupted view across the estuary in times of threat, Rochester Castle is a fine example of Norman military architecture. However, Crown surveys reveal that it was beginning to collapse in the 14th century and attempts by Richard III in the following century could not halt its decline.

Keep

Forebuilding

The keep and forebuildng

Access to the keep itself was via the forebuilding, the antechamber that served as an additional defense in that the entrance was located on the second floor. The original ramp is still in evidence, although the floors and roof of the keep are gone.

The Baronial Hall Keep

Castle Rising, Norfolk

Castle Rising in Norfolk began life as a baronial castle (as opposed to a royal one) and, like many towers of its type, it seems to have been built to advertise the newly elevated status of its owner. The man in question was William d'Aubigny, a Norman baron who rose by marrying the widow of King Henry I at some time between 1138 and 1139, at which point he was also created Earl of Arundel. Work at Rising probably began soon after.

Compared with the great towers that came before it, Castle Rising has a somewhat more homely feel. Unusually, for example, it incorporates a kitchen within the keep itself, which in turn suggests that its other rooms may have served the kind of domestic functions which in other castles were carried out in the bailey. Yet it remains a large and impressive building. It has close affinities with the royal keep at nearby Norwich, built slightly earlier, and may therefore have been worked on by the same team of masons. Although it was built during the civil war of King Stephen's reign (1135–54), the decorative stonework known as blind arcading on the exterior at Rising (*see below*), and the grandeur of its main staircase (*see opposite*), not to mention the complete absence of arrowloops, serve to remind us that there was more to life for Norman aristocrats than a ceaseless round of fighting.

19th-century notes
In 1884 the historian G. T. Clark was able to observe: "The Keep is a very noble example of the rectangular Norman type. Not that its area, still less its height, would place it in the first rank, but to considerable dimensions it adds a degree of ornament rarely bestowed upon military buildings, and though a ruin, its parts are unusually well preserved, and excellent both in materials and workmanship."
Today, much of the roof is missing although some sections of the castle are in remarkably good condition, including, on the second floor, the small chapel.

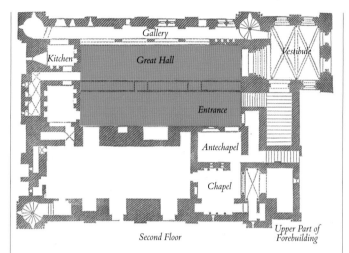

Gallery

Kitchen

Great Hall

Vestibule

Entrance

Antechapel

Chapel

Upper Part of
Forebuilding

Second Floor

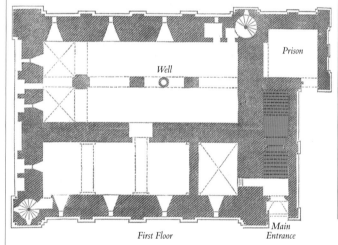

Well

Prison

First Floor

Main
Entrance

Plan of the hall keep

It is likely the stone rectangular keep
replaced an earlier wooden structure,
possibly a hall. The keep provided living
accommodation on three levels. Most of
the principal rooms, including the great
hall, were on the second floor. Both the
hall and chapel were ornately decorated
and included carved Norman arches,
columns, and paintings. The first floor,
apart from its prison and well, was
mainly used for storage purposes.
The castle has served as a hunting
lodge, a royal residence, and, most
notoriously, as the home of exile of
Queen Isabella, daughter of the king
of France and wife of Edward II. She
was exiled for her part in conspiring
to murder Edward. Ironically, she
developed a great fondness for the place.

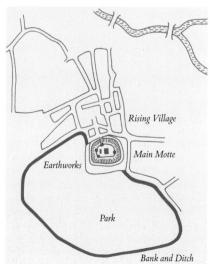

Rising Village

Earthworks

Main Motte

Park

Bank and Ditch

Impressive earthworks

Castle Rising was
probably modeled on
Norwich Castle, which
had a similarly huge
motte. Entry to the
central motte was from
the east, where a road
crossed the formidable
ditch by bridge. The
heavily defended keep,
originally ringed by walls
and towers, stands at the
center of massive, artificial
earthworks that pre-date
William d'Aubigny. Such
massive earthworks
ensured that surprise
attack by an enemy was
very unlikely.

Imposing stairs

Formal access was via
the forebuilding, which
contained two broad
flights of steps that
provide the means to
make a grand,
ceremonial entrance.

The Earl's New Tower

Hedingham Castle, Essex

Just as William d'Aubigny was proclaiming his new-found status at Castle Rising (*see pages 68–9*), another Norman magnate was doing exactly the same at Hedingham in Essex. Aubrey de Vere was one of many men who rose at the start of Stephen's reign as the King tried to outbid his rival, Matilda, in their struggle for political support. After the death of his namesake father in 1141, Aubrey was created Earl of Oxford, and construction of the great tower at his castle at Hedingham is reckoned to have been started soon after to mark this occasion.

Although smaller than the giant keep at Rochester, it is architecturally similar, and may therefore have been designed by the same person. Apart from its massive internal arch (*see opposite page*), the tower's most notable feature is its top floor, which is a 15th- or 16th-century conversion. Originally, this floor was a dummy: the external walls simply concealed a countersunk roof. While the desire for additional height might have been down to defensive concerns, it speaks more eloquently of the anxiety of a newly ennobled man to announce how high he had risen.

Hedingham's tower-keep
The four-story keep is over 110 ft (33 m) high with walls 12 ft (3.5 m) thick. These are constructed from flint rubble, bound with lime mortar, and faced with Barnack stone, a very high-quality limestone from the Barnack quarry near Stamford, Northamptonshire, and a valuable and expensive building material of the time. This was sculpted into rectangular blocks with square edges and smooth faces—a form of construction known as ashlar masonry. Very few Norman barons could afford this building technique; in most other castles, cut stone was only used around doors and windows.

Keep floor plans

The castle was built as a stronghold for the de Vere family. Its walls are uniformly 12 ft (3.5 m) thick on three faces, those on the eastern side are 13 ft (4 m). This is believed to be either to keep out the cold easterly winds that are common in this part of the country or to be for extra protection against a possible attack coming from the gatehouse side of the keep. A spiral stone staircase climbs up the northwest tower, originally built in stone, and replaced by bricks in the 16th century.

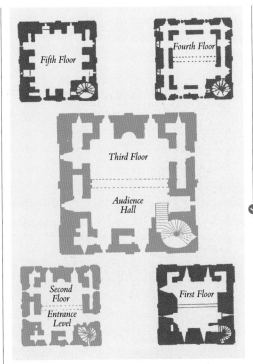

Layout of the castle

An artist's impression of the castle at the time the keep was built. A large ringwork ditch cut into a natural spur surrounds two raised baileys which are linked by a bridge. The artist exaggerated: there is no motte at Hedingham, though the keep and other buildings in the inner bailey did have a stone curtain wall. The larger outer bailey on a lower mound is similarly fortified, with a gatehouse providing the access point to the castle complex. The medieval town of Castle Hedingham was subsequently built on the southwestern side of the outer bailey.

Ceremonial hall

The keep's finest interior feature is the remarkable hall, which is spanned by the largest Norman arch in Europe—28 ft (8.5 m) in diameter. The hall extends upward from the second to the third floor, where a gallery, tunneled through the thick walls, runs around the central space. Such a grand space, endowed with so many windows, may have been used for ceremonial purposes.

The Siege of Hedingham

A medieval dynasty

Medieval magnates had to produce male heirs to perpetuate their power, and most managed a run of three or four generations. The record of the de Veres, who came with the Conqueror to England in 1066 and lasted until the early 18th century, is therefore a remarkable dynastic achievement, particularly in light of their participation in the sanguinary battles of Crecy, Poitiers, Agincourt, and Bosworth.

In 1216 Robert de Vere (son of Hedingham's builder, Aubrey) found himself and his castle facing the wrath of King John. The previous year Robert had joined the rebellion against the king, and had been one of the 25 men responsible for holding him to his promises in the Magna Carta. When John repudiated the Charter, the rebels offered the English crown to Louis, the son of the king of France, and some French troops were holding nearby Colchester at the start of 1216. At that point, however, John moved into Essex, retaking Colchester and laying siege to Hedingham, which surrendered after just three days. When Louis finally arrived in person in 1217 he retook the castle, but by this stage John was dead and support had swung behind his son, the nine-year-old Henry III. Earl Robert was returned to favor and his castle and lands were restored. Such was the luck that enabled the de Vere family to survive for five and a half centuries.

Mobile defenses

Archers besieging a castle employed wheeled shields or mantlets of wood and wickerwork. Illustrated here by Eugène Viollet-le-Duc (*see pages 144–45*), they had been used since ancient times. They offered protection from archers on the castle walls and could be staked together to form a barrier. Cylindrical cages or *gabions* filled with earth were also used to protect miners digging beneath a castle tower.

Wooden Mantlets

Wickerwork Mantlets

Catapult

Wheeled bridges, siege towers, and various forms of catapult were among the medieval warrior's armory. Castle attackers even attempted biological warfare against the occupants, using catapults to hurl the corpses of horses over the walls to spread both fear and disease among the troops inside.

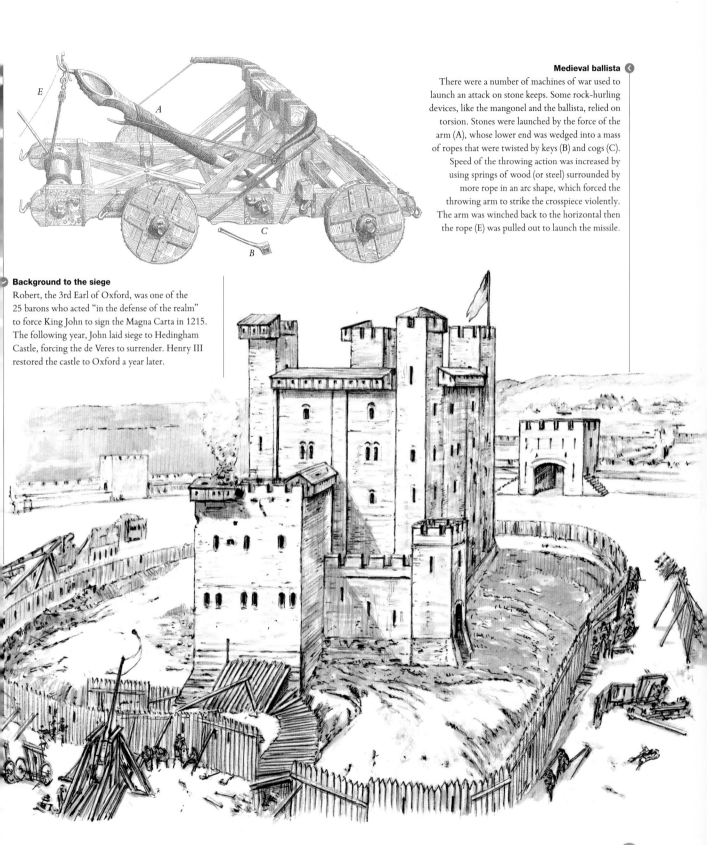

Medieval ballista

There were a number of machines of war used to launch an attack on stone keeps. Some rock-hurling devices, like the mangonel and the ballista, relied on torsion. Stones were launched by the force of the arm (A), whose lower end was wedged into a mass of ropes that were twisted by keys (B) and cogs (C). Speed of the throwing action was increased by using springs of wood (or steel) surrounded by more rope in an arc shape, which forced the throwing arm to strike the crosspiece violently. The arm was winched back to the horizontal then the rope (E) was pulled out to launch the missile.

Background to the siege

Robert, the 3rd Earl of Oxford, was one of the 25 barons who acted "in the defense of the realm" to force King John to sign the Magna Carta in 1215. The following year, John laid siege to Hedingham Castle, forcing the de Veres to surrender. Henry III restored the castle to Oxford a year later.

The Innovative Castle

Conisbrough Castle, Yorkshire

By the second half of the 12th century, great towers were becoming ever more architecturally exuberant. One famous example is the whimsical keep built in the 1160s by King Henry II (1154–89) on the Suffolk coast at Orford. Another is the tower built a decade or so later at Conisbrough by the king's illegitimate brother, Hamelin. Conisbrough had been established soon after the Norman Conquest by William de Warenne (*see page 60*, Lewes). It had come to Hamelin, probably in 1164, by virtue of his marriage to Warenne's great-granddaughter, Isabel, along with the rest of the Warenne inheritance and the title of Earl of Surrey.

Henry's tower at Orford is polygonal, with round rooms on the inside, and is supported on the outside by three great buttressing towers. Hamelin's keep at Conisbrough has similar round rooms and six exterior buttresses, while its exterior is completely cylindrical.

Historians were once inclined to interpret these features as experiments in military science, intended either to deflect missiles or to provide more angles from which to launch them. More recently, Orford has been shown to be something altogether different: a playful exercise in geometry. Conisbrough would seem to be a building in much the same mold. Such towers, because of the thickness of their walls, had an inherent resilience, and therefore were of military value. But they were also homes for the super-rich, designed by masons who prized inventiveness for its own sake.

> **The five-story stone keep**
> Conisbrough's keep stands 90 ft (27 m) tall and has walls 15 ft (4.5 m) thick built of high-quality limestone ashlar blocks. Its few windows are relatively small and positioned high in the walls. Such a formidably strong keep was able to withstand attack by men or by the hurled missiles of the war machines and siege engines of the time.

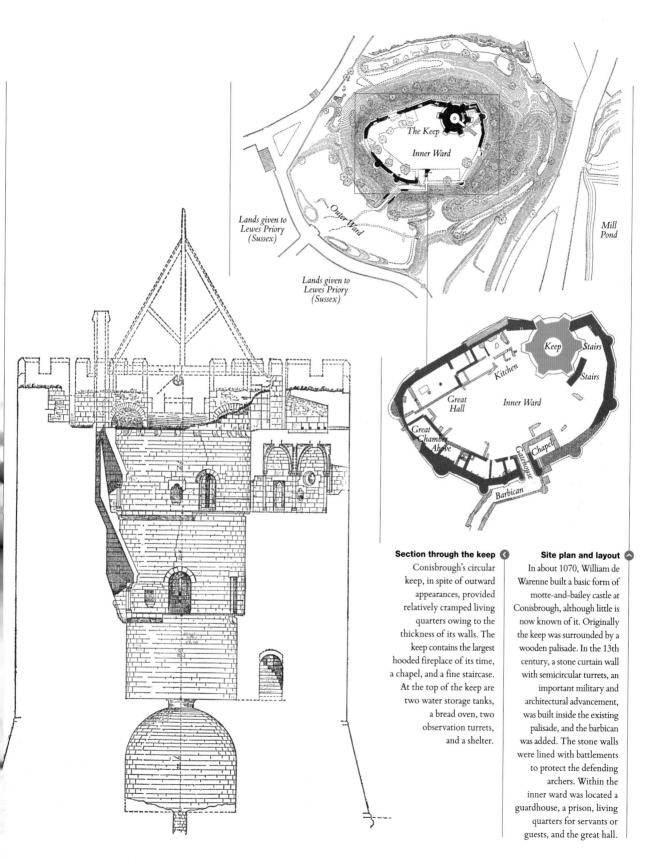

*Lands given to
Lewes Priory
(Sussex)*

The Keep

Inner Ward

Outer Ward

Mill
Pond

*Lands given to
Lewes Priory
(Sussex)*

Keep   Stairs

Kitchen   Stairs

Great
Hall

Inner Ward

Great
Chamber
Above

Gatehouse   Chapel

Barbican

Section through the keep

Conisbrough's circular
keep, in spite of outward
appearances, provided
relatively cramped living
quarters owing to the
thickness of its walls. The
keep contains the largest
hooded fireplace of its time,
a chapel, and a fine staircase.
At the top of the keep are
two water storage tanks,
a bread oven, two
observation turrets,
and a shelter.

Site plan and layout

In about 1070, William de
Warenne built a basic form of
motte-and-bailey castle at
Conisbrough, although little is
now known of it. Originally
the keep was surrounded by a
wooden palisade. In the 13th
century, a stone curtain wall
with semicircular turrets, an
important military and
architectural advancement,
was built inside the existing
palisade, and the barbican
was added. The stone walls
were lined with battlements
to protect the defending
archers. Within the
inner ward was located a
guardhouse, a prison, living
quarters for servants or
guests, and the great hall.

The Innovative Castle

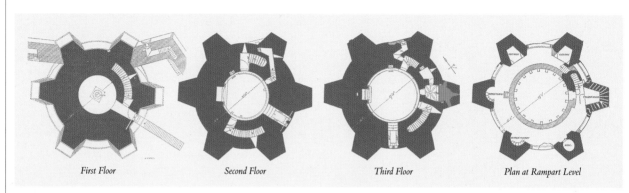

First Floor   *Second Floor*   *Third Floor*   *Plan at Rampart Level*

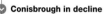

Conisbrough in decline

The fact that this remarkable keep survived the English Civil War of the 17th century, when numerous castles were deliberately damaged to prevent their military use, was due mainly to the fact that the south wall had collapsed in the 1530s, rendering the castle indefensible. It was decommissioned shortly after and, as a result, all the usable timber and lead was stripped from the roof, further accelerating its decline. Thereafter, the keep was not restored until the mid-1990s, when a new wooden roof was added and two floors were rebuilt.

Conisbrough's floor plans

Conisbrough's circular keep was built in advance of the fashionable movement to replace rectangular keeps with round ones. In addition, it was reinforced with a ring of wedge-shaped buttresses, which may have provided a lofty platform for archers but also served other purposes. Four of them are hollow and are believed to have housed a pigeon loft, an oven, and water cisterns. The fourth contained a tiny chapel.

The living quarters
Despite its impressive fireplaces, the keep was hardly agreeable as a permanent dwelling owing to constant drafts. The last person thought to have lived here was Maud, Countess of Cambridge, grandmother of Edward IV, who died here in 1446.

Private chapel
Each story in Conisbrough's keep consists of one single large room but of the six buttresses the four that were hollow contained side chambers. Within the fourth of these was a beautifully arched chapel that led off the lord's great chamber.

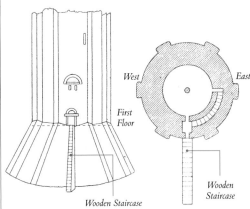

West

East

First
Floor

Wooden Staircase

Wooden
Staircase

Wooden staircase
The single entrance to the keep is at first-floor level—a common feature of Norman keeps. Access was via a wooden staircase, which could be burned by the occupants in times of siege to ensure their attackers had no means of entry.

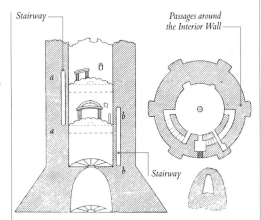

Stairway

Passages around
the Interior Wall

a

a

b

b

Stairway

Unconventional stairways
Unusually, Conisbrough has no spiral staircases. The upper stories are approached only by entering each main room to ascend to the next level by a single stairway set in the keep's immensely thick walls (shown above by the lines a–a and b–b. Originally there may have been passages around the interior circular walls of each room to protect the occupants' privacy.

Royal Hospitality

Dover Castle, Kent

The famous White Cliffs of Dover have long been defended. The headland on which Dover Castle now stands had first been fortified during the Iron Age, and subsequent ages also left their mark. Shortly after the Battle of Hastings in 1066, William the Conqueror seized the existing fortress and, in the words of his biographer, "spent eight days adding the fortifications that it lacked."

The castle as it appears today began with Henry II, who in 1179–89 constructed a giant keep, reminiscent, no doubt intentionally, of the Tower of London, ringed with walls. Like the Tower, it is a massive building, virtually impregnable, and the circuit of walls, studded with towers, made it eminently defensible.

Yet at the time of construction, defense of the Straits was probably not the King's primary concern. In 1170, Henry II had notoriously, if inadvertently, caused the murder of his friend, Thomas Becket, and immediately the archbishop's tomb at Canterbury became a destination for European pilgrims. In 1179 the King of France himself arrived at Dover and an embarrassed Henry had nowhere to accommodate him. A few months later, building work on the new castle began, so future royal guests could be received more hospitably.

Strategic position

The clifftop overlooking the narrow Straits of Dover was recognized for its defensive significance before the Norman invasion. Earthworks that do not appear to match the medieval stone castle suggest that, prior to the Roman invasion in 43 CE, the site may have been an Iron Age hill fort. The Romans located a lighthouse (*pharos*) here and the remains of this and an Anglo-Saxon church lie within the castle's confines.

The Great Keep

Dover's keep is on three levels, accessed by spiral staircases in its corner turrets. The entrance to the keep is protected by the biggest forebuilding of its day. A well-chamber opens into the forebuilding—a distinct advantage during times of siege. Three towers provide cover for the open stairs that lead into the keep itself. The keep has chambers at every level and, at the top, has a gallery which includes a prison cell. The vaulting in the second-floor gallery is brickwork, and not original.

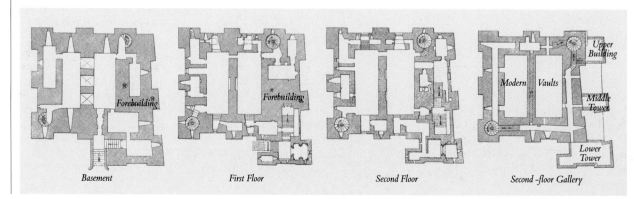

Basement   First Floor   Second Floor   Second-floor Gallery

Defensive role

Dover possesses one of Britain's most famous and iconic keeps, seen at its uncompromising best on the promontory overlooking the Straits of Dover. It has played a prominent role in England's history since the Norman invasions in the 11th century. Remarkably it retained a garrison until 1958, a span of almost 900 years of use matched only by Windsor Castle and the Tower of London.

Concentric fortifications

In the 1170s and 80s, Henry II's military engineer transformed the site. Its central feature was a massive stone keep, thought to have been one of the strongest of the century. It stands almost 95 ft (29 m) tall with walls that are up to 21 ft (6.5 m) thick at their base. An encircling wall with 14 open-backed flanking towers protected the inner bailey. Despite a breach in defense made by the French during the siege of 1216, Dover did not fall.

THEN & NOW

A Windsor Residence

Windsor Castle, Berkshire

Windsor Castle is the largest inhabited castle in the world and the longest occupied palace in Europe. It was founded at an unknown date by William the Conqueror (1066–87) to guard a strategically important stretch of the River Thames. Its elongated design—a central motte with two flanking baileys —was the Normans' solution to building on a long ridge with a commanding view of the river.

In area the castle covers some 26 acres (11 hectares) with three separate wards or courts. Its motte is 50 feet (15 meters) high, made primarily of chalk, and was originally topped by a wooden fortress. During the reign of Henry II, the original fortress was replaced by a stone keep, known as the Round Tower, which, along with the original outer wall, dates from 1170. Today, Windsor is one of Her Majesty the Queen's official residences.

Map of Windsor by John Norden, 1607

The fortifications of Windsor were expanded by both Henry I and Henry II, but it was Edward III in the 14th century who succeeded in making it England's most costly secular building project of the entire Middle Ages. It was Edward who began building the remarkable St. George's Chapel in the Lower Ward (completed by Henry VIII in 1528) and a suite of royal apartments in the Upper Ward. In the Tudor period Henry VIII made increasing use of Windsor as a royal court and Elizabeth I added the famous North Terrace. In 1607, James I commissioned topographer John Norden to create several bird's-eye views of the Royal Parks, including one of Windsor Castle itself. Norden compiled these into his *Description of the Honour of Windsor*, dedicated to James I. In 1612, the king made Norden surveyor of the royal castles.

Modern splendor

The medieval structures that form the skeleton outline of the castle were expanded and elaborated by successive monarchs to create the remarkable royal residence of today. Windsor is no longer a medieval castle but a modern palace. St. George's Chapel contains the tombs of 10 sovereigns, among them Henry VIII and his wife Jane Seymour, Charles I (who was also held prisoner during the English Civil War), Elizabeth the Queen Mother, and her husband George VI.

IF THERE WAS A MAJOR CHANGE in castle-building in western Europe during the Middle Ages, it occurred around the year 1200, when the technology of attack caught up with that of defense. With the advent of the throwing machines known as trebuchets, owners of great stone towers no longer felt quite so invulnerable. After the siege of Rochester in 1215, according to one contemporary chronicler, "few dared put their trust in castles."

CHAPTER 4

Late British Medieval Castles, 1200–1500

But castle builders fought back with new ideas of their own. Rather than trusting to a single tall tower, they invested in great circuits of stone walls. These walls were studded with multiple towers, typically round rather than square, and their gatehouses were enlarged and elaborated. Typical also was the trend toward multiple lines of defense: moats, ditches, and walls-within-walls, creating the effect of "concentricity." The result, by the late 13th century, was some of the greatest and most redoubtable buildings ever created.

Conventional wisdom once held that the age of castles was ended by the coming of guns and gunpowder and in Europe, perhaps, this theory may still hold some truth. But in the British Isles, and in England in particular, castles declined for different reasons. England was unusually peaceful in the later Middle Ages, so there was little need for aristocrats to invest in serious fortifications. What we increasingly see in the 14th and 15th centuries are castles built (or rebuilt) for what are clearly social reasons: to accommodate and entertain the grandest people in the grandest possible way. They may have moats, but only to magnify their towers; their portcullises, drawbridges, and battlements are intended to advertise aristocratic status rather than to deter military assaults. Windows grew larger, gardens grew grander: in England, at least, the castle grew old gracefully.

Bodiam Castle, Sussex, 1385
With its classic construction of four squat crenelated walls, set square, meeting at round corner towers and reflected in a formidable moat, Bodiam embodies the archetypal English castle. Fortified by Sir Edward Dallingridge in 1385, it does not actually feature a keep, the chambers being set into the defensive walls. Bodiam's military history does not live up to its appearance, its biography being one of a magnificent manor house rather than a monument to any notable sieges (see page 102).

ANATOMY OF
A Concentric Castle

The Defenses of Dover, Kent

The complex concentric castle, with its many levels and layers of defense, was the ultimate expression of medieval fortification. In the later medieval period, castles lost much of their original military function and became increasingly lavish palaces, ostentatious and luxurious homes for the richest and most powerful families of the land.

The example of the concentric structure shown here is Dover, which, through the efforts and vast expenditure of the great castle builder Henry II and his military engineer, and subsequently by his successors John and Henry III, was developed into one of the most powerful of all medieval castles.

What made Dover such an impregnable fortress was its concentric design: its great tower is surrounded by not one but two sets of curtain walls, set between high banks and deep ditches. The outer circuit, although not completed until John's reign (1199–1216) had been started during the 1180s, giving Dover a good claim to be the first concentric castle in Western Europe.

Strategic location
Dover is believed to have been the site of an Iron Age hill fort, selected for its command of land and sea. It was used by the Romans, who developed Dover as a port in the second half of the first century CE and erected a lighthouse there, one of three used to guide ships across the Channel. William the Conqueror likewise chose the highest point of the cliff as the location for his first earthwork castle following the Conquest.

The Great Keep
Square or rectangular keeps at the center of a castle are a feature of 12th-century military architecture. Dover's dates from the 1170s and 1180s and was part of Henry II's refortification of the site. Ultimately the keep was enclosed by two rings of walls and projecting towers. The inner bailey is protected by 14 square wall towers. Such powerful defenses ensured that the keep, although a formidable stronghold during a siege, could also serve as occasional royal residence.

An architectural triumph
None of the work undertaken during William the Conqueror's reign survives today. This reconstruction of Dover castle shows its likely appearance in the late 13th century after Henry III had completed the reconstruction begun by Henry II in the 12th century. The combination of its massive keep, concentric defenses, regularly spaced towers, and strategic cliff-top location from which both land and sea could be surveyed, earned it the epithet "the key of England."

Outworks
Outer defenses were often added if a particular aspect of the defenses proved vulnerable. In the case of Dover, this was its northern gate, which was almost breached during the siege of 1216–17. In its place a new tower was added, linked to a new outwork projecting from the enceinte to give a better command of the high ground.

Secret tunnels

Extending from the enceinte into the moat, a three-story tower, St. John's, was built to protect the weakest part of the castle after it was undermined during the siege. Bowmen in the tower could cover the outwork while defenders from the interior of the castle were able to access the spur undetected by means of an underground tunnel in order to launch a surprise attack.

Entrance and barbican

In the walls of the outer bailey Constable's Gateway replaced the north gate in the 1220s. It forms an elaborate entrance, protected by six round towers and originally linked by drawbridge to a barbican, another outwork, making it strongly defensible. At the rear of the gateway were quarters for the constable who was charged with supervising the safety of the castle.

Evolution of tower design

The towers constructed by Henry II's engineers were rectangular but later ones, added by Henry III in the 1220s, were D-shaped. This military advance meant their curved form was better able to withstand the stone-hurling siege engines, and defenders on the wall walks were more effectively covered by fire from the defendants within.

The Iron Ring

Subjugating North Wales

When Edward I of England invaded and conquered Wales in the late
13th century, castle-building in Britain reached its culmination. After
his first campaign (1276–77), Edward contained his rival, Llywelyn ap
Gruffudd, by building new castles at Rhuddlan, Flint, and Aberystwyth.
After his second campaign (1282–83), during which Llywelyn was
killed, the king cemented his conquest with even greater fortresses:
Harlech, Conwy, and Caernarfon. With the addition of Beaumaris
after a further Welsh revolt in 1294–95, Snowdonia was completely
encircled. Each castle was deliberately built on the coast, so they
could be kept supplied at all times by ships. As such, they
were virtually impossible to besiege, and all future attempts
to shake off English overlordship ultimately failed. Edward's
"Iron Ring" ensured that his conquest was never reversed.

Harlech, the enclosure fortress

At Harlech the twin-towered, three-story gatehouse was a
stronghold in itself. The gateway was protected by a succession of
obstacles, including three portcullises, and the sides of the passage
were flanked by guardrooms. The upper floors of the gatehouse
provided the main private accommodation, including a suite of
rooms for visiting dignitaries.

**Master James of St. George
(ca. 1230–ca. 1306–9)**
The "Iron Ring" was an extraordinary medieval
building project—the most ambitious, intensive,
and expensive of its day. Behind it was a master
mason, James of St. George, who was involved
in the majority of Welsh castles that Edward
built from scratch or reconstructed. Beaumaris
Castle was St. George's final work.

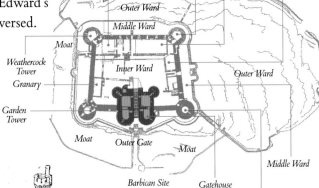

Harlech's concentric plan

The innate strength of the castle rock
and cliff face meant that only the east
side was open to possible attack. The
high curtain wall of the inner bailey is
defended on the angles by huge circular
towers and dominated by the massive
gatehouse. The lower outer curtain
wall is flanked by open bastions, and
twin-turreted gateways. At the foot
of the cliffs are two further gates: an
upper gate and a water gate defended
by two artillery platforms.

Conwy's construction

Constructing Conwy required the input of up to 1,500 craftsmen and laborers during intense periods of building activity between 1283 and 1287.

Conwy's location

The seemingly impregnable position selected for Conwy was a rocky outcrop overlooking the River Conwy estuary on the coast of North Wales. The fortifications comprise a castle and a town within a circle of walls that extend for over $1/2$ mile (1 km), studded with 21 towers and three gateways. The idea of a town and castle mutually dependent on each other for protection and trade was taken from the bastide towns of Gascony in southwest France, where Edward I was duke.

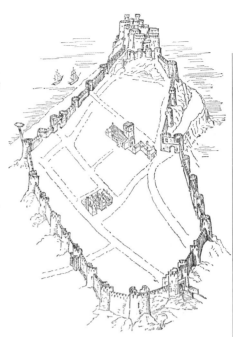

Conwy's defenses

Conwy Castle is surrounded by cliffs above water on three sides and perched on a linear rocky outcrop. The rectangular form of this massive castle with its eight enormous towers differed markedly from other Welsh castles built by James of St. George.

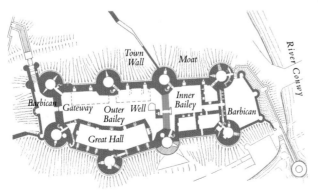

Town Wall · Moat · Barbican · Gateway · Outer Bailey · Well · Inner Bailey · Barbican · Great Hall · River Conwy

Conwy's linear plan

The linear design of Conwy features two entirely separate baileys, divided by a cross-wall that ensured that should one fall, the other bailey could continue to defend the site. The outer ward housed the garrison while the smaller, inner bailey contained the king's private quarters and thus was additionally protected from attack. Unusually, Conwy had a barbican at either end.

The Iron Ring

Caernarfon as capital

Caernarfon was intended as a nucleus of English influence in a region rich in anti-English sentiment. Edward desired it to be the capital of his new dominion and so incorporated a town and a market within its massive 20-ft (6-m) thick walls. Its position ensured that supplies could be received by sea, including building materials and the requirements and supplies of a permanently housed garrison. A 17th-century antiquarian traveler John Taylor said of Caernarfon: "If it be well manned, victualled, and ammunitioned, it is invincible."

Caernarfon, 1283

The colossal fortress of Caernarfon was strategically sited at the southern end of the Menai Strait from where it could service both Harlech and Aberystwyth. Its seven formidable towers gave Caernarfon an impressive aspect, as well as awesome military capability, a symbol of the English king's dominance over the subdued Welsh. Four of Caernarfon's towers provided accommodation on several stories.

Plan of Caernarfon

The initial building of Caernarfon began in 1283. Material for the castle, walls, and gates, and key supplies were brought in by sea. Only one tower, the triple-turreted Eagle Tower, was built during the initial phase where the emphasis was on making the site defensible. Using the castle and town walls provided up to two lines of defense. The twin-towered King's Gate was added during the second phase and the intention was to have a drawbridge, several doors, and portcullises, although the work was never completed.

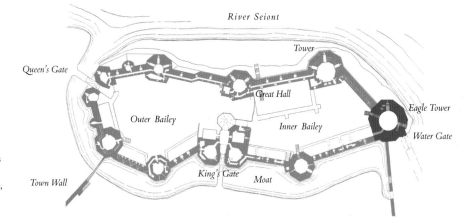

River Seiont

Queen's Gate

Tower

Great Hall

Outer Bailey

Inner Bailey

Eagle Tower

Water Gate

Town Wall

King's Gate   Moat

Beaumaris: the perfectly symmetrical concentric plan

The square inner bailey at Beaumaris was surrounded by an enclosing ward set within a second ring of fortified walls and towers. The whole was entirely encircled by an 18-ft (5.5 m) wide moat—the first great line of defense—that was fed by tidal waters.

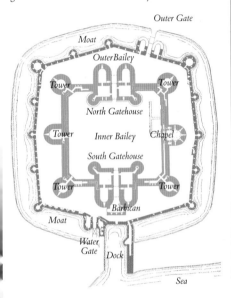

Outer Gate
Moat
Outer Bailey
Tower
Tower
North Gatehouse
Tower
Chapel
Inner Bailey
South Gatehouse
Tower
Tower
Barbican
Moat
Water Gate
Dock
Sea

Beaumaris barbican
The twin-towered south gate flanked by the projecting Gunners Walk faced the sea. A shooting deck on the walk protected the all-important dock.

Beaumaris Castle, Anglesey, 1295
Located on the northern entrance to the Menai Strait, which separates the isle of Anglesey from mainland Wales, Beaumaris was the final link in the chain of defense provided for the north Wales seaboard. It was the last—and largest—of Edward's great castles, begun in 1295 but never completed. Its perfectly symmetrical courtyard is surrounded by an enclosing ward, with round towers at the corners, D-shaped towers centered on the east and west sides, and twin-towered gatehouses to the north and south.

A South Wales Stronghold

Kidwelly Castle, Carmarthenshire

Established in the 12th century and continually adapted during the two centuries that followed, Kidwelly in South Wales is a chronicle in stone of the castle's evolution. The original ringwork castle was one of a series built by the Normans to secure their southern Welsh conquests. In the mid-13th century, the de Chaworth family constructed a square inner ward with four round corner towers and portcullis gates to the north and south, thus transforming Kidwelly into a concentric castle, with an inner and outer ring of defenses. In the early 14th century, the present outer defenses were constructed. The semicircular outer wall was heightened and strengthened to form a stone curtain wall with a wall walk and a series of semicircular towers. A small gate was inserted on the north side, while on the south the Great Gatehouse was constructed, massively strengthening the defenses. So tall was the new curtain wall that the four inner towers had to be heightened to maintain an effective field of fire. Although captured several times by the Welsh in the 12th and early 13th centuries, the castle proved impregnable thereafter, surviving intact into the Tudor period.

Structure of the gatehouse

The Great Gatehouse forms an architectural highlight of Kidwelly. Built on three stories, it is designed as a self-sufficient structure that can be held independently if the rest of the castle is captured. The gate passage has a tower on either side with basements that function as storerooms or prison cells. The first floors have guardrooms at the front and one has a prison situated to the rear. On the second floor is a large hall, accommodating the inner portcullis and the murder hole. The quarters of the constable are sited on the third floor.

Engineering prowess—using the land

Like other well-constructed castles, Kidwelly is built in a location that enhances its defensive capabilities. The original ringwork castle was founded on a steep ridge overlooking the River Gwendraeth at its upper tidal limit. The river provides a natural defense, and little further strengthening is needed on that side. The river is also useful as a means of access to the sea, so forming a link in a chain of new strongholds controlling a major coastal route.

Organic logic

Kidwelly Castle was part of a larger Norman settlement, covering around 8 acres (3 ha). The settlement's line of defenses can still be traced in the form of an earthen bank and ditch that surrounds it on all sides except for the east. The plan of existing roads probably follows the original layout.

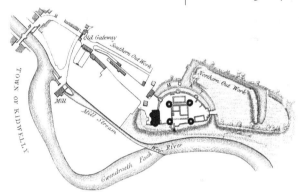

The concentric walls

A square inner bailey was defended by four round towers, which overlook a semicircular curtain wall on the landward side, with the massive gatehouse next to the river. The river prevents this being a truly concentric plan. However, a jutting tower, as well as the river itself, protects the riverside walls, and the final plan is very strong. As with all concentric castles, Kidwelly's strength lies not in its keep but in its walls, which are set with strongly fortified gatehouses and with towers at regular intervals around their circumference.

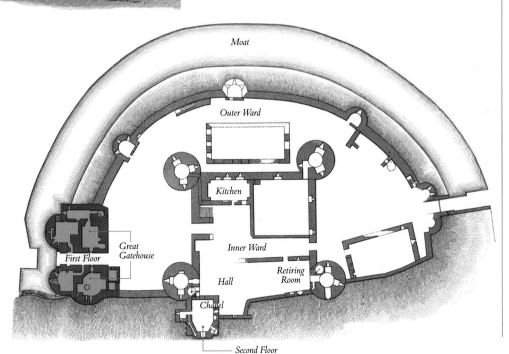

Moat

Outer Ward

Kitchen

Great Gatehouse

First Floor

Inner Ward

Hall

Retiring Room

Chapel

Second Floor

The Defensive & the Domestic

Goodrich, Herefordshire

Goodrich Castle, established in the 11th century, is evidently named after Godric, its owner at the time of the Domesday Book. Since Godric's name indicates that he was almost certainly English, it is a pity we know nothing else about him: quite how an Englishman came to be holding a castle immediately after the Norman Conquest would have been a story well worth hearing.

What stands today at Goodrich, apart from a 12th-century keep of uncertain sponsorship, is largely the work of a 13th-century magnate called William de Valence, a half-brother of King Henry III, who acquired the castle by marriage shortly after his arrival in England in 1247. Valence was close to his cousin, Edward I, accompanying him on Crusade and fighting for him in Wales, and his castle is stylistically similar to those built by the king in the wake of Wales's conquest. Standing so close to the Welsh border, high above the River Wye, the castle obviously had to be tough, yet equally striking is the refinement of its interior: Goodrich boasts one of the best-preserved suites of accommodation of any English castle of its age.

Section through the gatehouse
Built in ca. 1300, this remarkable asymmetrical, twin-towered structure forms the north-east corner of the castle. It formed a second line of defense in case the barbican, which occupied a front-line position on the other side of a moat, was breached. Attackers would then have to cross an exposed stone causeway to reach it. The gatehouse itself is housed in the lower part and consists of a long, vaulted corridor, protected by a portcullis at both ends. From here access to the main tower, which housed a chapel on the first floor serving the garrison billeted in rooms on the floor below.

Ruins and domestic buildings

William de Valence's work was expanded by his son, Aymer. He was responsible for constructing an additional line of outer defenses, including a barbican, to create a concentric castle. The Valence family not only strengthened the fortifications but successfully created luxurious living quarters in a way that was highly influential on many other castle conversions. Goodrich was besieged in 1646 during the English Civil War, when a huge mortar known as "Roaring Meg" succeeded in demolishing the castle's northwest tower. From that time on, the castle descended into ruin. Its picturesque nature inspired William Wordsworth to write "We are Seven" (1798). Despite the work of the great mortar the domestic buildings at Goodrich, believed to have been rebuilt by the de Valences, survived surprisingly intact.

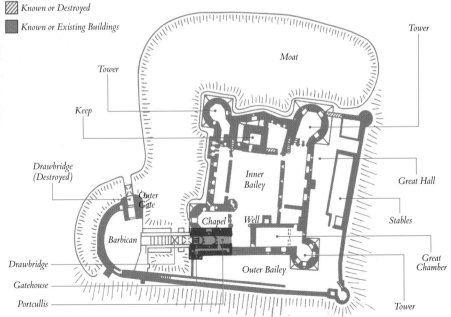

Known or Destroyed

Known or Existing Buildings

Tower

Moat

Tower

Keep

Drawbridge
(Destroyed)

Outer
Gate

Inner
Bailey

Great Hall

Chapel

Well

Stables

Barbican

Drawbridge

Outer Bailey

Great
Chamber

Gatehouse

Portcullis

Tower

Plan view

Goodrich's compact, 25-ft (7.5-m) square keep, still largely preserved, consisted of three stacked rooms, linked by a staircase in the northwest corner. Entrance was on the second floor, accessed by a flight of external stairs. The walls and corners of the keep were protected by clasping buttresses. The 70-ft (20-m) square courtyard area, built 1270s–1290s, contained many domestic buildings (still extant) around its walls, including a kitchen, buttery, and pantry, and a great hall—measuring 65 × 27 ft (20 × 8 m)—with the lord's private chambers, solar (sitting room), and small chapel attached. At Goodrich additional accommodation was built into the large corner towers.

Tough yet Sophisticated

York Castle & Clifford's Tower, Yorkshire

To subdue northern England in the years immediately after 1066, William the Conqueror built two motte-and-bailey castles in the city of York. The one to the west, now known as the Baile Hill, soon fell into disuse, but the one within the city itself became York Castle. In William's day it was a crucial military instrument, guarding the region not only against further English insurrection but also the threat of Danish invasion.

By the mid-13th century, however, this was all a long time in the past. The north no longer resisted rule from the south, and the Vikings were ancient history. The greatest threat to York Castle, which was still built of wood, seems to have been the weather: royal records reveal that in 1228 it was "blown down by the wind."

This clearly struck King Henry III, who visited in 1244, as a poor state of affairs; the following year he ordered the castle to be rebuilt in stone. Unlike his son, Edward I, Henry was an entirely un-martial monarch, but he did appreciate architecture: arguably his finest achievement was the rebuilding of Westminster Abbey. His new tower at York was created by the same master mason, Henry of Reims, who seems to have borrowed the quadrilobe design, unique in England, from an older example at Étampes. The result was a near perfect balance of toughness and sophistication.

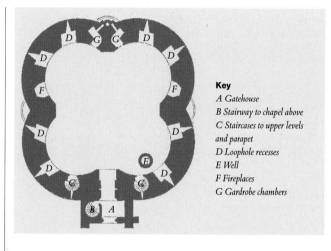

Key
A Gatehouse
B Stairway to chapel above
C Staircases to upper levels and parapet
D Loophole recesses
E Well
F Fireplaces
G Gardrobe chambers

The quatrefoil plan of Clifford's Tower
The tower has an interesting and unusual plan, which is unique in England—four circular lobes, each over 20 ft (6.5 m) across, with walls almost 10 ft (3 m) thick. Loopholes of a design unique to York Castle provided shooting points. A chapel was constructed over the gatehouse, doubling as a portcullis chamber.

Map of York castle, 1750
The commanding position of York Castle and Clifford's Tower over the Fosse and Ouse rivers is depicted on an 18th-century map by P. Chassereau. There is no indication of the existence of the Norman castle on Baile Hill, although its motte survives.

Cutaway of Clifford's Tower

King's Tower became known as Clifford's Tower after Roger de Clifford, a rebel baron who was hanged there in 1322. At its widest, the tower is 79 ft (24 m) in diameter. A square gatehouse measuring over 20 ft (6.5 m) wide protected the entrance on the south side between two of the circular lobes. There are defensive turrets between the other lobes. Large corbels and a central stone pier helped to support the huge weight of stone and the second floor, but the new stone keep suffered repeatedly from subsidence and required heavy investment to maintain its value as a military fortification.

Reconstruction of York Castle and Clifford's Tower

The base of the mound topped by Clifford's Tower is 200 ft (over 70 m) wide. On William the Conqueror's orders hundreds of houses were razed from the site chosen for the artificial motte. The King's Tower, later renamed Clifford's, was the first stone keep on the mound, erected as part of an extensive reconstruction on the orders of Henry III, between 1245 and ca. 1270. This included the building of a curtain wall with D-shaped towers, three gatehouses, and a chapel. Only the tower survives today.

Victorian barbican

An 1846 engraving of the crenelated Tudor Gothic gatehouse of the new prison at York Castle, an addition built in 1825 alongside Clifford's Tower.

A Castle in the Park

Restormel Castle, Cornwall

The story of Restormel Castle is similar to that of York—a motte and bailey castle, built for military reasons by the Normans, but later rebuilt by owners with an altogether different agenda. By the 13th century it was the property of the earls of Cornwall, an immensely rich family on account of their close connection with the English crown—Earl Richard (1227–71) was the younger brother of King Henry III, which made his son and successor Edmund (1271–1300) a first cousin of King Edward I.

Sadly no records survive to tell us exactly when Restormel was refashioned, but on stylistic grounds it seems that Earl Edmund was the likelier patron. The building he created can be usefully compared with the giant fortresses his cousin Edward was simultaneously raising to subjugate the Welsh—set against the likes of Conwy, Harlech, or Caernarfon, Restormel stands revealed as a wholly ineffectual castle in military terms. Edmund was sufficiently rich to build on such a royal scale, but evidently felt no need to do so. When the earl came to Cornwall, it was for recreational purposes—Restormel was located in the middle of the county's largest deer park, and its large windows offered splendid views across the valley of the River Fowey.

A reconstruction of Restormel

Viewed from above, Restormel's stone shell keep has been likened to a Roman amphitheater. An inner courtyard is bounded by a circular wall from which a ring of wedge-shaped, curved buildings made of stone and wood extend. These included a great hall, a kitchen, a guard-house, the *solar* (the luxurious private quarters used by the lord's family), and guest chambers. In the 13th century a chapel was added, built in a tower that projects beyond the curtain wall on the west side. Within the courtyard a well chamber provided the original water supply, but a spring that issued from higher ground beyond the castle itself was used as an additional source.

Plan of the shell keep

The perfectly circular 125-ft (38-m) diameter stone shell keep surrounds a vast courtyard. Built in local shillet stone, its 8-ft (2.5-m) walls are sunk into the motte. They butt up against the original gate tower and stand 25 ft (7.5 m) tall, topped by a wall walk and a parapet. The wall walk is still passable via stairs leading up to it on either side of the entrance. Originally entry was via a drawbridge. There is evidence to suggest the former existence of a second drawbridge within the square gate tower.

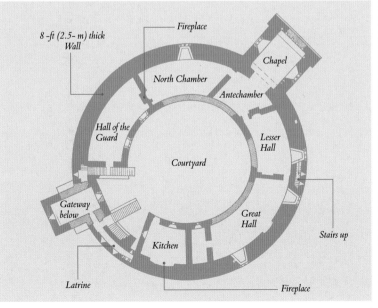

8-ft (2.5-m) thick Wall

Fireplace

Chapel

North Chamber

Antechamber

Hall of the Guard

Lesser Hall

Courtyard

Gateway below

Great Hall

Stairs up

Kitchen

Latrine

Fireplace

18th-century engraving

At the beginning of the 14th century, ownership of Restormel reverted to the crown and it was rarely used as a residence. Henry VIII removed the park status from the area surrounding the castle, returning it to ordinary countryside. Restormel saw military action only once, when it was used as a garrison during the Civil War, after which it was neglected and left to decay. By the 1740s, the castle had fallen into a state of picturesque ruin, covered with ivy and hidden from view by woodland. As a result, it became a popular visitor attraction.

The Fortress Palace

Kenilworth Castle, Warwickshire

Originally built in the 12th century by the Clinton family, Kenilworth already had its impressive great tower and inner curtain walls by the time it was confiscated by Henry II in 1174. Massively enlarged during the troubled reign of King John, who began the outer curtain and created the giant mere, the castle was further enhanced by Simon de Montfort, who, according to a contemporary chronicler, added "marvellous buildings" and "previously unheard-of machines." Its military effectiveness was amply shown in 1266, when Montfort's die-hard supporters endured a six-month siege by their royalist opponents—the longest in English history prior to that time.

But if the emphasis at Kenilworth up to this point had been on the military side, thereafter it was firmly on the domestic. In the late 14th century the castle was owned by John of Gaunt, third son of Edward III and one of England's richest-ever aristocrats, who constructed the huge great hall, as well as new kitchens and living quarters. Henry V, meanwhile, for all that he was a fearsome warrior king, added a pleasure palace or "pleasance" at the opposite end of the mere, equal in size to the site of the castle itself. Most famously of all, Robert Dudley, Earl of Leicester and favorite of Elizabeth I, made huge additions in order to host the queen, including a new gatehouse, a new accommodation block, and extensive gardens.

The prospect from the south

Considered by architectural historian Anthony Emery to be "the finest surviving example of a semiroyal palace of the later middle ages, significant for its scale, form, and quality of workmanship," it is fortunate that Kenilworth survived. In 1649 Parliament ordered the "slighting" of Kenilworth and significant parts of it were destroyed and some parts used as farm buildings. It was still a ruin in the 18th and 19th centuries but became known as a romantic Elizabethan location after publication of Sir Walter Scott's book *Kenilworth* in 1821. The castle is now protected as a nationally important archaeological site and its gardens have been much restored to their Elizabethan form.

13th-century defenses

King John was responsible for building a new outer curtain wall with towers that encompassed the original castle, earthworks, and an area of surrounding land to form an outer court. These defenses were further improved by the addition of a substantially enhanced gatehouse (Mortimer's Tower) and Lunn's Tower. By damming the local brooks King John also surrounded Kenilworth with a huge lake, half a mile long and a quarter of a mile wide—known as the Great Mere.

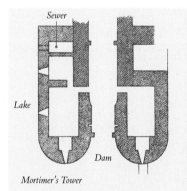

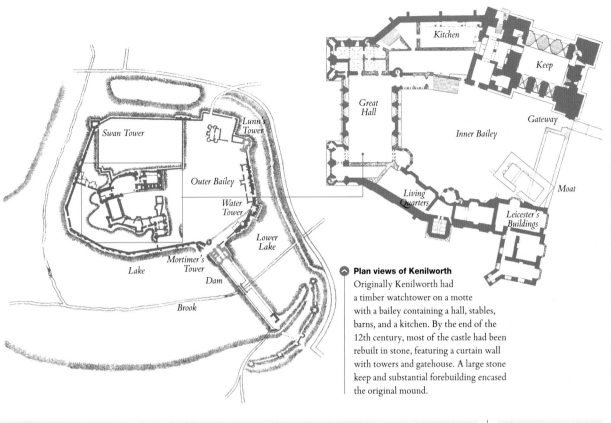

Plan views of Kenilworth

Originally Kenilworth had
a timber watchtower on a motte
with a bailey containing a hall, stables,
barns, and a kitchen. By the end of the
12th century, most of the castle had been
rebuilt in stone, featuring a curtain wall
with towers and gatehouse. A large stone
keep and substantial forebuilding encased
the original mound.

Garden Door and Alcove

Garderobe Tower

Well

Forebuilding

First Floor

Second Floor

Key

1 Wooded parkland
2 The Great Mere
3 The Pleasance
4 Swan Tower
5 Wall toward the Mere
6 The Strong Tower
7 The Hall
8 Lancaster's Buildings
9 Caesar's Tower
10 Leicester's Buildings
11 The Great Gatehouse
12 Lunn's Tower
13 Mortimer's Tower
14 Houses in Kenilworth

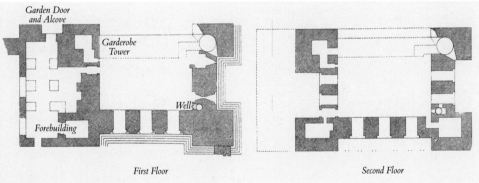

Rooms with a View

Warwick Castle, Warwickshire

Established as a wooden motte-and-bailey by William the Conqueror in 1068, and rebuilt in stone at some point during the 12th century, Warwick Castle conforms to what has become a familiar pattern. In the 14th century, however, the castle was transformed almost out of recognition by its latter-day owners, the Beauchamps—Earls of Warwick.

The transformation was the work of Thomas Beauchamps I and II, father and son, who between them held the earldom from 1329 to 1401. Wealthy landowners in their own right, their fortunes—like those of many Englishmen of the day—received a substantial boost from fighting in the Hundred Years War (1337–1453). During the Battle of Poitiers, for example, Thomas I captured the Archbishop of Sens, extracting sufficient ransom to meet the cost of building Caesar's Tower. This tower, and Guy's Tower added by Thomas II, could serve as defenses, but their main function was to increase the castle's accommodation—well-appointed rooms, with large windows, fireplaces, and ensuite latrines are found on every floor.

> ### Residential grandeur
> Antonio Canaletto was commissioned to paint Warwick Castle in 1747 and the landscape architect Lancelot "Capability" Brown, in addition to landscaping the grounds and gardens, was responsible for rebuilding the exterior entrance porch and stairway of the Great Hall, one of the residential buildings that face the River Avon on the eastern side of the castle. A century later the Hall was reroofed and repaired in Gothic style by the English architect Ambrose Poynter.

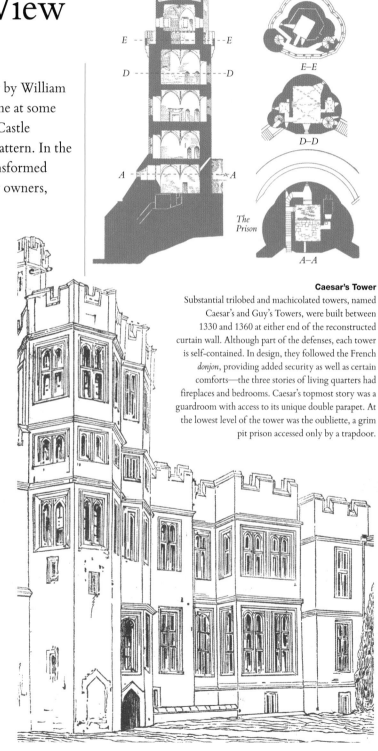

The Prison

Caesar's Tower

Substantial trilobed and machicolated towers, named Caesar's and Guy's Towers, were built between 1330 and 1360 at either end of the reconstructed curtain wall. Although part of the defenses, each tower is self-contained. In design, they followed the French *donjon*, providing added security as well as certain comforts—the three stories of living quarters had fireplaces and bedrooms. Caesar's topmost story was a guardroom with access to its unique double parapet. At the lowest level of the tower was the oubliette, a grim pit prison accessed only by a trapdoor.

Plan of the grounds

Warwick Castle was rebuilt in the reign of Henry II to a new design with buildings against the curtain walls. On the northern side, unprotected by the river or the old motte, the perimeter walls are further protected by a dry moat. The gatehouse, located centrally in the northwest wall, flanked by two gun towers, was a 15th-century addition. These two towers—named Clarence and Bear—formed an independent stronghold from the rest of the castle, equipped with their own ovens and wells.

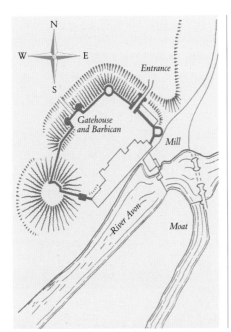

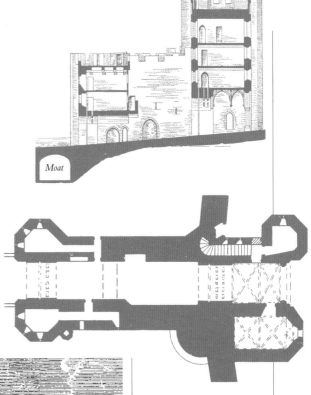

Plan and section of the barbican

Warwick's barbican consists of a two-story forebuilding and two flanking walls that enclose an open court between the forebuilding and the gatehouse. There are three tiers of battlements—on the roofs of the barbican and the gatehouse, and on the corner turrets of the gatehouse itself, all linked by spiral staircases.

Lavish facade

The southeastern facade overlooks the River Avon and houses the Great Hall, library, chapel, and residential quarters. Its elaborate design is indicative of a visible trend toward display in 14th-century English castle architecture. For example, the number and size of the windows were far more a statement of the wealth and power of the Beauchamps than a defensive measure.

The Water Castle

Bodiam Castle, East Sussex

Like Warwick, Bodiam was built from the profits of the Hundred Years War but, unlike the Beauchamps' castle, its builder was not from an established aristocratic line. A few generations before his birth, Edward Dallingridge's family had been mere foresters. Edward himself, however, was an ambitious man, and ended his days as the owner of what is arguably the most picturesque castle ever built.

Having made a fortune fighting in France, in 1385 Edward received royal permission to rebuild his existing manor house at Bodiam (a so-called "licence to crenelate"). In the event he abandoned the old building and started from scratch on a brand-new site. What he built was clearly a castle. Besides its famous moat, Bodiam was equipped with all the defensive paraphernalia one could expect—drawbridges, portcullises, battlements, machicolations, and murder holes—as well as the very latest development: gun loops, not arrow loops.

But do these defenses work? The general consensus among historians today is that they do not, and are in any case contradicted by the castle's large windows and ill-defended rear entrance. The conclusion is that the impressive military features were included purely for social reasons. Edward had no real fear of being attacked at Bodiam, but desperately wanted a home with all the aristocratic trimmings to cement his meteoric rise.

Signature moat
Bodiam's impressive moat is supplied by several springs. Unfortunately, the castle's 28 latrines also once drained directly into it, making it an open sewer. The moat was drained and cleared in 1919, which revealed the original footings of the bridges to the castle. Further excavations to the interior led to the discovery of a well in the basement of the southwest tower.

Picturesque ruin
The earliest known drawings of Bodiam date from the mid-18th century, when it was depicted as an overgrown ruin. Its romantic associations as a medieval castle aided the cause for the rescue and restoration of medieval structures. The first detailed survey was undertaken in 1864, and, although repairs got underway, the fashion for ivy-clad ruins meant that the vegetation was not removed despite its detrimental effect on the masonry.

Plans after excavations, 1919–20

Substantial renovations at Bodiam were carried out in the early 20th century by its then owner Lord Curzon, who commissioned a detailed investigation of the site in 1919. In his words, "so rare a treasure should neither be lost to our country nor desecrated by irreverent hands." Further study in modern times suggests that the castle was considered more ornamental than militaristic, the originally extensive water features and landscaping adding aesthetic emphasis to the fortification itself. This rings true, considering its location so far from the medieval coast—it would have been unable to defend Sussex against raids by the French. For all that, in the eyes of many, Bodiam represents the popular ideal of a medieval castle.

Splendid isolation

Bodiam is one of the best-surviving examples of a quadrangular castle. Its design is typical of 14th-century defensive architecture. It has no central keep; instead, circular towers form the four corners, with square central towers in the south, east, and west walls. The moat, with the castle sited roughly at its center, served to emphasize its splendid isolation.

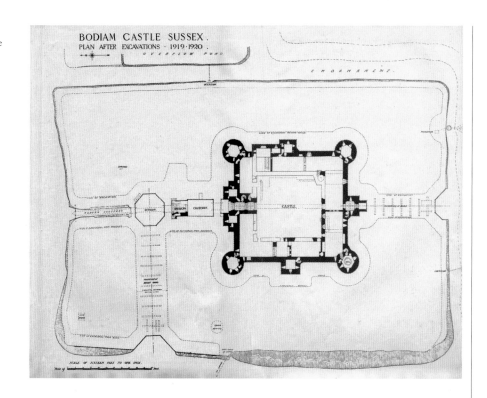

BODIAM CASTLE SUSSEX.
PLAN AFTER EXCAVATIONS · 1919·1920.

The Enduring Castle

Skipton Castle, Yorkshire

Probably established in the 11th century, rebuilt in stone during the 12th and extensively remodeled in the centuries that followed, Skipton has a fascinating medieval history. It also, like almost every other castle in the British Isles, suffered serious damage during and after the civil wars of the 17th century. On the order of Oliver Cromwell, large sections were torn down to make it indefensible (a process known as "slighting").

What makes Skipton doubly fascinating is that it belongs to a far more select group of castles that were rebuilt in the wake of this destruction. Thanks to the enthusiasm of Lady Anne Clifford (1590–1676), Skipton was restored, and survives as a residence to this day. Appropriately, the letters in stone above the gatehouse spell DESORMAIS: "from this time forth."

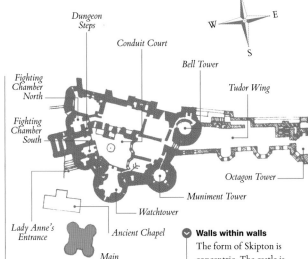

⌄ Layers of history

Skipton's gate is Norman; its watchtower medieval. Dating from 1536, the Tudor wing encloses the bell tower and links the original castle to the Octagon Tower. The Conduit Court is a set of early Tudor domestic buildings that survive intact. After Cromwell's slighting, the castle was restored by Lady Anne Clifford, who was born here in 1590. The current main entrance, built out over the former moat, bears her name.

⌄ Walls within walls

The form of Skipton is concentric. The castle is surrounded by an outer curtain wall with towers and an impressive twin-towered gatehouse. The structure of the castle itself is D-shaped, incorporating a curve of high curtain walls linking six substantial round towers, which back on to the steep cliff edge behind.

Lower gatehouse
The massive twin-towered gatehouse dates from ca. 1311 when the castle was granted by Edward II to Robert Clifford. It provided access to the outer bailey, which contains the chapel and the castle itself. The single-word motto of the Clifford family—Désormais—is an apt choice for a castle that was actively repaired, rather than being left to decline. The gatehouse itself was restored in the 17th century by the Countess of Pembroke.

Ordnance Survey map of Skipton Castle, 1891
With rising ground in front and a sheer precipice dropping away to the river behind, Skipton Castle occupies a naturally defensive site that proved its worth during the Civil War, when the castle was held by the Royalist Sir John Mallory. He and his garrison of 300 men were besieged by Parliamentary forces for three years before finally surrendering in 1645.

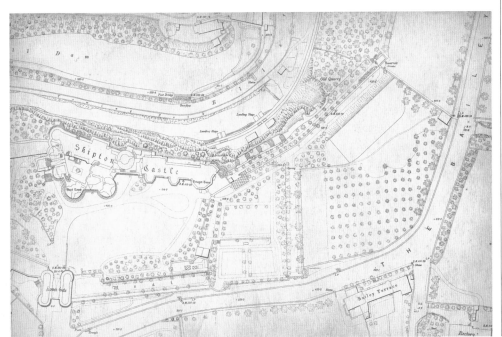

Towers of Power

Threave and Borthwick, Scotland

At the time when, increasingly, English medieval castles were starting to resemble courtyard houses (Tattershall in Lincolnshire is a notable exception), castles in Scotland evolved completely differently. From the late 14th until well into the 17th century, Scottish aristocrats tended to invest in "tower-houses". Designed to provide protection against armed raiders, these thick-walled vertical houses were cheaper to construct than larger curtain-walled castles and thus were built by a wider social range of landowners. Variation in design was considerable but most were two- to five-stories, with space for animals on the first floor, windowless living quarters above, and a crenelated top floor with a wooden or stone roof. They were sometimes surrounded by wooden buildings, often ringed with a smaller curtain wall. Some later versions were rectangular with an additional building added to the main tower, often containing an entrance and main staircase, to form an L-shape.

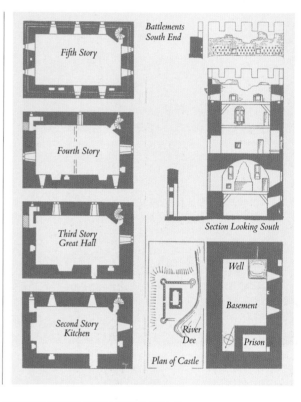

Fifth Story

Fourth Story

Third Story Great Hall

Second Story Kitchen

Battlements South End

Section Looking South

Well

Basement

Prison

River Dee

Plan of Castle

▶ Threave, Dumfries and Galloway

Threave Castle, set on the edge of an island in the River Dee, was built ca. 1369–90 by Archibald the Grim, 3rd Earl of Douglas, and one of the most distinguished warriors and noblemen of his age. He formed Threave as his main residence and stronghold in a troublesome district he was determined to rule. This rectangular structure, 61 × 41 ft (18.5 × 12.5 m) across and 70 ft (21 m) high, had five stories with walls 8 ft (2.5 m) thick. Toward the end of the 15th century it was enclosed by a protective curtain wall surrounded by a ditch.

▲ Plan of Threave

The entrance to Threave Castle was via the second floor, a vaulted chamber with a fireplace, that served as the kitchen. The only access to the ground floor, which contained a well and a latrine (known as a prison or pit), was via a trapdoor from the room above. The second and third floor were well-lit living rooms with fireplaces and latrines; the second floor also served as the Great Hall. At the top level the position of strong wall ties is shown, without which the stability of the tower at this height would have been greatly compromised. Only two stories of the tower remain.

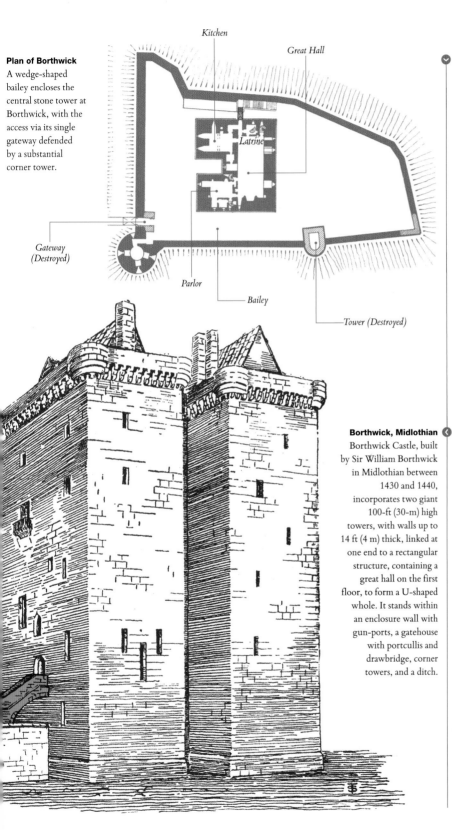

Plan of Borthwick
A wedge-shaped bailey encloses the central stone tower at Borthwick, with the access via its single gateway defended by a substantial corner tower.

Kitchen

Great Hall

Latrine

Gateway (Destroyed)

Parlor

Bailey

Tower (Destroyed)

Borthwick, Midlothian
Borthwick Castle, built by Sir William Borthwick in Midlothian between 1430 and 1440, incorporates two giant 100-ft (30-m) high towers, with walls up to 14 ft (4 m) thick, linked at one end to a rectangular structure, containing a great hall on the first floor, to form a U-shaped whole. It stands within an enclosure wall with gun-ports, a gatehouse with portcullis and drawbridge, corner towers, and a ditch.

Section and layout of Borthwick
The central tower, vaulted at various points, contains all the living quarters. There are two entrances, one directly connecting to the Great Hall by means of a bridge that linked it to the curtain wall (*shown below left*); the second, set immediately below it, provided access from the courtyard to the basement.

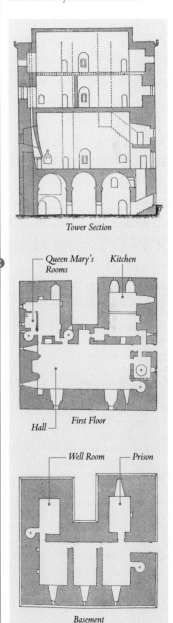

Tower Section

Queen Mary's Rooms

Kitchen

Hall

First Floor

Well Room

Prison

Basement

THEN & NOW
Edinburgh Castle

The seat of ancients

There is archaeological evidence of habitation on the 350-million-year-old plug of volcanic rock that Edinburgh Castle crowns since at least the first and second centuries BCE, and evidence of continuous occupation from at least 600 CE throughout the early Middle Ages. Some large timber buildings existed on the site by 1140, where the first meeting of the Scottish Parliament took place. Edinburgh became the royal residence during the reign of David I (1124–53) during which time St. Margaret's Chapel was built on the summit where it still stands, the oldest surviving building in the city. It may be a remnant of a larger stone keep.

When William "the Lion" was captured by the English in 1174, Henry II forced him to sign a treaty to obtain his release, which involved surrender of Edinburgh Castle along with others. The English held the castle until 1186, when it was returned to William as part of a marriage dowry, and from where he reigned until 1214. When Edward I launched an invasion of Scotland in 1296 he captured the castle

Edinburgh in 1544
This map depicts Edinburgh Castle and part of the Royal Mile in 1544, after further additions had been made to David II's reconstructed castle which was completed in the 1370s after his death. The 15th-century additions included the first royal apartments, the Great Hall, and the Crown Square, laid out over stone vaults. David's Tower, completed in the 1370s, after the death of David II, and these later works were virtually destroyed in savage cannon bombardments by the English, following the so-called Lang Siege of 1571.

after three days of bombardment and installed a garrison of 300 soldiers. The castle was recaptured during a surprise attack in 1314 by 30 of Robert the Bruce's men. Bruce ordered its destruction to avoid the English reoccupying it. In 1333, Edward III invaded Scotland, captured the castle, and refortified it but in 1341 it was in Scottish hands once more. David II ordered the rebuilding of the castle in 1356 and made it his main seat of government.

Edinburgh Castle and part of the city today

With the unification of the Scottish and English thrones, the castle was rebuilt and, from 1660, a garrison was continually maintained at the castle until 1923, when it became a military prison and, latterly, the site of a number of military museums and the backdrop to the Edinburgh Military Tattoo. Much restoration and new building work was carried out in the 19th century by Edinburgh architect Hippolyte Blanc. Today the castle is looked after by Historic Scotland and is a Scheduled Ancient Monument. Edinburgh Castle dominates the city and is its most iconic symbol, attracting more than a million visitors a year.

FOR MUCH OF THE PERIOD 1066–1204 the duke of Normandy and the king of England were the same person, and even thereafter the top people in English society shared a common culture with their peers across the Channel. England's rulers and aristocrats spoke French as their first language until the end of the 14th century, and links were equally strong in terms of literature, art, and architecture. Unsurprisingly, castles built in the two countries were also fundamentally similar.

CHAPTER 5

French Medieval Castles

Such differences as we find between the two nations occur chiefly in the period after 1204, when England and Normandy parted company. In France, for example, the great tower does not seem to have fallen out of fashion to the same extent it did in England, and they continued to be built throughout the 13th century and beyond. Unlike the towers built in England, moreover, those in France—particularly the ones built by the French crown—tended to be round rather than square, probably as much for reasons of fashion as for any perceived defensive advantage.

Advancing into the later Middle Ages, the major factor that was responsible for a difference in castle design was the contrast in political fortunes. France did not enjoy the same domestic peace as England in the 14th and 15th centuries—apart from anything else, the Hundred Years War was overwhelmingly fought on French soil. Consequently, while English castles could be rebuilt more or less exclusively for pleasure, in France they had to remain functional as fortresses. Naturally, however, this did not mean that French aristocrats suffered their fortresses to be any less luxurious than those of their rivals. Behind their towers and battlements, French castles, like English ones, grew ever more palatial.

Château de Bonaguil, Lot-et-Garonne

Château de Bonaguil marks the end of the era of building great fortified castles in France. Although by the late 15th century it boasted every defensive innovation to protect itself—perimeter defensive walls, tall towers, and a deep moat and drawbridge, and the ideal location, high on a rock spur between two rivers—that attack never arrived. In the north of France the shift from fortress to ducal residence was taking hold and Bonaguil had missed its finest hour. The castle has been described as perhaps the most magnificent folly in France.

The First French *Donjons*

Nerra III, the Great Builder, 972–1040

If you had to pick one man as the pioneer of castle-building in France, or even in Europe, it would probably be Fulk Nerra. At the turn of the first millennium, when the ancient kingdom of the Franks had collapsed to an extent that it was every man for himself, Fulk carved out his own little empire along the Loire Valley, creating the county of Anjou. He did this, naturally, by building castles.

In this respect, of course, Fulk was by no means unique. What raises him head and shoulders above the crowd of early castle-builders was his huge investment in stone, erecting the oldest great towers in Western Europe. In his effort to seize the city of Tours from his rivals, the counts of Blois-Chartres, for example, the count of Anjou is said to have raised no fewer than 13 *donjons*, several of which have survived. Over a thousand years on, his castles at Langeais and Montbazon, and above all the soaring tower at Loches, still retain their power to overawe and impress.

Merciless visionary
Fulk Nerra was a savage warlord yet he left a substantial legacy in the form of a network of *donjons* and castles in Anjou as well as a number of abbeys. Estimates vary from 50 to 100 buildings, among them the first stone castles in France.

Château de Montbazon, Touraine
Situated above the Indre River in the Loire Valley, Montbazon has the oldest stone keep in France, built for Fulk Nerra in 991–94. He also fortified the town, the first of a score of such structures—including Montrésor, Montrichard, and Semblançay—that he created across Anjou. The 80-ft (25-m) high rectangular three-story stone keep still survives today. Conceived as a form of attack rather than defense, Montbazon was a successor to several flimsier fortresses—built in solid stone, it still stands tall today.

Château de Loches, Indre-et-Loire
The tower at Loches used to be dated ca. 1100, but has recently been scientifically redated to the early 11th century, which is the time of Fulk Nerra. The same analysis suggests it took a little over 20 years to build. During the 12th century the castle's defenses were added to by the kings of England, and further additions were made after the French conquest of Normandy in 1204.

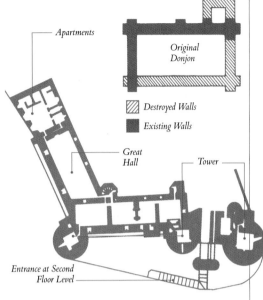

Apartments

Original
Donjon

Destroyed Walls

Existing Walls

Great
Hall

Tower

Entrance at Second
Floor Level

Château de Langeais, Indre-et-Loire

Built in the 990s and one of the first stone castles, Langeais was sited on a promontory not far from Tours created by the small valley of the River Roumer opening into the Loire Valley. These early *donjons* had a simple, heavy design, mainly built to a basic rectangular layout. Over the next 40 years Langeais was held variously by the successive counts of Blois and Anjou. In 1044, Fulk Nerra's son, Geoffrey II, regained control of Langeais once more. The original site was rebuilt by Louis XI in the 15th century (*see left*). The three round towers, and "pepperpot" style slated roofs are typical features of castle building in that century.

Château d'Angers, Maine-et-Loire

The existing structure of Château d'Angers, which sits on a ridge above the River Maine in the Loire Valley, was built on the site of Fulk Nerra's original stronghold. Nearly 655 yd (600 m) in circumference, the castle's dominant feature is its distinctive shale and limestone curtain walls, interspersed by 17 massive towers, that were constructed ca. 1230–40 during the reign of Louis IX. These were originally 130 ft (40 m) high but were lowered during the reign of Henry III in the 16th century, and fitted out with artillery terraces. He used the stone from the castle to create streets and buildings in the village of Angers.

The Conqueror's Birthplace

Château de Falaise, Calvados, Normandy

Around the turn of the first millennium, government in Normandy was stronger than elsewhere in France, and hence castle-building was restricted to the dukes of Normandy themselves and a handful of their leading men. One of the earliest castles we hear about was the ducal fortress at Falaise, first mentioned around the year 1027 and later said to be the birthplace of William the Conqueror.

The earliest buildings that stand at Falaise today were created by the Conqueror's youngest son, King Henry I of England, who began the castle's large square keep in 1123. A second, smaller keep was later added to protect the western front of the fortress and to provide additional accommodation.

After Normandy was lost to France in 1204, its conqueror, King Philippe Auguste, constructed a third keep at Falaise, but unlike the two earlier examples this one was round—a design choice characteristic of the French king's castle-building in the wake of his victory. At 115 feet (35 meters), it also dwarfed the earlier Norman towers.

Further defensive improvements, including cannon-ports in the ramparts, were carried out between 1417 and 1450 when the English occupied Falaise during the Hundred Years War, at which time the round keep was renamed the Talbot Tower after the castle's governor.

In 1590, the troops of the French King Henri IV besieged Falaise, reportedly destroying its western wall with a barrage of 400 cannon shots. The castle was bombarded again in World War II during the battle of the Falaise Packet (12–21 August 1944), the decisive engagement of the Battle of Normandy. Despite much damage elsewhere, the three keeps survived unscathed.

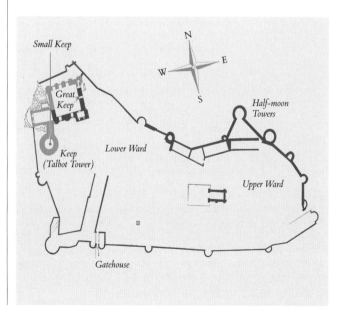

Plan of Château de Falaise
The extraordinary survival of the three keeps of Falaise (see, in addition, the view, right) is the result of two major restoration projects. The first, after the castle was listed as an ancient monument in the 19th century, was led by the architect Victor Ruprich-Robert, a disciple of Eugène Viollet-le-Duc, and ran from 1864 to 1911. At that time, the eastern façade of the Great Keep had partly fallen down, the vaults of the chapel had been destroyed, the roofs and floors of the two square keeps had disappeared, and the top of the Talbot Tower was threatening to collapse. Robert saved the keeps and made them accessible to visitors.

Detail of castle window
While the first priority of early castle architecture was defense of the structure, some attention was also paid to the convenience of those living within, with relatively large windows, set high off the ground, providing light and air.

"William the Bastard" ca. 1028–87

The illegitimate son of Robert I, Duke of Normandy and Herleva of Falaise was born in Falaise. At age seven he was recognized as the official heir after his father's death. He reportedly survived several attempts on his life during his early years, and eventually crushed opposition to his rule in Normandy by his late 20s. He married Matilda of Flanders in ca. 1051 and they had nine children. He led the Norman invasion of Britain in 1066 and was crowned King of England that Christmas. He spent much of the next two decades suppressing rebellions and crushing any resistance to his rule, invading Scotland, and marching into Wales. One of his most lasting legacies is the Domesday Book, a survey of his kingdom, produced in just seven months in 1086.

Bombardment

The heavy damage inflicted during World War II reduced much of the castle's walls to rubble and the subsequent general neglect of the site eventually necessitated a further major restoration if the castle was to survive. Bruno Decaris was the chief architect of this 10-year project (1986–96), which was funded by the town council of Falaise. During this the Talbot Tower and the square keeps were restored and reroofed and a forebuilding was rebuilt with scrupulous historical accuracy. Restoration of the original castle walls is ongoing.

The invincible keeps

Falaise is located on the River Ante. The town is famous for being the Conqueror's birthplace and its castle was where, in December 1174, the Treaty of Falaise was signed between the captive William I, King of Scots, and the English king Henry II Plantagenet. Almost two-thirds of Falaise was destroyed by Allied bombing but the town was largely restored after the war.

A "Rampart of Pride and Folly"

Arques La Bataille, Seine-Maritime, Normandy

During the troubled minority of William the Conqueror, the strict control that earlier dukes of Normandy had maintained over the construction of castles collapsed. "Many Normans, forgetful of their loyalties, built earthworks in many places," explained a contemporary chronicler, "and erected fortified strongholds for their own purposes."

None of these private castles was more impressive than the giant example created by the Conqueror's uncle, William of Arques, on a promontory near Dieppe. "A rampart of pride and folly," said another contemporary, "he had built it with great toil and difficulty on the high hill of Arques." The scale of its surviving earthworks suggests how strong this early fortress must once have been. When in 1053 the count subsequently raised a rebellion against his nephew, it took a year-long siege before Arques was surrendered.

Over the centuries, the castle passed through many hands and was the scene of many battles. In 1589 the French king Henri IV, supported by troops sent by Elizabeth I of England, successfully held the castle against the forces of the Duke of Mayenne by employing artillery to devastating effect. During World War II, German troops occupied the castle and thus made it a target for Allied bombs. When they retreated, the Germans blew up their ammunition dump in the castle, further destroying the remaining ruins.

Defensive fosse

The fosse that surrounds the walls was impressively deep, steep, and wide. The outline of the fortress is oval but irregular and studded with towers placed at unequal distances of varying forms, both round and square, which appear in character to be buttresses as much as towers. Within the bailey was the great keep, a watchtower, as well as the seigneur's house, a garden, and stabling.

Plan of the citadel

The citadel is located on a hilltop southwest of the village of Arques some 6 mi (10 km) inland from Dieppe. The ridge of chalk hills that rise to the west of Dieppe terminates at considerable height here, giving an unbroken, commanding view of the valley below. The gateway to the walled defenses was further reinforced by François I in the 1540s by adding four towers armed with artillery. Internally, the castle is divided into two wards, of which the outer is far smaller. The larger inner ward, approached by a square gatehouse with embattlements, contains a massive quadrangular keep.

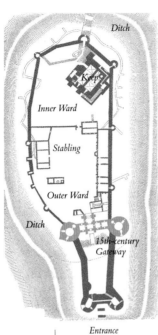

Ditch

Keep

Inner Ward

Stabling

Outer Ward

Ditch

15th-century Gateway

Entrance

The keep

At the south end of the citadel, stands the quadrangular keep, rebuilt, along with the walls, by the English king Henry I in 1123. In its original construction the walls of the keep were carefully faced with large square stones, but today only the shell is visible. Beneath the castle are labyrinthine tunnels leading to spacious crypts.

Elevation of the keep

The ground floor of the great keep housed two stores, a well, and prison cells. The first floor provided further storage while the top floor provided the living accommodation. François I made frequent stays here during 1544 and 1545 to oversee the construction of his reinforced barbican.

Fortress mentality

The design of the solid, square keep towers at Arques, in common with other early strongholds at Loches, Falaise, and Montbazon, proved invincible in the face of attack by arrow, crossbow, and other 11th- and 12th-century weapons of war, which were found to be capable of inflicting only superficial damage.

Anglo-Norman Frontier Fortress

Château de Gisors, Eure, Normandy

The kings of France did not like the fact that their neighbors, the dukes of Normandy, were also kings of England. From 1051, when Duke William was promised the English throne, to 1204, when Philippe Auguste finally conquered Normandy, relations between the two sides, once extremely cordial, were rarely anything other than hostile. As such, the disputed border region between them (the Vexin, *see box*) was filled with fortifications.

The castle at Gisors was begun in 1097 on the orders of the Conqueror's son, William Rufus, and strengthened with an octagonal stone keep during the reign of Henry I. Towards the end of the 12th century Henry II increased the keep to twice its height, encircled it with a stone "*chemise*" and built an extensive stone curtain wall around the bailey. In 1193, however, the castle was seized by Philippe Auguste and, despite the best efforts of Richard the Lionheart, remained in French hands for more than two centuries. King Philippe, as was his wont, added a new round *donjon* to the castle to mark his triumph. It was not until 1419, in the context of the Hundred Years War, that Gisors was once again besieged and recovered by English forces, who held it for a further 30 years, during which time further changes were made, including the construction of earthen ramparts to protect it against artillery fire. The castle was decommissioned around 1559 and declared a historic monument in 1862.

The Vexin

The Vexin is a former region of France, originally the territory of the Veliocasses, a Gaulish tribe. It was divided into two parts by the Treaty of Saint-Claire-sur-Epte (911) which fixed the boundary between the Duchy of Normandy and the territory of the Kingdom of France along the River Epte—a small tributary of the Seine. Over time, both banks bristled with castles: on the Norman side, the châteaux Gisors, Château-sur-Epte, Neaufles-St.-Martin; on the French side Sorts, Boury, and Chaumont (Oise).

Section through the site, viewed from two sides
The stone chemise wall that encircled Gisors' keep was polygonal, its 24 sides supported by flat buttresses. The weight of the new stone keep probably required the motte to be reinforced to support it.

Keep
Curtain Wall
Ditch
Motte
Ditch

Keep
Motte
Ditch
Curtain Wall

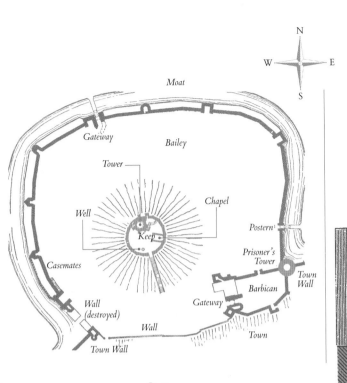

Motte-and-bailey

Situated on a hilltop with a commanding view over the Epte Valley and the Vexin countryside, Gisors consisted of a large conical motte almost 100 ft (30m) high, 230 ft (70 m) in diameter at the base, with a total circumference of 720 ft (220 m). The motte was topped by a wooden tower and fence, and the whole contained within a bailey comprising a number of buildings including a chapel and a secret dungeon.

Gisors

Gisors was a key component in the Dukes of Normandy's defense of their territory. The castle also has significance as a stronghold of the Knights Templar. Philippe II Auguste, who in 1180 succeeded Louis VII, left from Gisors, en route for the Holy Land. Richard the Lionheart was victorious in the Battle of Gisors (1198). Once Gisors was in the hands of the kings of France it was no longer of strategic significance as a frontier castle.

Section through the Prisoner's Tower

A second keep, cylindrical in shape, was later added to the outer wall of the castle by Philippe II Auguste. This substantial construction—90 ft (28 m) high, 45 ft (14 m) in diameter with walls 13 ft (4 m) thick—was known as the Prisoner's Tower. Its most famous inmate, Jacques Molay, Grand Master of the Order of the Templars, was imprisoned there in 1314. The tower has ribbed vaults and bas-reliefs believed to have been carved by inmates.

A Fortified Trade Center

La Tour César, Provins, Champagne

There were, of course, other regions of France besides Normandy and the French royal demesne, and these too had castles. Provins, for example, was once one of the largest cities in France after Paris and Rouen, surrounded by three-quarters of a mile of medieval fortifications built between 1126 and 1314. Within its walls are 58 listed historic monuments, principal among them being the unique Caesar's Tower, which still stands intact.

The town is located in the former territory of the powerful counts of Champagne, on the axis of two vital trade routes linking northern Europe and the Mediterranean. A document signed by Charlemagne in 802 indicates that the site was already fortified. In 996, the remains of a saint were found in the town, believed to have been hidden there by monks evading the Normans, a discovery that caused the surrounding marshland to be drained and various religious edifices to be built. As the city's political and commercial importance grew, the octagonal tower, perched on a hill above the city, was built in the 12th century, by various counts of Champagne.

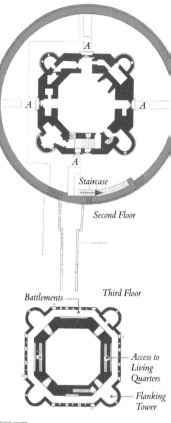

Plan of Caesar's Tower
Caesar's Tower sits on a square base with a turreted tower on each corner. It contained a hall, a chapel, and a room for the lord, but only limited further accommodation to suit a household. The top of the tower had a terrace and a crenelated parapet that served as a watchtower over the surrounding plains. The first floor consisted of a vast vaulted room above which was a similarly dimensioned room that served as the communication center. From the second floor only, four postern gates (A) connected the tower with the outer wall. Stairs leading off this hub connected to the living quarters, and to the battlements.

Second Floor

Staircase

Battlements — *Third Floor*

— *Access to Living Quarters*

— *Flanking Tower*

Tower in Section

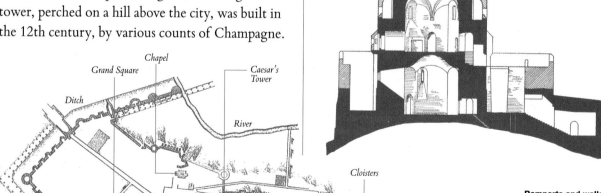

Chapel

Grand Square

Caesar's Tower

Ditch

River

Cloisters

Church

Ditch

Cloisters

Ramparts and walls
Ramparts dating from the 12th century still surround the upper part of Provins on three sides. During the Hundred Years War, the town was occupied by the English from 1417–33 who built a heavy wall of masonry to improve its defenses.

T. E. Lawrence

One of Provins' most famous visitors was T. E. Lawrence who, on visiting in July 1908, commented that its great tower was "a most puzzling keep with the remains of town walls. I was in and around them for hours and came to the conclusion that the architect was making experiments."

Tower of Prisoners

Caesar's Tower tops a motte that was once the site of a Roman fortress. It replaced an earlier fortification that is documented as being on the site in 1137. The tower sits on square base and becomes octagonal at mid-height. In the 13th century, the tower served as a prison and became known as the Tower of Prisoners. The curtain wall that now surrounds it was constructed by the English during their occupation of the town in 1432 as a platform for their artillery.

A wooden roof

A later addition to the Caesar's Tower was the timber-framed roof, added initially in 1554 and rebuilt in the 17th century to accommodate six bells taken from the local church of St. Quiriace, which collapsed in 1689. Five of these were melted down between 1793 and 1798; the one remaining bell has a diameter of 5 ft (1.5 m). Caesar's Tower was declared a national monument in 1846.

The Royal Arsenal

Palais du Louvre, Paris

The vast complex known as the Palais du Louvre originated as a fortress, built from 1190 by King Philippe II Auguste, who in that same year constructed a rampart around Paris to protect it from the Anglo-Norman threat. The fortress had at its center one of the king's trademark cylindrical *donjons* which served at once as a treasury and a prison. The Louvre underwent frequent renovations throughout the Middle Ages and, under Louis IX in the mid-13th century, it became the home of the royal treasury and a residence of the king and his court.

Successive kings until the time of François I occupied themselves very little with the Louvre, and scarcely ever lived there. In 1527, François decided to take up residence in Paris, ordering the medieval keep to be demolished to create more light and space and instructing the architect Pierre Lescot and sculptor Jean Goujon to create a new Renaissance palace.

François acquired what would become the nucleus of the Louvre's holdings, among them Leonardo da Vinci's painting *Mona Lisa*. The Louvre as a museum of art was founded by the revolutionary regime in 1793.

A palace of towers

The Louvre was originally built in the form of a quadrilateral, 255 x 235 ft (78 x 72 m), studded with towers. Each one was designated a name, according to its history or purpose. At the center the Grosse Tour was also called the Ferrand tower, after the Count of Flanders who was confined there. The library tower was where Charles V amassed 959 volumes that formed the nucleus of the National Library. Others were the tournament tower, from which the king could view jousts and tournaments; a clock tower, an artillery tower, a falcon tower, the hatchet tower, and the towers of the Great Chapel and the Little Chapel also had their distinct roles.

First (ground) floor plan

A The Great Tower
B Inner moat
C Entrance to *donjon*
D Linking gallery
E Queen's quarters
F Fountain
G Games court
H Staircase
I Chapel
J Tower guarding approach by river
K Principal gate, protected by small outer castle
L Outer castle, beyond main moat
M Guard room
N Artillery services
O Outer courtyard
P West gate, deemed the most likely to be attacked
Q Menagerie
R Gardens
S Thirteenth-century corner towers
T Thirteenth-century twin-towered main gate

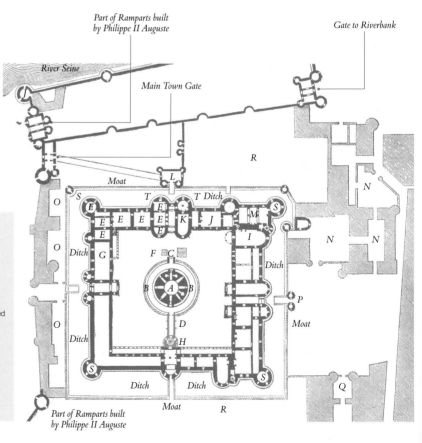

Part of Ramparts built by Philippe II Auguste

Gate to Riverbank

River Seine

Main Town Gate

Part of Ramparts built by Philippe II Auguste

From fortress to residence

In 1364 the work of Raymond du Temple, the royal architect to Louis IX, transformed the former fortress into a sumptuous royal residence. The interiors were decorated with sculptures, tapestries, and rich paneling, and contained a majestic spiral staircase. His work was progressively ruined in the course of the Hundred Years War.

Formidable fortress

Philippe II Auguste's fortress was not a royal palace but a sizable arsenal consisting of a moated quadrilateral with round bastions at each corner and in the center of the north and west walls. Defensive towers flanked narrow gates in the south and east walls, while two inner buildings abutted the outer walls on the west and south sides. At the center stood the independently fortified Great Tower (La Grosse Tour)—50 ft (15 m) in diameter and 100 ft (30 m) high. The gardens of the Louvre, though not extensive, were greatly admired. They included aviaries and a menagerie, and provided for tournaments. Charles VI increased the fortifications of the Louvre, sacrificing some of the gardens.

Connecting gallery

Under Charles V a number of buildings were added as the function of the Louvre changed from being purely an arsenal to become a palace. A gallery at second-floor level connected the tower to the north wing, accessed by du Temple's vast staircase.

The Cave Castle

Château de La Roche-Guyon, Ile de France

The site of La Roche-Guyon—a large, tongue-shaped peninsula, almost entirely enclosed by a loop in the River Seine—must have seemed the perfect place to plant a castle. On the opposite bank a high limestone plateau forms a sharp elbow, providing a perfect choke-point from which to guard the river and control its traffic. The top of the plateau, meanwhile, affords a commanding view of the landscape.

It is no surprise, therefore, that the site exhibits signs of having long been inhabited. A cave chapel was created here in the third century CE, and local settlers (and river pirates) subsequently carved out cave dwellings. It may have been fortified as early as the ninth century, when Vikings were sailing up the Seine to Paris, but the first castle on the site dates to the start of the 11th century, and is built directly into the foot of the cliff. The ingenious fortifications on top of the cliff were added during the reign of Philippe Auguste, probably around the year 1190,

as part of his ongoing struggle against the Anglo-Norman empire—La Roche-Guyon lies close to the border on the French side.

The *donjon* the king created was, inevitably, a round one, but had two original features. First, its walls on the side facing away from the river are thickened to a point, creating a tower with a beaked profile, much like the more famous example created by Richard I at Château Gaillard a few years later. Second, the *donjon* is linked to the earlier castle at the foot of the cliff by a tunnel and flight of 100 steps, laboriously carved into the rock.

The castle came briefly into English hands after the battle of Agincourt, but by the 16th century it was considered of negligible strategic value and used only as a royal hunting lodge. It was not until World War II that La Roche-Guyon was again put to military use, when Field Marshall Rommel established his headquarters there, utilizing the castle's caverns as barracks.

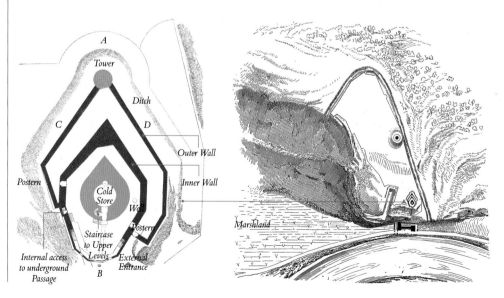

Detailed plan of the donjon
The double-walled keep was well-appointed in case of siege. As well as latrines, tucked into the thickness of the curtain wall, it had a well and, at its heart, a cold store for preserving salted provisions. Two posterns (small doorways) hidden in the interior flanking wall allowed the occupants to enter or exit the keep unobserved; a third was subsequently added in the end tower. The main approach to the castle was protected by an encircling ditch hewn into the rock and by parapet walls at right angles to the entrance.

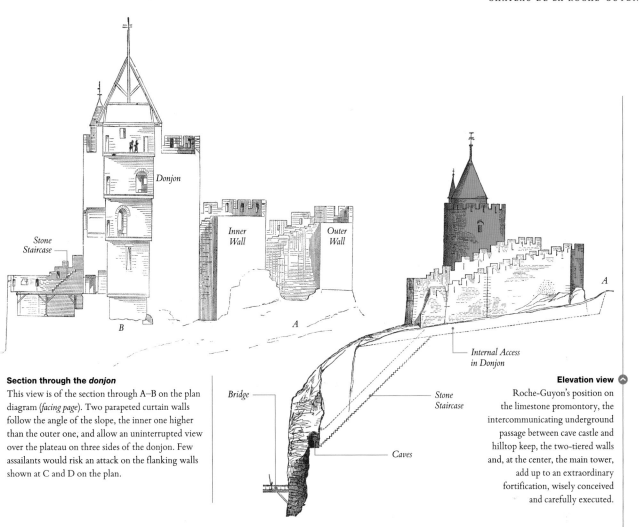

Section through the *donjon*

This view is of the section through A–B on the plan diagram (*facing page*). Two parapeted curtain walls follow the angle of the slope, the inner one higher than the outer one, and allow an uninterrupted view over the plateau on three sides of the donjon. Few assailants would risk an attack on the flanking walls shown at C and D on the plan.

Elevation view

Roche-Guyon's position on the limestone promontory, the intercommunicating underground passage between cave castle and hilltop keep, the two-tiered walls and, at the center, the main tower, add up to an extraordinary fortification, wisely conceived and carefully executed.

Strategic location

The fortress at La Roche-Guyon was hidden in the cliff at river level where it guarded a strategic crossing point. On the hill above was a defensive mound and lookout tower—with the whole area enclosed by a curtain wall. Between two- and three thousand men positioned on the peninsula and a further 400 to 500 stationed in the castle itself were sufficient to stop a large army and paralyze its movements on both banks of the river. These days the defenses built at the water's edge act as flood protection.

Richard the Lionheart's Castle

Château Gaillard, Eure, Normandy

This remarkable stronghold played a pivotal role in the struggle for control of Normandy waged between the French and English kings. Constructed on a naturally defensible site overlooking the River Seine, it was the creation of Richard the Lionheart (King of England and Duke of Normandy) and was completed in just two years, as was the town of Petit Andeley to which it was linked.

Château Gaillard was subsequently captured by the French King Philippe II Auguste after a lengthy siege (*see pages 128–9*), a key victory that led to his final conquest of Normandy, which, for the first time since 911, came under the direct rule of the French king. The castle's ownership later changed hands many times during the Hundred Years War before finally being restored to permanent French ownership in 1449. By 1573 it was uninhabited and in ruins but was still considered a threat should it be repaired. As a result, Henri IV of France ordered its demolition in 1599, completed in 1611.

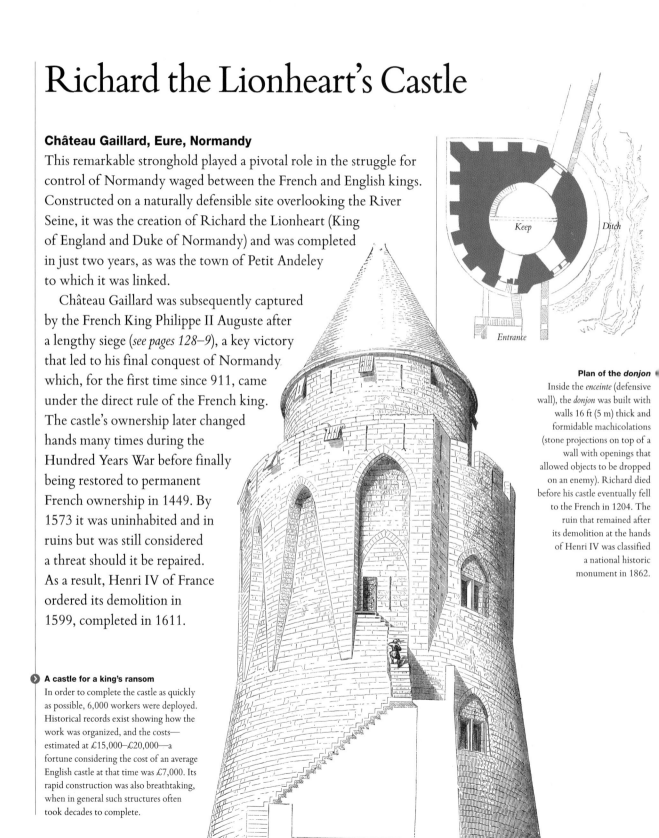

Keep   *Ditch*

Entrance

Plan of the *donjon*
Inside the *enceinte* (defensive wall), the *donjon* was built with walls 16 ft (5 m) thick and formidable machicolations (stone projections on top of a wall with openings that allowed objects to be dropped on an enemy). Richard died before his castle eventually fell to the French in 1204. The ruin that remained after its demolition at the hands of Henri IV was classified a national historic monument in 1862.

A castle for a king's ransom
In order to complete the castle as quickly as possible, 6,000 workers were deployed. Historical records exist showing how the work was organized, and the costs—estimated at £15,000–£20,000—a fortune considering the cost of an average English castle at that time was £7,000. Its rapid construction was also breathtaking, when in general such structures often took decades to complete.

Architectural novelty

The rampart is the most original architectural feature of Richard the Lionheart's fortress. It consisted of 19 arcs of a circle pierced by arrow slits. The design of the inner ward or bailey, with its wall studded with semicircular projections, was unparalleled. This innovation had two advantages: first, the rounded wall absorbed the damage from siege engines far better than square walls; second, the arrow slits in the curved wall allowed archers to shoot their arrows from varying angles.

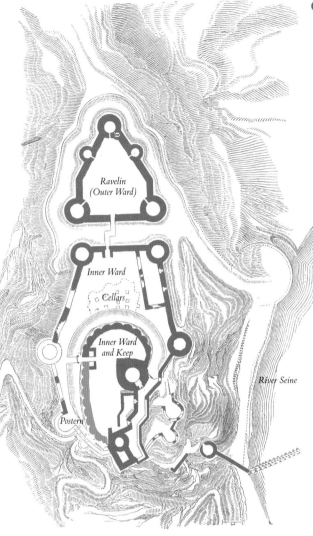

Strategic location

Richard chose the site of his fortress carefully, positioning it where the Seine makes a sharp curve at Les Andelys. In the curve in front of the peninsula, a 330-ft (100-m) high cliff juts provocatively over the river. This triangular spur is linked only by a narrow strip of land to the plateau beyond—this way the castle could only be attacked from one angle. The castle consisted of three enclosures, separated by dry moats, with a keep in the inner enclosure. It was one of the earliest examples of concentric fortification, a form that would be refined and developed by Edward I in the late 13th century (*see pages 86–7*).

Defensive detail

Château Gaillard's defensive architecture included several features that reflect the design of Middle Eastern castles—which displayed a combination of Muslim, Byzantine, and European influences— he would have seen during the Crusades.

Siege of the Lionheart's Castle

Under siege: September 1203–March 1204

This decisive military action was a key part of a campaign by the French king Philippe Auguste to sever the link between England and Normandy and bring the duchy under his own control. Symbolically and militarily, the capture of Château Gaillard, Richard's former stronghold, was vital to his success.

Arrow loops and hoardings

Slits in the tower walls gave defenders a clear line of fire without exposure to counterfire, while rocks could be dropped on the heads of attackers through gaps in the wooden floor at the top of the tower (*see below left*).

Richard the Lionheart, 1157–99

Richard was the third son of Henry II and his French wife Eleanor of Aquitaine. His epithet was earned through his successes in battle, crusades, and siege warfare. In 1172, age 14, he was invested with his mother's inheritance of Aquitaine and Poitou. On the death of his older brother Henry in 1183, Richard became heir to the entire Angevin empire. By 1189 he was King of England, Duke of Normandy, and Count of Anjou. Following his coronation, Richard joined the Third Crusade to free the Holy Land from Saladin, leader of the Saracens. Despite reports of his successes, he failed to regain control of Jerusalem. The last phase of his life was spent strengthening his Angevin empire against Philippe Auguste, King of France. He had several victories over the French, including the Battle of Gisors (1198) but met an untimely death from an arrow wound.

Mangonel

The *mangonel* was a machine of war, usually of great size, that relied on torsion. It required several men to hurl its charge of rocks against enemy walls. Some could be loaded with clay pots filled with flaming materials aimed at igniting the besieged castle.

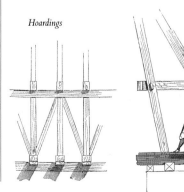

Hoardings

Section View

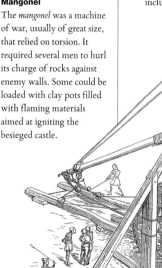

Belfrey

Belfries (mobile siege towers) enabled attackers to approach the outer walls in number. The French gained access to the castle by undermining one tower, setting fire to the chapel, and lowering the drawbridge. The defenders retreated to the inner ward and, when that was breached, to the keep, which was under the control of a castellan, Roger de Lacy. Lacy and his troops—20 knights and 120 other soldiers—were forced to surrender on March 4, 1204.

Besieged then evicted

The French began by attacking Les Andeleys so that the population was forced to seek refuge in the castle. It was well-equipped for a siege but the influx of some 2,000 villagers put a strain on the castle's resources. De Lacy was forced to evict a thousand of them in two groups, both of whom passed safely through French lines before Philippe called a halt. The next evicted group were shot at and had to take shelter in the shadow of the castle walls, where they stayed for several months, many dying from cold and starvation.

ANATOMY OF
French Medieval Defenses

The key points for defense

Before the arrival of gunpowder in the late
15th century, permanent fortifications were the
predominant means of both controlling and defending
territory and property. During the medieval period,
tried and tested defensive features, from drawbridges
to ditches, were imitated and adapted for use in a
variety of fortified structures, including castles,
walls, towns, cities, monasteries, ports, and harbors.

Vincennes

*The Château de Vincennes is one of the most important castles
in French history and one of the biggest and best-preserved castles
in Europe. The major building works were undertaken in the
14th century, beginning with the construction of a 165-ft (50-m) high
donjon (keep), surrounded by its own enceinte, built between 1361
and 1372. When this was complete, Charles V decided to extend
his project and ordered the construction of a vast enceinte aimed at
protecting the cluster of buildings that existed on the site. These
included the original manor house, the St.-Martin chapel and various
residential and utility buildings.*

Enceinte

*A strong stone wall is built around
the outside of the keep. The area
between the keep and the enceinte
is known as the bailey. The enclosed
area at Vincennes is the size of a
small medieval town.*

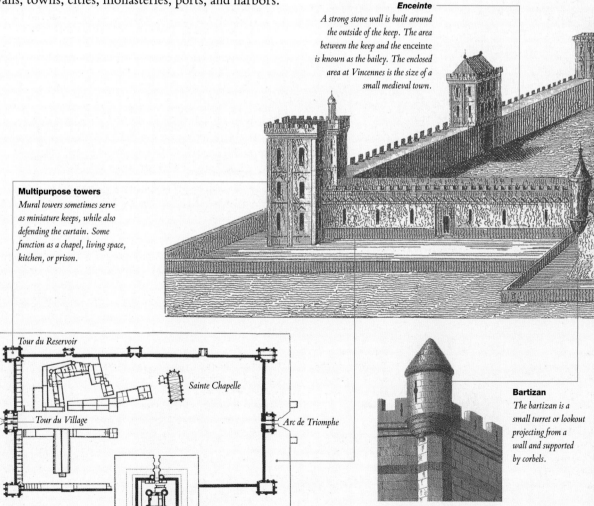

Multipurpose towers

*Mural towers sometimes serve
as miniature keeps, while also
defending the curtain. Some
function as a chapel, living space,
kitchen, or prison.*

Tour du Reservoir

Sainte Chapelle

Tour du Village

Arc de Triomphe

Bartizan

*The bartizan is a
small turret or lookout
projecting from a
wall and supported
by corbels.*

Keep

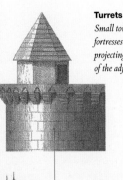

Turrets

Small towers project vertically from fortresses. They are used to provide a projecting defensive position to allow cover of the adjacent wall.

Arrow loops

Arrow loops allow defenders to fire bows from cover. Rare before 1190, they begin as a simple vertical slot, less than 2 in (5 cm) wide at the outside, and average between 3 and 12 ft (1 and 3 m) in length. In the late 12th century, a splayed foot is introduced, which widens the defenders' field of shot.

The Keep

The central tower of the castle is usually the most well-defended area. It often provides the main living quarters, storage for arms and food, and a well. Vincennes' keep is the highest remaining structure of its kind in Europe.

Stairs

Interior rooms often have wooden staircases, while walls and towers have stone stairs. The newel stair, in which a spiral stair revolves around a central column, is common.

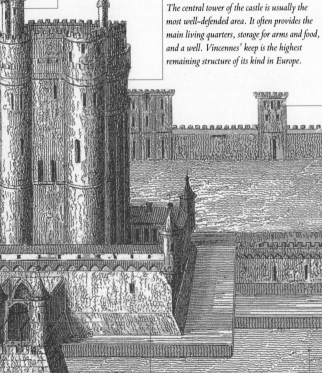

Gateway

The castle's entrance is its weakest point, so priority is given to building a strong gatehouse. Often this is the first part of the castle to be rebuilt in stone. Placing the gatehouse near a moat or keep gives it added protection.

Drawbridge

Defenders raise the far end of the drawbridge by hauling on ropes or chains.

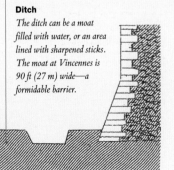

Ditch

The ditch can be a moat filled with water, or an area lined with sharpened sticks. The moat at Vincennes is 90 ft (27 m) wide—a formidable barrier.

Oubliette

The oubliette (from the French oublier, "to forget") is a type of hidden dungeon accessible only from a hatch in a high ceiling.

131

A Fortified City

Carcassonne, Aude

The fall of Normandy to Philippe Auguste in 1204 was a crucial tipping point in the fortunes of medieval France. In the 13th century, more and more outlying territories were brought under direct royal rule. One of the brightest jewels added to the French crown during this period was the southern city of Carcassonne.

Like many frontier towns, Carcassonne, which lies close to the modern Franco-Spanish border, often had to adjust its loyalties: the Romans, the Visigoths, and the Saracens held it successively during the first millennium CE, each adding to its fortifications. From the later 11th century it was an independent lordship ruled by the local viscounts, who constructed the present inner ring of walls as well as the Château Comtal.

This independence was curtailed in the 13th century, initially as a result of the religious war known as the Albigensian Crusade, and decisively in 1247 when the town was taken over by the French crown. The outer defenses seen today were constructed by Louis IX (1226–70) and Philippe III (1270–85), and proved effective. In 1355, during the Hundred Years War, Edward, the Black Prince, tried but failed to take Carcassonne.

A circle of towers and ramparts

Carcassonne's medieval defences are mainly built in rough-cut yellow sandstone with roofed round towers. When the city's strategic value dwindled in the 17th century its fortifications fell into disrepair, to such an extent that the French government decided in 1849 that they should be demolished. The mayor of the city and a prominent writer Prosper Merimée, who had been appointed the first inspector of ancient monuments, led a campaign for its preservation and appointed military architect Eugène Viollet-le-Duc (*see pages 144–5*) to oversee the renovation of Carcassonne's towers and ramparts.

Barbican and St. Nazaire Gate

Basilica of St. Nazaire

Narbonne Gate and St. Louis Barbican

Barbican and Aude Gate

Château Comtal

Town

Plan of the citadel

Carcassonne's ramparts, studded with 53 towers, contain the city, the Château Comtal, and the Basilica of St.-Nazaire. Its eastern flank was protected by a great semicircular barbican (St. Louis) through which everyone had to pass in order to reach the main gate, while a round keep defended the entrance on the western flank. The compound within could support a permanent garrison and reinforcements in times of siege.

Defense of the west face

The highest, western face of Carcassonne, where the castle was located, was virtually impregnable by reason of the steep terrain and the huge, circular moated barbican, through which any attackers would have to pass to enter the city. Its walls had two tiers of arrow slits and a further upper gallery from which bowmen could defend their city.

A Fortified City

Tours de force

The medieval architect of Carcassonne's defenses, whose identity is unknown, relied heavily on the fixed *enceinte* originally constructed around the hilltop by the Romans in around 100 BCE. The inclusion of so many towers built at close intervals was an integral part of the strength of the city's walls, making them impregnable to the siege engines of the time.

The Aude Gate and Château Comtal

The entrance in the western walls leads to the rectangular towered castle that dominates Carcassonne. This image dates from after the restoration work carried out by Viollet-le-Duc, and reflects the way the city looks today. In his lifetime, Viollet-le-Duc attracted much criticism for restoring the tower roofs with pointed cones in slate instead of following the local vernacular style of low-pitched terracotta tiles (*seen right*). His achievement was subsequently recognized, despite its lack of strict authenticity.

Responses to an attack

Carcassonne's encircling ramparts are studded with 53 towers but connection by means of the walkway on top of its walls could also be severed at each tower in times of attack. Each one was built as an independent, readily defended fort, which made an assault on the walls from the exterior doubly difficult. In the tower itself access to the floors was by wooden ladders which could be pulled up to thwart attackers, while supplies of ammunition could be winched up to the defenders.

Construction of the towers

The towers built into Carcassonne's walls presented a cylindrical front to the exterior but the interior, city side, was square. Access from within the citadel was via a staircase from ground level to the tower at the level of the walls. Entry into the tower itself was further impeded by means of two ditches (shown at A and B on the section drawing), over which wooden drawbridges could be raised or lowered.

The Walled Port

Aigues-Mortes, Petite Camargue, Gard

The walled town of Aigues-Mortes is one of the finest and best-preserved examples of 13th-century military architecture, and a further instance of the expanding authority of the French Crown at the time. In 1240, King Louis IX was seeking a southern port from which to launch his Crusade to the Holy Land. Since the rest of the towns along the Mediterranean coast were owned by other powerful rulers, Louis settled on Aigues, an ancient settlement owned by the local monks at the Abbey of Psalmody.

Having struck a deal with the monks, the king began by building a road to the town through the salt marshes and a separate tower (the Tour Carbonnière) to guard it from attack, while a canal was dug to connect it to the ocean. In 1242, work began on the King's Tower (later renamed the Tour de Constance), which served as a lighthouse, stronghold, and symbol of royal power. After a century of success, the town's port began to silt up and Aigues-Mortes fell into decline. Today the huge Tour de Constance is all that remains of the castle.

Grid layout

Aigues-Mortes is constructed along neat, rectilinear lines within the confining walls. The Tour de Constance forms the northern corner of the walls, from which it is separated by a water-filled moat and spanned by a fixed-frame bridge.

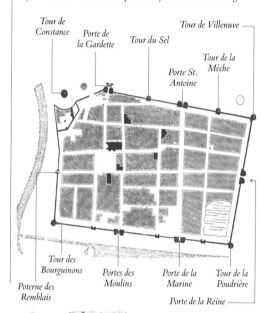

Tour de Constance
Porte de la Gardette
Tour du Sel
Tour de Villenuve
Tour de la Mèche
Porte St. Antoine
Tour des Bourguinons
Poterne des Remblais
Portes des Moulins
Porte de la Marine
Porte de la Reine
Tour de la Poudrière

Watery world

Aigues-Mortes is a derivation of *aygas mortas*, meaning "dead waters," referring to the swamps and salt marshes that surrounded the site. The town is enclosed by a mile of crenelated walls, with five towers and 10 fortified gateways. These were largely built in two phases during the reigns of Philippe III (the "Bold") and Philippe IV (the "Fair"), between 1272 and 1300.

La Tour de Constance, 1248

The huge cylindrical construction that became known by the name of Louis' daughter was built on the ruins of a previous tower (La Tour Matafère) built by Charlemagne in 791. With walls 100 ft (30 m) high and 6 ft (2 m) thick, it was designed to protect the town and the port. The tower is the town's only defensive structure but was expertly designed. A first door has a solid casement and a portcullis. A second conceals the stairway leading to the upper levels and a final door is secured by both lock and cross-beam. The higher-level platform is mounted on an ornamental openwork cage of forged iron, which is topped by a conical roof in lead.

Section

South Elevation

Well

Gateway   Postern

Moat

Plan at A–A

Plan at Gallery, B–B

The tower in section and plan view

At ground level the guardroom is equipped with a bread oven and a well. Access to the upper level is via a spiral staircase and rainwater collected on the roof is run down the tower to a tank. The central aperture of the vaulted ceiling opens into the Salle des Chevaliers above, which matches it in dimensions and architecture. Regular-sized holes in the walls of the knights' room indicate the former presence of beams suggesting there was once a floor level here. Access to this room is through a vaulted vestibule that would once have served as a room where Louis IX granted audiences.

The Porte de la Gardettte

The fortification of Aigues-Mortes continued until 1310, by which time it formed a quadrilateral enclosure with a mile-long perimeter of yellow ocher limestone 35 ft (11 m) high, and 8 ft (2.5 m) thick, topped by a parapet with corner towers to defend the main doors. The infamous tower was surrounded by a moat, and its formidable construction —177 ft (54 m) high with walls 20 ft (6 m) thick and 72 ft (22 m) in diameter—makes it the epitome of medieval defensive construction and, later, ideal as a place of incarceration.

A Fortified Palace

Coucy-le-Château, Aisne, Picardy

Castle-building in late medieval France was not, of course, the exclusive preserve of the monarchy. Many fortresses were built by French aristocrats, perhaps partly in reaction to the expanding power of the crown. The giant castle at Coucy, midway between the cities of Amiens and Reims, can certainly be read in such a way, for it is—or rather, was—one of the most formidable fortifications of the medieval Western world.

The castle in its prime was constructed by the lords of Coucy, a long succession of men named Enguerrand. It was Enguerrand III (d. 1242) who, in the 1220s, instituted a massive rebuilding and expansion of the existing castle, creating a curtain-wall enclosure defended by great towers at each corner, as well as the largest *donjon* ever built in Christendom. The adjacent city of Coucy was surrounded by an *enceinte* with 13 towers and 3 portals. In the 14th century Enguerrand VII (d. 1397) transformed the castle again, making it into a still more sumptuous palace.

In ca. 1540 Coucy's fortifications were adapted for the age of artillery. It survived for another century before being made "militarily unusable" by royal order. Much-plundered in the ensuing centuries, the castle was rescued and restored in the 19th century by, among others, Viollet-le-Duc (*see pages 144–5*), and became a popular tourist destination. Sadly, however, this splendor was not to last (*see opposite*).

Apartments *Buildings in Curtain Wall*

Escarpment

D *C*

Upper Ward

A

Donjon

Ditch

B

Ramparts

Gate connecting to Town via Drawbridges

Chapel of Enguerrand III

A formidable defense
When threatened with attack, wooden extensions, or hoardings, were added to the top of the castle towers to shield the archers from counter-fire. At Coucy, even the secondary towers surrounding the court were as big as the *donjons* being built at that time by the French monarchy: indeed, the entire fortification was seen as a challenge to the crown.

Plan of Coucy
Coucy's architects conceived their castle as a whole, not a set of individual elements. The entire project was a massive undertaking in terms of its execution and expense. The result was a castle of extraordinary defensive capability. It was built on an irregularly shaped plateau, towering over steep scarp slopes some 165 ft (50 m) above a valley between the towns of Noyon and Chauny. Its surface area was some 12,000 sq yd (10,000 m²). Between the town and the castle itself was a vast fortified lower ward, separated from the castle by a 65-ft (20-m) wide ditch. (The chapel was one of the buildings of the lower ward.) Access to this ward and the town was by a single gate, heavily protected by the huge *donjon* and flanking towers A and B.

The mighty tower

At the time of its construction Coucy's tower outranked anything else built in Europe, measuring 115 ft (35 m) wide and 180 ft (55 m) tall, with walls 25 ft (7.5 m) thick and its construction was a remarkable feat, achieved by building a spiral ramp around its great girth. In 1652 the engineer, Métezeau, brought in to render the castle militarily unusable, succeeded in destroying the gates, the curtain wall, and the keep's vaults, but the Grand Tower remained a symbol of power for knights for almost seven centuries.

Majestic construction

Perched on a rock dominating a vast outlook, the fortified castle forms an irregular trapezoid of 300 x 115 x 165 x 260 ft (92 x 35 x 50 x 80 m). At the four corners are cylindrical towers 65 ft (20 m) in diameter, and originally 130 ft (40 m) in height. Between two towers on the line of approach was the massive keep. The rest of the bluff or *falaise* was covered by the lower court of the castle, and the small town. What remains of the castle today is the ruins of the palace erected by Enguerrand III in 1220. During World War I, Coucy became headquarters for German troops, as it lay just 8 mi (12 km) from the front line. When the Germans retreated in March 1917 they dynamited the keep and the four other major towers. This act of "barbarity" moved the government to preserve the ruins as a national monument.

A Ducal Fortress

Château de Pierrefonds, Oise, Picardy

A castle was first built at Pierrefonds in the 12th century by the lords of Nivelon. Two hundred years later, Charles VI bestowed the property on his brother, Louis, Duke of Orléans (1372–1407). From 1393 until his death, with his court architect Jean Le Noir, Louis set out to create a new castle that was both a sumptuous residence and an impregnable fortress. Pierrefonds was inaugurated in 1406 with a royal wedding but the duke was assassinated the following year, an event that triggered a civil war. In the centuries that followed Pierrefonds was attacked, taken, and retaken by the English, the Spanish, by French rebel forces, and by the French monarch. In March 1617, after a six-day siege, the castle was taken by the forces of Louis XIII, who ordered its demolition—a task that was never fully completed. The castle remained a ruin for two centuries.

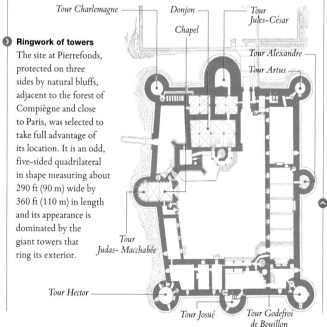

Tour Charlemagne · Donjon · Tour Jules-César · Chapel · Tour Alexandre · Tour Artus · Tour Judas-Macchabée · Tour Hector · Tour Josué · Tour Godefroi de Bouillon

▶ Ringwork of towers
The site at Pierrefonds, protected on three sides by natural bluffs, adjacent to the forest of Compiègne and close to Paris, was selected to take full advantage of its location. It is an odd, five-sided quadrilateral in shape measuring about 290 ft (90 m) wide by 360 ft (110 m) in length and its appearance is dominated by the giant towers that ring its exterior.

▶ From ducal ruins to imperial residence
Napoleon I bought the remains of the castle in 1810 and it acquired distinction as a romantic ruin, leading to its classification as an historic monument in 1848. In the 1850s Napoleon III instructed Eugène Viollet-le-Duc (*see pages 144–5*) to undertake its restoration. As work progressed it was clear that a simple repair job was not feasible. The ambitious decision was made in 1861 to keep the ruins intact and create an entirely new castle as an imperial residence. Viollet-le-Duc's grand romantic folly was the result, a masterly reimagining of the medieval castle of yesteryear.

The emperor's castle

Funded largely from the emperor's purse—the total estimated cost was 5.8 million francs—work on the new castle at Pierrefonds proceeded at a furious pace. The number of laborers who were working seven days a week increased from 100 in 1863 to 300 in 1865. The project halted when the empire collapsed in 1870 and resumed in 1873. Viollet-le-Duc died six years later and his work was continued by Maurice Oadu and Juste Liche until 1885 when the project ended.

Hallmarks of Gothic revival

Viollet-le-Duc's involvement with the exteriors of the new castle at Pierrefonds is acclaimed as an accurate portrayal of 14th-century military architecture, although his interiors are considered more a work of invention rather than historically scrupulous restoration.

The Fortified Abbey

Mont St. Michel, Manche, Normandy

The celebrated abbey of Mont St. Michel began life on October 17, 709 CE, with the consecration of a small church on a rocky island off the coast of Normandy. The earliest buildings on the site today, including the abbey church itself, date from its Romanesque rebuilding in the 11th century. At the start of the 13th century King Philippe II, flushed with his recent conquest of Normandy, paid for a new set of Gothic buildings called "La Merveille." This was partly a fortified structure, but the period that saw the most extensive fortification at Mont St. Michel was the later Middle Ages, when Normandy became a major battleground during the Hundred Years War. King Charles VI (1380–1422), for example, is credited with adding numerous structures to the abbey mount, building towers and strengthening the ramparts. During this period the English besieged the island for 30 years but, thanks to these military improvements, were unable to take it. Declared an historic monument in 1874, Mont St. Michel was listed as a UNESCO World Heritage Site in 1979.

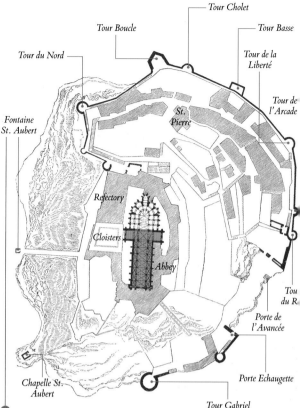

Tour Cholet — Tour Boucle — Tour Basse — Tour du Nord — Tour de la Liberté — Tour de l'Arcade — Fontaine St. Aubert — St. Pierre — Refectory — Cloisters — Abbey — Tou du R — Porte de l'Avancée — Chapelle St. Aubert — Porte Echaugette — Tour Gabriel

Constructing a platform

In 1017, Abbot Hildebert II began the scheme, by Italian architect William de Volpiano, of buildings around the rock to create a huge platform level with the summit, on which the church might stand. Two lower stories form vast irregular rings, entirely enclosing the natural rock. The third rests partly on the lower two and partly on the apex of rock immediately beneath the pavement of the abbey church. The church is cruciform with a Norman nave. Originally seven bays in length, the three western bays were destroyed in 1776.

Linked by a causeway

The Mont (mount) is a cone of rock that rises 300 ft (100 m) above the sea. The rock is nearly a mile offshore, but in 1880 a causeway was built across the dangerous quicksand that separates the island from the mainland to aid the pilgrims visiting the holy site. The abbey was used as a prison during the French Revolution (1789), and in 1836 Victor Hugo was one of many influential figures to launch a campaign to restore this architectural treasure. Restoration work continues to the present-day.

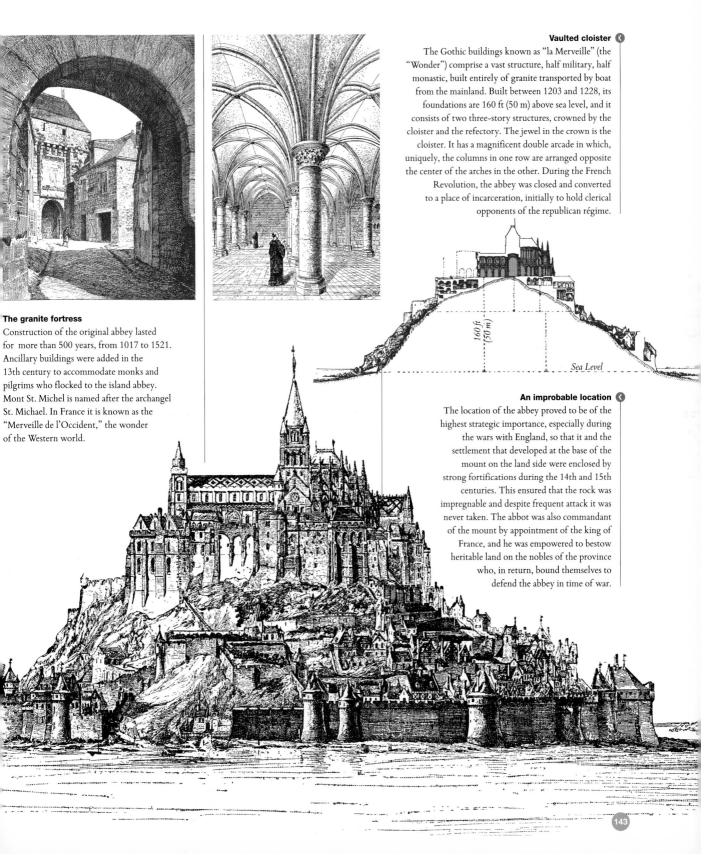

Vaulted cloister

The Gothic buildings known as "la Merveille" (the "Wonder") comprise a vast structure, half military, half monastic, built entirely of granite transported by boat from the mainland. Built between 1203 and 1228, its foundations are 160 ft (50 m) above sea level, and it consists of two three-story structures, crowned by the cloister and the refectory. The jewel in the crown is the cloister. It has a magnificent double arcade in which, uniquely, the columns in one row are arranged opposite the center of the arches in the other. During the French Revolution, the abbey was closed and converted to a place of incarceration, initially to hold clerical opponents of the republican régime.

160 ft
(50 m)

Sea Level

The granite fortress

Construction of the original abbey lasted for more than 500 years, from 1017 to 1521. Ancillary buildings were added in the 13th century to accommodate monks and pilgrims who flocked to the island abbey. Mont St. Michel is named after the archangel St. Michael. In France it is known as the "Merveille de l'Occident," the wonder of the Western world.

An improbable location

The location of the abbey proved to be of the highest strategic importance, especially during the wars with England, so that it and the settlement that developed at the base of the mount on the land side were enclosed by strong fortifications during the 14th and 15th centuries. This ensured that the rock was impregnable and despite frequent attack it was never taken. The abbot was also commandant of the mount by appointment of the king of France, and he was empowered to bestow heritable land on the nobles of the province who, in return, bound themselves to defend the abbey in time of war.

The Gothic Revivalist

Eugène Emmanuel Viollet-le-Duc, 1814–79

Eugène Viollet-le-Duc was an architect best known for his restoration of medieval buildings and for his remarkable multivolume work, *Dictionary of French Architecture from the 11th to 16th Century*, which is beautifully illustrated with his own drawings.

Viollet-le-Duc was a leading figure in the Gothic Revival, an architectural movement that began in England in the 1740s and spread throughout Europe. It coincided with the rise of medievalism, a movement that viewed preindustrial society as a golden age and fostered a fresh appreciation of the arts and crafts of that period.

In 1833, the newly established Commission des Monuments Historiques commissioned Viollet-le-Duc to restore the Romanesque abbey at Vézelay. Work got underway in 1840 and continued in stages for two decades, the beginning of a lifetime of restoration work on some of France's most famous buildings including Notre Dame de Paris, Mont St. Michel, the medieval city of Carcassonne, and numerous medieval castles.

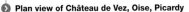

Plan view of Château de Vez, Oise, Picardy
The *donjon* (A) of Vez is constructed at the angle formed by two curtain walls of which B (*see inset plan*) dominates an escarpment while that labeled C is separated from an outer bailey (D) by a wide ditch. Only a single flanking tower remains of the entrance. At its center are the ruins of a former lodge (E).

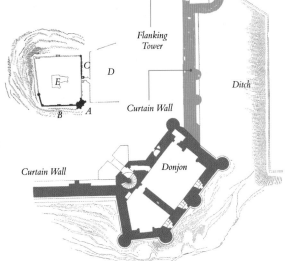

Flanking Tower

Ditch

Curtain Wall

Curtain Wall

Donjon

The *donjon* of Vez
An imposing medieval fortress, Vez has Gallo-Roman origins, when it was used as a military camp to defend Gaul against the barbarians. After the Battle of Soissons in 486 CE, Vez became the capital of the Valois for the following five centuries. The five-sided tower dates from 1360. It came to the attention of Viollet-le-Duc in the 19th century, who oversaw its restoration.

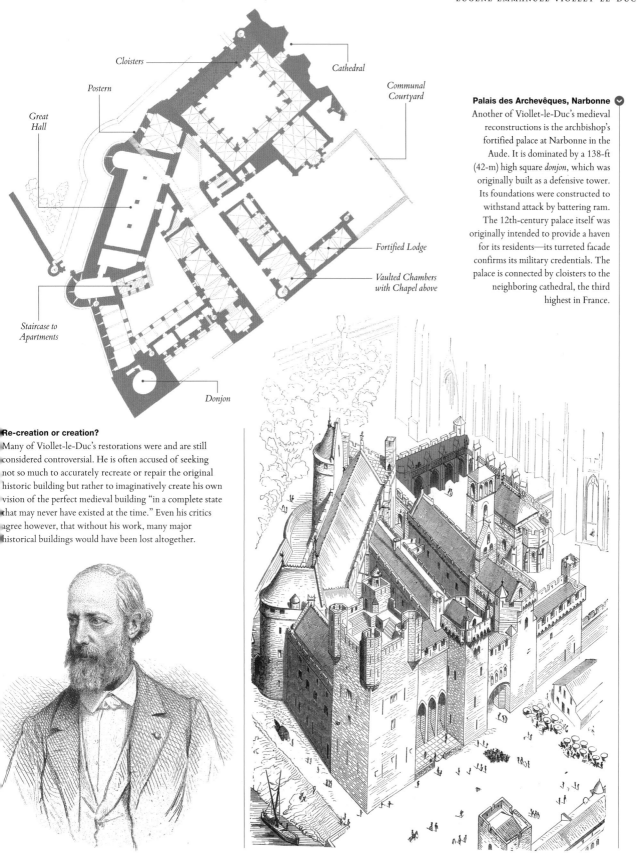

Cloisters

Cathedral

Postern

Communal
Courtyard

Great
Hall

Palais des Archevêques, Narbonne ⊙

Another of Viollet-le-Duc's medieval
reconstructions is the archbishop's
fortified palace at Narbonne in the
Aude. It is dominated by a 138-ft
(42-m) high square *donjon*, which was
originally built as a defensive tower.
Its foundations were constructed to
withstand attack by battering ram.
The 12th-century palace itself was
originally intended to provide a haven
for its residents—its turreted facade
confirms its military credentials. The
palace is connected by cloisters to the
neighboring cathedral, the third
highest in France.

Fortified Lodge

Vaulted Chambers
with Chapel above

Staircase to
Apartments

Donjon

Re-creation or creation?

Many of Viollet-le-Duc's restorations were and are still
considered controversial. He is often accused of seeking
not so much to accurately recreate or repair the original
historic building but rather to imaginatively create his own
vision of the perfect medieval building "in a complete state
that may never have existed at the time." Even his critics
agree however, that without his work, many major
historical buildings would have been lost altogether.

The Last Castle

Château de Bonaguil, Lot-et-Garonne

Bonaguil derives its name from the French phrase *bonne aiguille* (meaning "fine needle"), in reference to the castle's location—a steep, rocky promontory that forms a natural defensible site. Located in a strategic position bordering several provinces, in Lot-et-Garonne in southwest France, it was the last great castle to be built at the end of the medieval period in that country.

Its original builder was a knight, Arnaud de la Tour of Fumel, who, in 1250, constructed a small stone keep with a barracks to house a garrison. He sided with the English in the Hundred Years War, during which the castle was taken and retaken several times before being burnt and abandoned.

Almost a century later, ownership had passed to Jean de Roquefeuil, who carried out extensive renovations and moved into the castle with his wife Isabeau de Peyre in 1444. Of their nine children, four were boys, only one of whom, Berenger, survived and inherited Bonaguil. He transformed the castle over a 40-year period into an imposing fortress—a marvel of military architecture with 13 towers and 1,500 feet (455 meters) of perimeter walls, stacked with artillery. Extensive earthworks ensured the enemy's cannon could not get within firing range. These elaborate defenses were never tested in Berenger's lifetime (d. 1530); the only time the castle briefly saw military action was during a battle between his two grandsons in 1563, who were fighting on different sides in the Wars of Religion (1562–98).

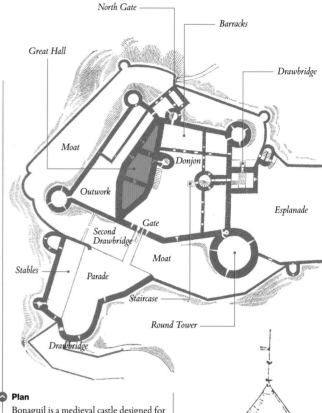

Labels on plan: North Gate · Barracks · Great Hall · Drawbridge · Moat · Donjon · Esplanade · Outwork · Gate · Second Drawbridge · Moat · Stables · Parade · Staircase · Round Tower · Drawbridge

Plan

Bonaguil is a medieval castle designed for an age of artillery and musketry. Such castles became obsolete as the power of artillery increased, leading to the birth of the modern fort. The castle is concentric in design, combining three levels of defense, each one higher than the other. The first is the outer curtain wall, linked to a fortified barbican that protects the main entrance to the castle. Behind this was a deep dry moat, in which were *caponiers* (fortified huts). The moat was spanned by a large drawbridge given access to the main castle.

Garrison headquarters

The second level of defense was formed by the castle walls which were crenelated, studded with embrasures to allow musket fire, and had machicolations. These were protected by a series of towers, the largest of which—the Great Tower— was 116 ft (35 m). The lower levels of these were used for artillery, including cannon, and the upper levels provided living quarters.

Defensive detail

The tower walls were 13 ft (4 m) thick at their base and were ringed with machicolated battlements supported by stone corbels, which offered better resistance to cannon fire. From these holes the defenders could drop stones or other objects on attackers at the base of the wall, or shoot them with arrows or muskets. The height of the walls and towers prevented the enemy using ladders to scale them. The unusual-shaped keep was the final line of defense and the tallest structure in the castle. It was the main observation post, with an artillery emplacement on the roof, which served as the headquarters for the castle's garrison.

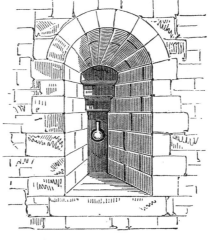

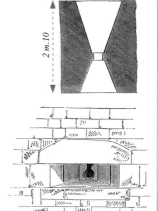

Embrasures

An embrasure is an opening in a crenelation or battlement, wider on the inside of the wall than the outside, which allows a defender to fire on an attacker whilst remaining under cover. Initially they were vertical arrow slits (also known as loopholes); a variation with both horizontal and vertical slits in the form of a cross was used, principally for crossbows. Embrasures were adapted for musket and cannon. A horizontal slit would allow the gun or cannon to be raised or lowered but its movement would be limited from side to side. Horizontal embrasures were useful for sweeping fire across a broad arc. Bonaguil had 104 embrasures built into its various lines of defense. As a result, artillery and musket fire could be used at long and short range to deter attackers from approaching the castle, to fire on siege engines, and to prevent any attempts to scale the walls.

THEN & NOW
The Illuminated Castle

Château de Mehun-sur-Yèvre, Cher

The *Très Riches Heures* is considered the finest illuminated manuscript of the 15th century, and one of the most magnificent medieval works of art in any genre—and it is no surprise that the castle is one of the most prominent subjects for illustration. The manuscript was one of many commissioned by Jean, Duke of Berry (1340–1416), the third son of John II of France. As the landowner of a large part of central France, the duke was immensely wealthy, and spent lavish amounts on all manner of beautiful things—rare jewels, exquisitely illuminated manuscripts, and the grand castles that guarded his estates and pronounced his status in bold statements carved in stone. The duke's friends and protégés included architects such as Guy de Dammartin, and sculptors, among them Jean de Cambrai, and the work of such luminaries in the form of his fortress homes is immortalized in the manuscript, illuminated by three brothers, Paul, Hermann, and Jean Limbourg. Such was the extravagance of the duke's patronage that even his vast estates were unable to sustain his expenditure, and he was deeply indebted on his death in Paris in 1416. But he left behind the castles built by his architects, and a wonderful record of their original appearance. The manuscript is now in the Musée Condé in Chantilly, France.

Château de Mehun-sur-Yèvre, ca. 1412
Like other works of its kind, the *Très Riches Heures* was intended as much to pay tribute to the dignity and wealth of its owner as to assist in his devotions. The manuscript page here, folio 161v, shows the temptation of Christ in the wilderness by the Devil, as told in the gospel of Matthew. Christ is offered all the kingdoms of the world if he will bow down and worship the devil. The temptation itself is relegated to the background, while all around the mountain upon which Christ stands rise the castles and cities of the duke's estates that symbolize the riches on offer; they have been identified as the castles of Poitiers, Bourges, Montlhéry, and the fortress of Nonette in Auvergne.

The illumination, painted by Paul Limbourg, is dominated by a representation of the Duke of Berry's favorite castle, Château de Mehun-sur-Yèvre, remodeled by the duke in 1367 from an early 13th-century fortress. Jean Froissart referred to the castle in his *Chronicles* as "*l'une des plus belles maisons du monde*" ("one of the most beautiful houses in the world"). The illuminators even found a place for the duke's symbols: swans glide along the waters of the Yèvre surrounding the castle and a bear has climbed into a tree to escape a lion. While the château is here raised to mythical proportions, it is accurately depicted, and it is fascinating to compare the castle in all its pomp to the ruins shown on the far right.

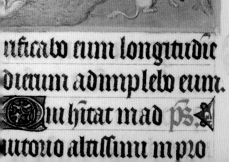

Fine detail

A drawing dating from 1737, when the castle still stood in its entirety, indicates how faithfully Paul Limbourg reproduced this magnificent château. The plan of the castle is trapezoid, with one cylindrical tower at each corner and a rectangular tower in the center of the longest wall. Its slender towers are solidly implanted in the glacis that borders the water. The rectangular tower can just be seen rising on the left, and the chapel with its steeple is shown situated over the main entrance. One tower, 36 ft (11 m) in diameter, was much larger than the others—25 ft (7.5 m) in diameter—and served as the keep. The castle was largely a ruin by the end of the 18th century, although the keep and the west tower still stand to their full height, each crowned with intricate defensive machicolations.

GALLERY OF
Western Medieval Castles

The medieval landscapes of Britain and Europe were dominated by feudal fortresses. Today, restored or ruined, many seem romantic, fairytale visions but in their time castles had an active and utilitarian role and remained a key military resource for much of the Middle Ages.

Hohenzollern, Germany ca. 1454
Ancestral home of the Hohenzollern princes and the Prussian royal houses.

Dubrovnik, Croatia
The walled defenses of Dubrovnik, a free state between the 14th and the end of the 19th century.

Ananuri, Georgia
The seat of the dukes of Aragvi, rulers of part of the Caucasus region during the 13th century.

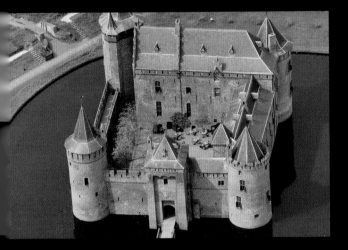

Loevestein Castle, Holland
Built in ca. 1360 at the confluence of the Meuse and Waal rivers, Loevestein was strategically placed to levy tolls on passing ships.

Castillo de la Mota, Spain
Dating from 1080, fought over by the rival kings of Aragon and Castile the fortress was rebuilt in 1433 and reconstructed in the 20th century.

Caerlaverock Castle, Scotland
A triangular, moated fortress built in ca. 1270, Caerlaverock was key in the defense of the realm, particularly against the English.

Walled towers and city of San Marino
A former refuge for the founding saint of San Marino, an independent enclave within Italy, and one of the oldest city-states in Europe.

3

Eastern Castles
of the
Middle Ages
& Early
Modern Period

Introduction

If castles began life in Western Europe in the form we usually understand them, the technology—and the know-how—soon began to spread eastward. There were soon similar structures as far as Poland and Russia, spread—as much as anything else—by the extraordinary meeting of European and Eastern cultures in the Middle East during the Crusades.

Furthermore, if castle-building reached a spectacular apogee in the Crusader kingdoms, first in Palestine and then in Cyprus, it was partly because the best inventive minds in Europe converged there and learned from their Muslim opponents, and vice versa. There is even evidence that some of the innovations used by both sides were built by the same groups of castle artisans.

If this was true of the Crusader and Islamic castles of the Middle East, it was even more so of those castles which were farther East. The Kremlin in Moscow was rebuilt by Italian architects. In the same way, the spectacular Indian forts used expertise from all over the international melting pot that the region around the Indian Ocean had become.

But there was a difference from the European tradition. In the vast spaces of India and Russia, the sheer firepower that the Europeans were able to bring to bear on castle walls was simply not available to attackers. This meant that the high walls were able to survive, as they still do so spectacularly in Moscow's Kremlin. In both places, the high walls also served a useful psychological purpose—impressing the local population.

In Russia, the kremlins have often taken on a continuing role as administrative and religious centers, protecting great cathedrals behind those walls, and providing a tradition of castle-building that looks very different from the original European inspiration.

Timeline

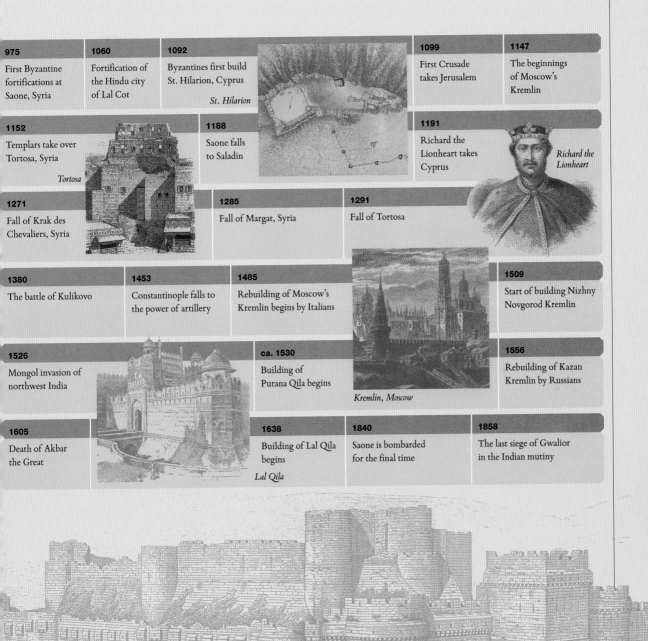

975
First Byzantine fortifications at Saone, Syria

1060
Fortification of the Hindu city of Lal Cot

1092
Byzantines first build St. Hilarion, Cyprus

St. Hilarion

1099
First Crusade takes Jerusalem

1147
The beginnings of Moscow's Kremlin

1152
Templars take over Tortosa, Syria

Tortosa

1188
Saone falls to Saladin

1191
Richard the Lionheart takes Cyprus

Richard the Lionheart

1271
Fall of Krak des Chevaliers, Syria

1285
Fall of Margat, Syria

1291
Fall of Tortosa

1380
The battle of Kulikovo

1453
Constantinople falls to the power of artillery

1485
Rebuilding of Moscow's Kremlin begins by Italians

1509
Start of building Nizhny Novgorod Kremlin

1526
Mongol invasion of northwest India

ca. 1530
Building of Purana Qila begins

Kremlin, Moscow

1556
Rebuilding of Kazan Kremlin by Russians

1605
Death of Akbar the Great

1638
Building of Lal Qila begins

Lal Qila

1840
Saone is bombarded for the final time

1858
The last siege of Gwalior in the Indian mutiny

Eastern Medieval & Early Modern

In terms of their architecture, castles and cathedrals were the pinnacles of achievement in the Middle Ages, while the cherished military goal of many a commander was to seize a medieval castle in order to capture—by force if necessary—the hearts, minds, and souls of a local population. Medieval castles typically occupied strategic points at frontiers, trade routes, sea ports, or river confluences, while others exploited natural advantages: a peninsula, clifftop, or island. Throughout the eastern Mediterranean and the Middle East defensive architecture displays a mix of ethnic and cultural backgrounds. The maps here show the castles from southern Turkey to modern-day Israel that embody elements of Christian, Muslim, and Byzantine design in their defenses and, on into Asia, the onion-domed Russian kremlins and the rock forts of India.

Krak des Chevaliers, Syria
See pages 160–3

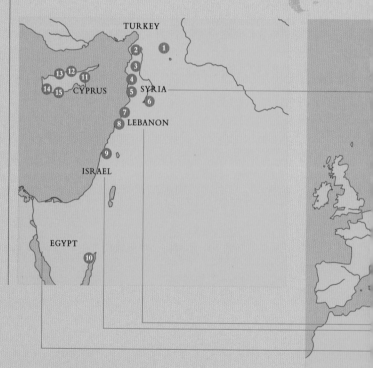

Antioch, Turkey
See pages 172–3

Kantara, Cyprus
See page 174

Moscow Kremlin, Russia
See pages 180–1

Islamic & Byzantine Fortifications

1 Aleppo
2 Antioch
3 Saone
4 Margat
5 Tortosa
6 Krak des Chevaliers
7 Byblos
8 Sidon
9 Acre
10 Pharaoh's Island
11 Kantara
12 Buffavento
13 St. Hilarion
14 Paphos
15 Kolossi

Russian Kremlins

16 Solovetsky
17 Ivangorod
18 Moscow
19 Rostov
20 Nizhny Novgorod
21 Kazan

Indian Fortresses

22 Jodhpur
23 Kumbhalgarh
24 Delhi
25 Agra
26 Gwalior

Gwalior, India
See pages 188–9

WHEN THE FIRST CRUSADE finally arrived in Jerusalem in the summer of 1099, at the end of an extraordinary trek across Europe, there was a final orgy of bloodshed when most of the Muslim population of the holy city was slaughtered. Several other cities, including Tyre, remained in Muslim hands for a further generation, but the entire western seaboard of the Holy Land was now a European colony: Outremer, the land "beyond the sea."

CHAPTER 6

Islamic & Crusader Castles

At its height the Outremer stretched from the Sinai Desert in the south to Lebanon in the north, and beyond that via its vassal states into areas that are now modern Syria and Jordan. As soon as Jerusalem was in European hands and the Crusader vows of the army fulfilled, most of the fighting force returned home. The new King of Jerusalem, Baldwin I, was left with only 300 knights to defend the whole area. He badly needed new fortifications, and there was also no time to lose. As early as 1102, a new tower he had built at Ramlah saved Baldwin and his army from humiliating defeat.

That is the main reason why he and his successors pursued a determined policy of castle-building for the life of the Kingdom of Jerusalem, the Kingdom of Acre which followed it and the other Crusader states. This was not just to deter attack. It was also to control the passage of trade, so that merchants and traders needed permission to pass by. The result is one of the most extraordinary collections of medieval fortifications anywhere.

It isn't that these castles are unlike those found anywhere else in the world, though their defining feature—the precarious way in which they so often blend in with rocks, perch on impossible crags, or emerge cut into living mountains—certainly makes them distinctive. What makes them so unusual is that they include features of castles in other parts of the world, but they meld together so many different features, from Byzantine or Islamic castles, as well as characteristics from the very different castle styles of northern France, England, Germany, or the regions between.

Pharaoh's Island, Egypt
On a tiny island in the Gulf of Aqaba is a Crusader fortress originally built by Baldwin I, in ca. 1116. Despite its diminutive size this rocky islet, also known as Coral Island, was selected for sound strategic reasons: it lay at the heart of a vast trade route linking Europe and the Far East; it was in the narrowest section of the Gulf; it was on high ground—Egypt, Israel, Jordan, and Saudi Arabia are all visible from its summit—and it was readily defensible because it was out of range of catapults on the mainland. The original fortress may have been considerably expanded toward the end of the 12th century after it was captured by Saladin, and then further enhanced by Mamelukes and Ottomans.

ANATOMY OF
Crusader Castle Defense

Krak des Chevaliers, Syria

Krak des Chevaliers, high in the mountains of southern Syria, is one of the most impressive castles of any age. It managed a long history of sieges, resisting Tancred of Antioch in 1102, Saladin in 1188, and eventually falling to Sultan Baibars in 1271 after a siege of only a month. But its features are typical of Crusader castle-building, in the way it used its mountain site and in its double walls of defense. Between the two sets of walls the castle had its own reservoir, which was vital in times of siege.

Towers
The round tower and the square towers at the southwest end were rebuilt by Baibars and the Mamelukes after their successful attack that caused a great deal of damage at that end.

Main entrance
The main entrance into the castle was a long, covered passage that led from the main gate deep inside the fortress, but it was also a death trap for anyone unwelcome. Along the length of its walls there are a series of holes and other hidden gaps where various projectiles could be dropped on or shot at anyone rash enough to attack that way.

Outer walls
The outer walls included deep slits so that archers were able to shoot downward. The brilliant mining techniques of the Muslims were known to be a major threat to walls of any kind and this was at least some defense.

Slot machicolations

The great towers have three slot machicolations through which stones could be dropped on attackers. These defenses were probably added after the earthquake of 1202.

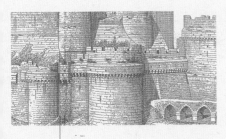

Square towers

Only one of the square towers built on the inner walls in the 12th century survives. The rest fell victim to the ravages of time or, more likely, the damage from the earthquake of 1202, after which it was widely rebuilt.

Extraordinary stonework

One of the most distinctive features of Krak was the extraordinary stonework that makes it appear as though the round towers grow naturally out of the sloped walls.

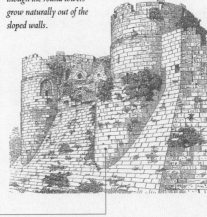

Box machicolations

There are box machicolations on the walls at Krak which are extremely distinctive, and the same features are obvious at the citadel of Aleppo and contemporary castles that were built and designed by Muslims. This is evidence either that the castle defenders copied each other widely, or perhaps that the same group of multinational craftsmen built several examples.

ANATOMY OF
Crusader Castle Defense

Siege tactics

Architects were required to balance defensive and domestic needs in their design. This included the provision of vast water and food reserves—enough for several years. Krak's huge cisterns held up to 2 million gal (10 million liters) of water. One of Krak's towers included a windmill in addition to millstones and ovens for preparing grain. Often the besiegers, camped in inhospitable terrain, were the first to suffer from lack of supplies.

Castle approaches

One tactic of the Crusaders' architects was to smooth the sides of the rock summit on which the castle was built to deny hand- or footholds to anyone attempting to scale the walls.

Multiple roles

The biggest castles were residential and administrative centers as well as fortified buildings. The huge inner spaces would include markets, meeting places, souks, and a chapel.

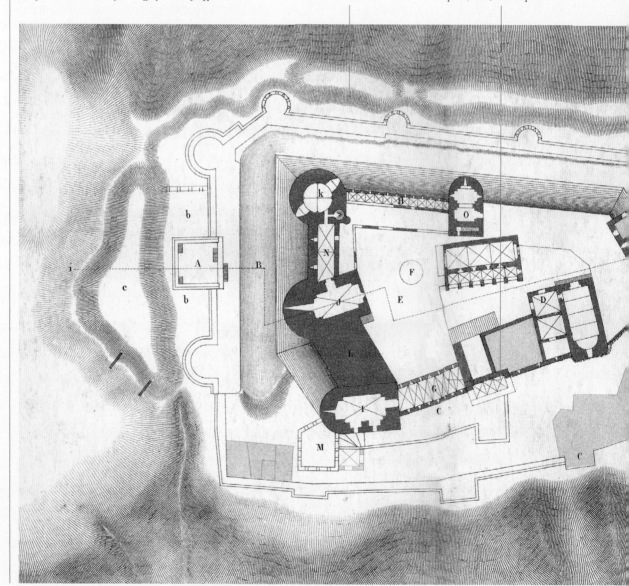

Confusing by design

Internally the castle layout was labyrinthine, designed to confuse anyone unfamiliar with it, and to provide the maximum number of angles from which anyone could be shot at. The enemy would thus be fatigued, bewildered, and thoroughly demoralized in their attempt to take such a formidable fortress.

Inner and outer walls

Launching a surprise attack was usually the only chance of a direct assault succeeding. To prevent this, the inner wall was always higher than the outer one, to provide a double line of fire. Walkways on top of the walls were accessible only from the flanking towers and the wards within the main defense were further subdivided by walls to defy any large-scale invasion.

"Bent" entrance

The entrance to Krak was a complicated affair. It rose between two gates by means of broad shallow steps which presented no difficulty to men or horses approaching slowly, but could not be taken at speed. Three consecutive changes in direction, one a hairpin bend, would slow an enemy fighting his way in, while rapid changes in lighting levels (from bright sunlight to dark shadow) added to the confusion, all the while being subject to overhead attack.

Projecting towers

Circular towers projecting from the curtain walls were a Crusader innovation. With arrow slits covering all angles, defenders in the towers could thwart any attempts at scaling the walls with ladders.

A Hospitaller Stronghold

Margat, Syria

Margat is built on a rocky spur that juts out into the sea from the Syrian coast, facing toward the territories of the Assassins. It is built as a triangle to suit the shape of the site, with a strong inner citadel and a much bigger outer fortress that has its own double defensive wall.

Like so many of the Crusader castles, Margat was built originally by the Islamic defenders and taken over—in this case after long negotiations—in 1118, after which it became a base for the Knights Hospitaller. It eventually surrendered in 1285 after Muslim sappers had forced the collapse of the southern tower, known as the Tour de l'Eperon. For centuries afterward it remained a stronghold, serving for a time as the prison for deposed governors.

The castle is built from black basalt rock—a black partner to Krak des Chevaliers, which is made from white sandstone. Margat is defended on the outside by a series of round towers, and on its most vulnerable side by a reservoir hewn from the rock. Like so many of the Crusader castles, the square defenses evolved into a round keep at the heart, which was less vulnerable to bombardment.

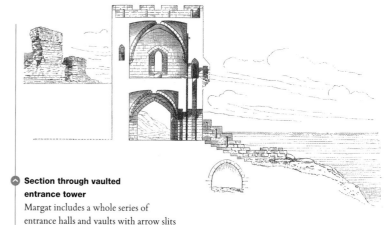

Section through vaulted entrance tower

Margat includes a whole series of entrance halls and vaults with arrow slits that doubled as stores or galleries from which to shoot arrows. Some of them are also built underneath a wide roof terrace which is thought to have been designed to allow siege engines to be used from within the castle. Such features played a major role in defending the castle in 1285, before it finally surrendered.

Round towers in basalt

The huge round towers on the outer wall were added by the Hospitallers when they took over the castle at the end of the 12th century. Margat was the largest of all the Crusader castles, virtually impregnable within its double concentric walls, and stocked with provisions to last a thousand men five years.

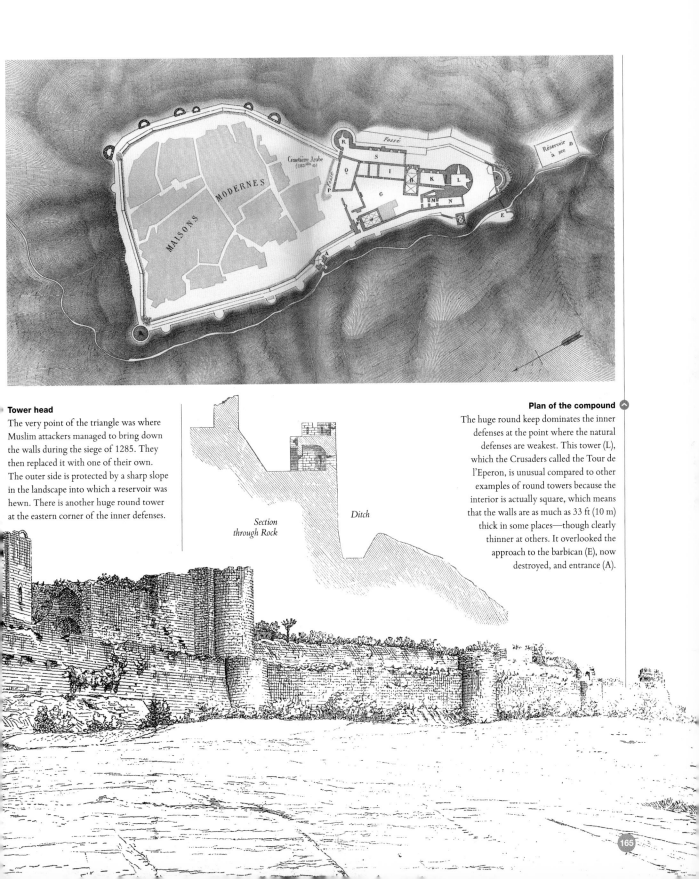

Tower head

The very point of the triangle was where Muslim attackers managed to bring down the walls during the siege of 1285. They then replaced it with one of their own. The outer side is protected by a sharp slope in the landscape into which a reservoir was hewn. There is another huge round tower at the eastern corner of the inner defenses.

Section through Rock

Ditch

Plan of the compound ⌃

The huge round keep dominates the inner defenses at the point where the natural defenses are weakest. This tower (L), which the Crusaders called the Tour de l'Eperon, is unusual compared to other examples of round towers because the interior is actually square, which means that the walls are as much as 33 ft (10 m) thick in some places—though clearly thinner at others. It overlooked the approach to the barbican (E), now destroyed, and entrance (A).

The Crusaders' Maritime Capital

Acre, Israel

Acre is one of the oldest inhabited places in the world. There is some evidence that it is the city recorded in an inscription dating back to the 16th century BCE. It is also one of the most besieged cities in history, from the ancient world right up until the most recent siege, which ended in 1948 with the expulsion of most of its Palestinian population. As such, the walls of Acre have a special fascination for military historians, and especially for their involvement in the two great Crusader sieges—when Crusaders under Richard the Lionheart took the city in 1191 and, exactly one century later, when they lost it again.

The events of those sieges, and the original struggle by the First Crusade to take the city in 1099 were illustrated over and over again by medieval monks, visualizing the history on the page without actually having seen the walls of Acre themselves. We have to see these medieval illustrations not as the walls actually looked, but as they believed they must have looked to have inspired such momentous events—though the great towers that were such a feature at the time are in the pictures too.

**Medieval Acre,
14th-century plan**

The old city of Acre, to the
southeast of the present city,
was entirely surrounded by
a double line of walls and
towers. At its center is the
citadel and, standing in the
bay, the fortress tower of
the Templars. Acre's modern
lighthouse, on the southwest
of the old city, is built over
the foundations of the
Templars' fortress.

Harbor defenses

Acre's harbor and
breakwater were built
by the Romans. Chains
connecting the sea
tower to the harbor
walls were used by the
Crusaders to prevent
enemy ships from
sailing into the harbor.
The Templars' fortress,
now submerged in
the shallow waters
of the bay, was once
connected by a tunnel
to the port itself.

The coastal citadel

Acre was inhabited during
the Bronze Age, expanded
by the Romans, and later
fortified by the Crusaders.
It is sited on the bay of
Haifa and throughout its
history it has been subjected
to conquest and siege.

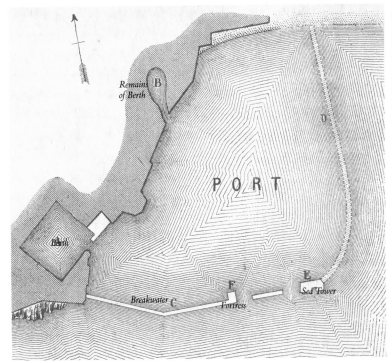

Remains
of Berth

B

D

PORT

Berth

Breakwater   C

F
Fortress

E

Sea Tower

Saladin's Fortress

Saone, Syria

Saone was built on an extraordinary natural defensive system, on a rocky ridge between two huge gorges in the mountains north of the port of Latakia. The site was captured by the Byzantines in 975 and most authorities believe that the first fortifications and the long outer walls were built after that. Unlike other castles of the period, Saone does not dominate the countryside. Quite the reverse, it is hidden away, but is just as fearsome despite that.

The slopes surrounding the castle site are terrifying, and there is even a natural ravine between the lower and upper bailey, linked by two small gates. The walls stretch around the top of the plateau that determines the size of the castle, but was itself a weakness, especially for a garrison that was almost bound to be too small. When Saladin laid siege to Saone in 1188, he was successful because the perimeter wall proved too long to be defended. The site was abandoned during the Middle Ages and the process of decay was speeded up by another serious bombardment in 1840.

Site plan
The rocky spur that juts out was always going to be vulnerable to attack and it was here that Saladin set up his siege machines and bombarded it until the garrison could no longer cope with the damage on such a huge site. This end of the castle site included a small town with at least two churches.

Ensuring the water supply
A huge cistern to store water was built by the Crusaders with a barrel vault. It is one of a number of storage areas built at that time, including the large stone hall between the keep and the west wall. This also served as somewhere where the residential population could shelter from bombardment, and women and children were among the survivors who must have sheltered here during the siege of 1188.

Natural advantages

The strategic potential of Saone was identified long before the Crusades. The site is believed to have been fortified at least since the Phoenician period in ca. 1000 BCE. Saone was built on a ridge between two vast canyons in the inhospitable Jebel Daryous mountain range east of Latakia and has an uninterrupted view of the entire coastal plain below. In the opinion of T.E. Lawrence, the castle was "probably the finest example of military architecture in Syria."

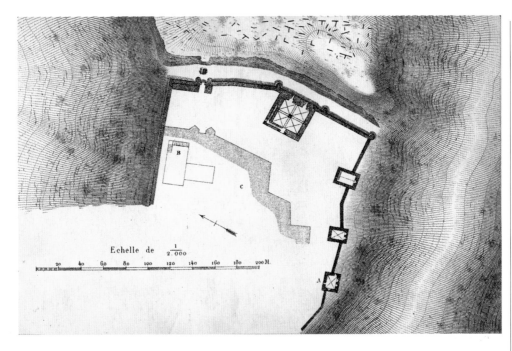

The Crusaders' keep

The central fortress dates from the Byzantine period, but the Crusaders added a large keep overlooking the great ravine in the eastern end of the castle, which seems to rise directly out of the rock. It was here that the surviving garrison retreated in 1188 and negotiated with Saladin, who let them escape to Antioch in return for a cash payment.

Ravine defense

The main entrance to the castle was over a huge gap known as a fosse, which was hacked out of the rock — about 170,000 tons (154,000 tonnes) of it, without the benefit of rock-breaking equipment or gunpowder— with a huge wall built by the Crusaders on the other side. The fosse was too wide for contemporary engineering to bridge in a single span and a drawbridge was supported by one thin pillar of rock, which is all that remains, and which is made higher by the addition of some masonry. The construction of such a chasm was useful in keeping siege engines such as the trebuchet a good distance from the walls.

A Templar Castle

Tortosa, Syria

Tortosa, modern-day Tartus, was an ancient port on the Syrian coast, with a strong citadel at the northwest corner of the fortifications of the town. Only the foundations of the huge keep still exist next to the sea, but the rest of the castle shows signs of the numerous times this town changed hands. It was captured by the Byzantines in the tenth century, and then by the Crusaders in 1099, only to be lost again immediately afterward. In 1152, it was taken over by the Templars.

The castle was attacked over and over again in the two centuries that followed. Saladin managed to take parts of the town but not the castle. In 1291, after a short siege, the garrison escaped to Cyprus, taking with them the famous icon of the Virgin Mary that had been lodged in the church of St. Mary next door. As late as 1518, Christian soldiers were still trying to take it back. Today there are houses built into the city walls.

An unexpected location
Unlike so many Crusader castles, Tortosa was built on a flat site with no natural protection other than the sea. It turned the location to its advantage by establishing terraced platforms beyond the walls on which to set catapults and other siege engines. The fact that Tortosa repelled so many attacks, notably in 1188 when the Templars held off Saladin from the safety of the keep, is a testament to its defenses. If defenders could physically hold off an attack, they could be supplied by sea.

Coastal citadel
Tortosa was established in the fourth century by Emperor Constantine. It formed part of Arab conquests in the seventh century and remained in Arab control until the Crusader invasion at the end of 11th century, with the Knights Templar assuming responsibility in 1152. At the end of the century the walls were further enhanced to form part of the defenses along the coastal strip held by the Crusaders. Most of the medieval town is outside the double walls and sea-filled moat. On the seaward side a slope or *glacis* was built at the foot of the walls to resist attack on the foundations.

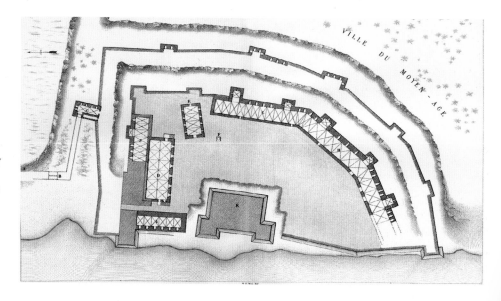

Concentric walls

Like so many other Crusader castles, and in contrast to most of the Islamic ones, Tortosa was protected by a double line of walls, with deep ditches on the outside of both concentric lines. The walls were as high as any other Crusader castle, on top of which ran wall walks that gave access to the archers so that they could shoot through the slits.

Architectural detailing

The sources of Crusader castle architecture are likely to be drawn from various influences and experiences of the Crusaders. Given that the European model was still evolving, Eastern designs were developed—borrowing particularly Muslim and Byzantine ones.

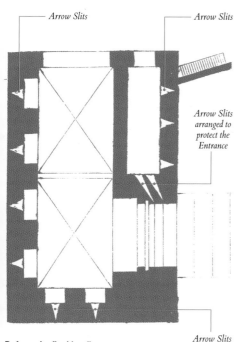

Arrow Slits — *Arrow Slits*

Arrow Slits arranged to protect the Entrance

Arrow Slits

Defense by flanking fire

When Wilbrand of Oldenburg passed through Tortosa on his way to Antioch in 1212, he was there a generation after Saladin's attack and a decade after the earthquake that damaged so many Crusader castles. He described it as a small city that had "a very strong castle with an excellent wall with eleven towers as if crowned by eleven precious stones". These towers were built by the Templars to provide the kind of flanking fire that was increasingly required.

The City on a Hill

Antioch, Turkey

The siege of Antioch during the first Crusade quickly attained the status of legend. Strictly speaking, the city endured two sieges—one where the armies of the First Crusade arrived and laid siege to the city in 1097 and a second the following year, once they were in control, where they were besieged in turn by the Muslims.

This second siege, and the battle that ended it, saw the intervention by the monk Peter Bartholomew, who claimed to have had a vision of the Holy Lance buried at the cathedral. The subsequent discovery of the lance—although it was greeted with skepticism by the crusader leaders—seems to have turned the morale of the defending troops and won them the battle. The hilltop city was the capital of the Crusader principality of Antioch for the next two centuries before it fell in 1268. It had been one of the great cities of the ancient world, with up to half a million people living in it, but by the 15th century there were only about 300 houses left.

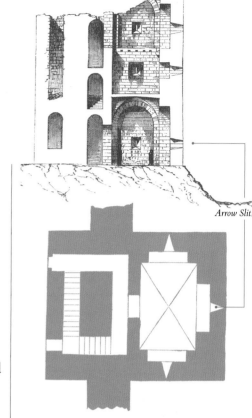

Arrow Slit

Elevation and plan view
Square towers are distinctive of the early Crusader style, with arrow slits on the sides as well as forward facing to enable the defenders to shoot along the walls at attackers. By the 13th century, Templars and other military orders were responsible for most of the castle-building in the region, and the same master builders may have been used for several castles.

The Principality of Antioch
On the River Orontes in what is now Turkey, Antioch was a critical objective on the way to the Holy Land. Once known as the "fair crown of the Orient," it was of great trading and religious importance. It became one of the Crusader states formed during the First Crusade and was a vast complex, ringed by walls with, it was said, 400 towers. In the 12th century it may have had a permanent population of 20,000, including a number of Crusaders of Norman or southern Italian origin.

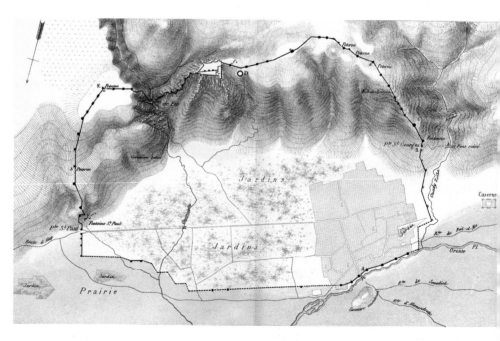

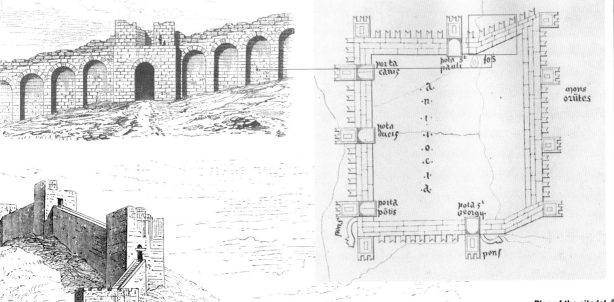

Plan of the citadel

The citadel of Antioch has been described by historians as "surprisingly modest" for such an exposed Crusader outpost, but it had important natural defenses, being built at the top of Mount Silpius, overlooking the city down below.

Defending a mountain

The walls and the citadel had been built originally after 969 by the Byzantines, but both were strengthened considerably by the crusaders in the 12th century, who added square defensive towers strung out along the side of the mountain. About 17,000 defenders were killed and 100,000 taken into slavery when the city fell in 1268, largely because the population had been weakened by endless disputes with Armenia and there were insufficient defenders to man the whole city wall.

Fortifying Cyprus

St. Hilarion, Kantara, Buffavento & Kolossi

Cyprus received its first brush with the crusading world in 1191 when Richard the Lionheart arrived on his way to the siege of Acre, and discovered that his sister and fiancé had been taken hostage by the local ruler, Isaac Comnenus. His response was to take the island, and Isaac took refuge briefly in Kantara Castle before being captured. From then on Cyprus played a key role in the defense of the kingdom of Acre and its castles were built along similar lines to the ones on the mainland.

The Crusader castles follow the same tradition as those on the mainland, but pushed somehow to an extreme, with dramatic mountain scenes or castles that appear to rise out of the living rock. St. Hilarion, for example, makes use of a dramatic mountain top. It had been built originally on the site of a monastery, at the end of the 11th century and was improved at the beginning of the 13th under the local regent Jean d'Ibelin. It was later used as a summer residence for the royal family.

The linked defenses
Kantara Castle is only 2,200 ft (630 m) up, with a watchtower on its very peak, but from the castle you could send and receive signals from Famagusta and Buffavento. It is believed that the Byzantines built it in the tenth century as a lookout post against raiding Arabs. The only way to avoid the rocks is via a small mountain pass toward the south side, defended by semicircular bastions.

St. Hilarion
The upper fortress of St. Hilarion dates from the Crusader period and it includes the royal palace with tremendous views across the harbor and the sea. Up here, the Crusader walls with square towers protect the safest and least accessible part of the castle. This replaced Byzantine walls with round towers around the 13th century. The Crusaders called this summit *"Dieu d'Amour,"* because of its security and cool breezes, but this may have been derived from the Greek *Didymos*, the Byzantine name for the twin peaks.

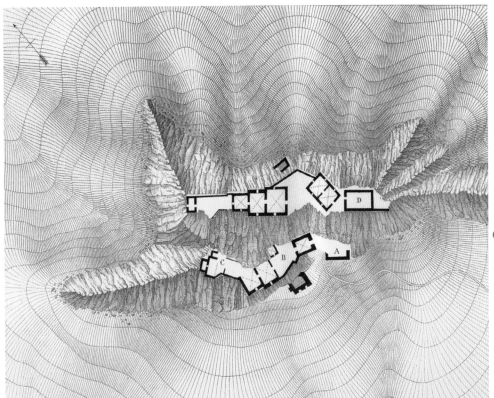

Buffavento

Like many of the other
Cypriot castles, which
seemed built to unique
designs because every
mountain top was a
different shape, the castle
of Buffavento, built at
an altitude of 3,000 ft
(900 m) on top of steep
crags, was used as a place
where bonfires could be lit
to signal that unidentified
ships were in sight.

Kolossi

The fortress at Kolossi was of
great strategic importance. It
controlled valuable holdings
that produced cotton,
wheat, sugar, and produced
a renowned sweet wine
known as *commandaria*.
The Hospitallers actively
encouraged the production
of wines and sugar, the
majority of which found
a ready market in Venice.

"God Wills It"

The Crusades were viewed as a just war. They were launched,
directed, funded, and managed by the papacy and had adopted
a cross as their emblem. The religious significance of the Holy
Land prompted various contingents of Crusaders to take up
the cause—to restore Jerusalem to Christian control. In 1489,
the kingdom of Cyprus was passed to Venice. Along with
many other mountain fortresses on the island, St. Hilarion was
taken apart by the Venetians in the 16th century to save money.

THEN & NOW
Aleppo

Saladin's citadel, Syria

The citadel of Aleppo dominates an ancient city that was for a time the Roman capital of Arabia, and has been regional capital ever since—although it has also been in Persian, Byzantine, Arab, and Mongol hands. It saw military action between the last Mameluke sultan and the Ottoman Turks as late as the 16th century.

The appearance of the castle owes most to Saladin and his successors, who rebuilt the walls and constructed the nine towers. Aleppo was redesigned again to cope with changing methods of siege warfare. Castles and their defense had become increasingly important during the Crusader period, rather than field battles, which could be unpredictable. Defenders had to protect themselves against siege engines and also needed to provide bases for trebuchets for bombarding the enemy camp. Towers gave them a far better range than just setting themselves up inside the walls.

One of Aleppo's mysteries is the sudden appearance of box machicolations, through which stones could be dropped onto attackers below. These were added to the walls here at about the same time—and in the same style—as they were added by Crusader castle designers at Krak des Chevaliers. This implies an interesting link between the two sides— they either were impressed by these features in action, or perhaps they employed the same craftsmen.

Aleppo, a 13th-century depiction

The palace was built by Sultan Baibars on top of the huge new gate that was built there by Saladin's son al-Zahir Ghazi. There were also palaces in Damascus and Bosra, the other magnificent Muslim castles of the period. Unlike the Crusader castles at the time, however, Aleppo was also an urban stronghold. The garrison could live in the town, so there was no need to build huge spaces inside the castle to house them. Muslim and Crusader castles of the period included towers that were far bigger than anything that had been used before. In contrast to the contemporary Crusader castles, however, Aleppo's Islamic builders did not use round towers.

The citadel and city today

The modern city of Aleppo is dominated by its citadel and its infrastructure has been built around it. Although not as large as the citadels of Cairo and Damascus, the limestone used to build the rectangular towers and walls on the summit of the great mound serve to exaggerate its visual impact. The moat surrounding the elliptical base is still a feature, and the entrance, via an arched bridge with its two-towered lower gate, has been renovated.

Tʜᴇ ᴡᴏʀᴅ *kremlin* means fort or fortress. The term is familiar to the rest of the world because of the famous Kremlin in Moscow but all fortresses in Russia are called kremlins. They were powerful bastions of defense, many of them devastated and rebuilt many times as the wars washed back and forth before the advent of gunpowder rendered high walls—hitherto the basis for defense—too vulnerable to attack.

CHAPTER 7

Russian Kremlins

The distinctive domes and ornate towers that loom above huge walls would be instantly recognizable as Russian castles, with their white-washed or red-brick defenses. Kremlins were often central to a Russian town or city in a way that the castles of Western Europe were not—and, as administrative centers, they continue to be so. These castles of Russia also emerged in a different environment, and a different kind of history, from those in the West. The terrifying winters, the frozen rivers, and the wastelands of ice provide a backdrop to warfare in the East. Russia was also subject to almost continual invasion for most of its history, from Tatars, Swedes, and Germans, but the great forces of history also swept to and fro across Russia, from the Mongols to the Poles. These were not small skirmishes. If the English mustered a force of little more than 5,000 men to fight the battle of Agincourt in 1415, the Battle of Kulikovo in 1380—the decisive battle against the Mongols—saw anything up to 400,000 Russians face down an army of possibly up to 700,000.

The kremlins of Russia also continued in use longer than their counterparts in the West, well into the 17th century—though it is true that the Welsh castles were adapted for service in the English Civil War at the same time. But while castles in Western Europe were being designed with low walls to provide mounts for artillery, the Russian castles continued the tradition of towers and high walls as their functions were still so much broader than those of their Western counterparts.

Rostov Veliky, Russia
The kremlin at Rostov Veliky (Rostov the Great) stands on Lake Nero in the Yaroslavl region. Its complex of palaces, churches, and onion-top towers was built between the Spaso-Yakovlevsky and Abraham monasteries. The town, one of Russia's ancient centers, is one of several recognized for the unique monuments of Russian architecture dating from the 12th to the 18th centuries. The kremlin itself is one of the finest outside Moscow.

A Seat of Soviet Power

The Kremlin, Moscow

Moscow's Kremlin is famous, not because it was a castle, but because it became a palace and then the seat of government for the Soviet empire and the Russian federation. It probably dates back to the founding of the city in 1147. The first wooden walls went up a decade later, but that kremlin was swept aside during the Mongol and Tatar invasion of 1238. In 1368, the wooden walls that replaced it were destroyed in the same fire that burned down the city. Its walls were rebuilt in limestone, dragged over ice by sledge and, as Moscow grew in power and prestige, these white defenses survived to form the foundations of the present triangular shape. The Kremlin was rebuilt in 1485–95 using Italian architects, including Pietro Solari who in 1500 developed a new kremlin construction method. The final towers were not finished until the 17th century. By then, the walls stretched for $1^{1}/_{3}$ miles (2.2 kilometers), making the Moscow Kremlin the most powerful fortification of its kind in Eastern Europe.

Beklemishevskaya Tower
Because the Kremlin continues to play such an important role, most of the walls, towers, and other buildings have been changed constantly. The exception is the Beklemishevskaya Tower, which has remained almost unchanged. It is also the most important of all the Kremlin towers, because it stands at the junction of the Moscow River and the Kremlin's moat, which made it the first point of attack. Even in the 18th century war with Sweden, the tower was strengthened to carry heavy cannon.

Wall and tower complex
The huge Kremlin walls were originally designed to be strengthened with 18 defensive towers. Another two were added in the 17th century, right at the end of the period when the walls were regarded as serious defenses. All but three of the towers are square. One of the most conspicuous is the Spasskaya Tower (seen on the left of this image), built in 1491 and now marking an entrance to the Kremlin. It was the first of the Kremlin towers to be given a roof, this one by Scottish architect Christopher Galloway in 1624.

Early Italian design

The Beklemishevskaya Tower was built from 1487 by the Italian architect Marco Ruffo in order to protect the ford that was the only available crossing over the river. The tower is also important because it included an underground "listening vault" to detect the sounds of enemy miners tunneling their way under the river.

Map of Moscow, 1739

The Kremlin walls remain impressive to this day. The triangle encloses as much as 68 acres (27 ha), with walls as high as 60 ft (19 m) and as thick as 20 ft (6.5 m) in places. They were built by the Italian architects brought in for the purpose between 1485 and 1495. The moat and river made them relatively safe from mining, but—when the cannon were removed in the 17th century—they lost their defensive role, along with the outer wall that had been built to protect them along the perimeter.

A Frontier Fortress

Nizhny Novgorod Kremlin

The city of Nizhny Novgorod was originally a frontier town for the Muscovites, founded in 1221 at the meeting point of two of the great Russian rivers, the Volga and the Oka. It was key to defending the frontiers of Russia from marauding Tatars, Mordvinians, and Cheremis. It is hardly surprising that it became known as one of the most powerful kremlins in Russia. It had to be powerful—there are records of Nizhny Novgorod having to withstand some form of attack an amazing 17 times.

The first wooden fortress on the site made use of the rivers, defended by a moat on one side and the steep cliffs of the river bank on the other. The great red kremlin that remains to this day was built in stone, beginning in the summer of 1509. The lineal link with the Moscow Kremlin is extremely strong because the architect at Nizhny Novgorod was the Italian Peter Fryazin who had worked on the stone walls of Moscow a decade before.

The supreme moment for the Nizhny Novgorod Kremlin came in 1612, when the city's volunteers—led by Kozma Minin and Dmitry Pozharsky—marched out of the fortifications to fight the Polish invaders. Minin's patriotic appeal went down in history: "Oh, brothers and friends, all folk of Nizhny! What can we do, when Moscow state is in great devastation?" and there is a commemorative statue of him in the main square. In 1932 Nizhny Novgorod was renamed Gorky in honor of the famous writer Maxim Gorky, who was born in the city. In 1991 the city regained its historic name.

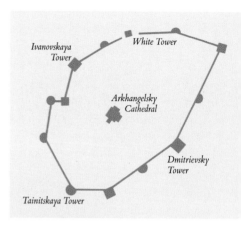

Layout of the kremlin
Nizhny's stone-walled kremlin, begun in 1509, was subsequently recognized as an outstanding example of Russian-style fortification art. As with Moscow's Kremlin the Italian architect Peter Fryazin was involved in its design. The perimeter walls contained 13 circular and rectangular red-brick towers. Like Moscow's Kremlin, Nizhny's originally had a detached *strelnitsa* (bastion) connected to the gate in the Dmitrievsky Tower by means of a stone arched bridge, built across a 100-ft (30-m) ditch, now destroyed. The Dmitrievsky Tower is now a museum.

Brick-built towers
The main feature of the city today remains the distinctive red towers of the Nizhny Novgorod Kremlin. But within the walls of the kremlin it is a different story. In the aftermath of the 1917 Revolution, the only historic building left standing was the Archangel Cathedral, which dates back to 1624.

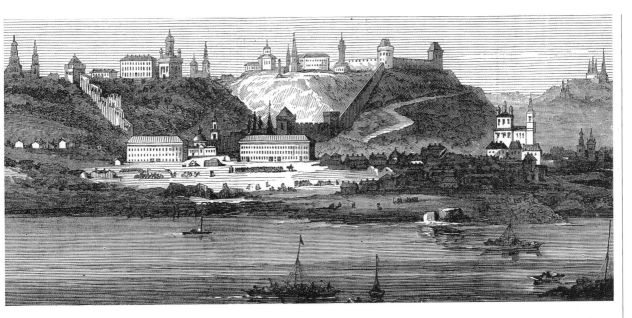

Frontier fortress

The walls and the long line of Nizhny's kremlin towers has been described as a "stone necklace" across the slopes of Chasovaya Hill. It withstood sieges by Tatars in 1520 and 1536. Legend has it that the 1520 siege was lifted after the besieging army encountered a local woman who killed ten of their scouts with the yoke with which she carried two buckets of water.

Town plan

The main square in front of the Nizhny Novgorod kremlin is called Minin Square after the local meat merchant who inspired the city volunteers to march out and tackle the Polish invaders. Minin is buried in the Kremlin and a statue of him is in the square, outside St. John the Baptist Church, from where he was believed to have issued his appeal.

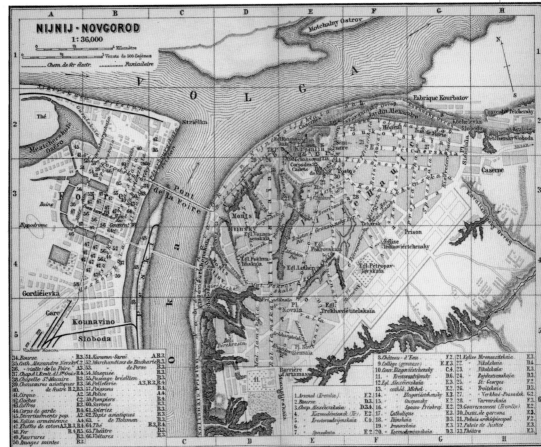

THEN & NOW
Kazan

Kremlin of the Tatars

Russian castles have a continuing afterlife that is rare compared with their equivalents in Western Europe. The Kazan Kremlin has certainly had one, and it is seen here in all its splendor—with buildings from Orthodox culture, as well as Muslim, Russian, Bulgar, and Tatar—when it had just become capital of the vast Tatar province of the Russian Empire. Like the Moscow Kremlin, it still has a role as the seat of power, but this picture shows the Kazan Kremlin at its most magnificent, and before the Stalinist architectural purges that demolished many of the monasteries and churches inside.

The origins of the castle are unclear but there was a stone fortress here in the 12th century, which was demolished by the Mongols and rebuilt during the 15th century by the Kazan Khans, part of the Golden Horde. The city was taken by Ivan the Terrible in 1552, and what happened to the buildings remains controversial to this day, given that Kazan has as a result an almost evenly balanced population of Orthodox Russians and Muslim Tatars. Depending on who you believe, Ivan then demolished either the entire kremlin or some of it and brought in Russian masons from 1556–58 to rebuild the walls and towers that we see today.

The outer defenses

The Russian style is to build and re-build these huge walls, along the lines of the walls of Kazan—though the Moscow Kremlin originally added an outer wall of defenses, since demolished. The medieval walls of Kazan were built of oak beams, but were rebuilt in stone by Ivan the Terrible, and over the centuries the stone was slowly replaced by brick. By the time the walls and defenses were completed at Kazan in the 16th century, there were also 13 towers to provide defensive positions and to watch out over the water. In fact, the natural defenses of Kazan were also impressive. The kremlin was, at one time, surrounded on three sides by water—the River Kazanka to the north, three large lakes to the east, and the Tatar Bulak Canal (an artificial waterway to link the city with Lake Kaban) providing a barrier to the west. Ivan the Terrible believed that the kremlin he had captured was beautiful. The one he built to replace it remains so; it was also for many years believed to be impregnable.

The distinctive watchtowers today ⌄

The Kazan Kremlin remains distinctive, partly because of the five domes of the Annunciation Cathedral inside, and partly because of Ivan the Terrible's new Spassky Tower, which came to mark the entrance to the kremlin. But most of all, it is because of the mysterious leaning Suyumbika Tower, which is controversial because it goes to the heart of the argument about how much Kazan blends Russian and Tatar influences. Officially, Ivan demolished the entire kremlin and ordered the tower to be built. But there is some evidence that it reflects the tastes of the exiled Khan Muhammad Amin, who lived in Moscow while Italian architects were rebuilding the kremlin there. That would mean that the tower was built before 1490, in the Italian style, and preserved by Ivan because of the Moscow connection and because—at seven stories high—it was an effective watchtower. Evidence for this is that the size of the bricks used for the tower matched that used by Moscow's Italian architects, rather than the size used for the rest of the walls and towers in the 16th century.

ORTH INDIAN CASTLES display a mix of Hindu and Islamic elements. In the 12th century invaders of Turkic and Afghan origin established the Delhi Sultanate, a series of five Islamic dynasties centered on Delhi which built a succession of forts in what is now the capital. In 1526 a Mongol invasion from Central Asia took control of northwest India and established one of the most powerful and wealthy Indian dynasties, the Mughal Empire.

CHAPTER 8

Indian Fortresses

The successive Islamic invaders made use of the fortifications that already existed in the territories they conquered, and although they would demolish temples and replace them with mosques, they generally retained and repaired the castles and city walls. Many north Indian fortifications are primarily Hindu in style, but with perhaps a characteristically Muslim arched gate, evidence of restoration after a siege. Like their European counterparts, the north Indian castles of the medieval period were also the palaces of the feudal lord of an area, and so their grandeur reflected the status of their princes. Gateways decorated with molded and sculptured ornament are common, and even the merlons on the parapets were cut into elaborate shapes.

As the Delhi Sultanate dissolved during the 15th century into separate principalities, numerous castles were built to defend these autonomous territories from their neighbors. Unlike fortifications in the West, which were increasingly designed to withstand artillery, Indian castles continued to be built following medieval principles, with high walls and towers, into the 18th century. It was only with the arrival of European invaders that fortifications began to take account of the increasing power of cannonry.

Mehrangarh Fort, Jodhpur, Rajasthan
The Mughal Empire was responsible for some of the finest architecture in India. The fort at Jodhpur, a city founded in 1459 at a strategic point on the route between Delhi and Gujarat, is one example. Jodhpur grew rich on profits from opium, copper, silk, and coffee and benefited from exposure to the wider world: new styles of art and architecture appeared. The Mehrangarh Fort, which towers above the city, is one of India's largest. It was founded when the 15th ruler of Rathore, Rao Jodha (1438–88) moved his capital to Jodhpur. Inside its immense walls are several palaces, courtyards, and a temple. Some of the walls are almost 120 ft (36 m) high and nearly 70 ft (21 m) wide in places, although much of what stands today dates from the 17th century.

The "Gibraltar" of India

Gwalior Fort, Madhya Pradesh

There has been a fort at Gwalior since at least the tenth century, although it is possible that its origins date back several hundred years before that. The fort was rebuilt and modified many times, and withstood numerous sieges, the last of which occurred during the Indian Rebellion in 1858, during which the Queen Lakshmi Bai, the Rani of Jhansi and one of the leaders of the Indian struggle for independence from the British, was killed.

The fort encloses numerous temples and six palaces, of which the finest is Man Mandir Palace, built by Raja Man Singh in the early 16th century. The fortifications were intended to impress visitors with their grace and beauty as well as their military power, and so the walls and gates were decorated with reliefs and carvings and faced with colored tiles. Reservoirs excavated at the southwest of the complex are fed by a natural spring that rises within the fortress walls.

Hathi Gate

At the top of the northeastern access road stood the magnificent Man Mandir Palace, which was entered through the Hathi Gate. This gate, whose name means "elephant," was so called because a statue of an elephant with a herder used to stand in front of it. There is a sharp right turn on the path immediately before the gate that prevented a swift charge by attackers using elephants.

Hilltop fortress

Gwalior occupies the flat-topped summit of a 2-mi (3-km) long rocky outcrop approached from west or east via the Urwahi or Gwalior gates, the latter dating from ca. 1660. The Urwahi Gate stands in a defensive wall built across the mouth of the Urwahi valley, a deep wedge-shaped gorge that cuts into the outcrop on which Gwalior stands.

Entrance road

The northeast entrance is accessed by a winding road that originally had seven gates, though only five remain standing. The gates were connected with curtain walls, so that attackers, having passed through one gate, would find themselves under fire from the walls on either side as well as from the next gate along. Most of the gates were quite simple in construction, though those at either end of the entrance road were more heavily fortified.

Impregnable position

The fort is built on a huge sandstone outcrop and dominates the surrounding countryside from a height of nearly 300 ft (90 m). The curtain wall runs around the entire perimeter of the rocky hill, enclosing an area of 1⅕ sq mi (3 km²), and it is punctuated at intervals by towers or bastions. In some places the slope of the hill was cut away to leave a sheer rock face.

Jain statue

On the southern side of the fort were huge figures cut into the rock that represented Jain *tirthankaras*, or "pathfinders." One of these statues is 40 ft (12 m) tall.

City of Nine Fortresses

Fortifications of Delhi

Delhi has been inhabited for about 3,000 years, and there are known to be about nine different cities around the site of the present-day city. The earliest, the Hindu city of Lal Kot, was built and fortified around 1060, and some fragments of its walls can still be seen. From the 14th century successive Muslim cities were built, of which Tughluqabad and Adilabad remain impressive examples of the fortifications of the period, despite being quarried for building materials over the subsequent centuries. These have masonry walls about 30 feet (10 meters) thick built from huge stones, reaching a height of 90 feet (28 meters) at the citadel itself. Later forts were Purana Qila, built around 1530, and Lal Qila, the fortress of the city of Shahjahanabad, founded by Shah Jahan in 1638.

> **Lal Qila**

The fort of Lal Qila was built largely to protect the palace and other buildings within. Its fortifications were constructed on a plinth of rubble above which rise walls of sandstone ashlar to a height of 100 ft (30 m). The wall is topped by a battlemented parapet with loopholes for small-arms' fire, and there is a deep ditch outside the walls. On the east side that faces the River Jumna the walls are only about a third of the height of the landward walls, so that the palace was vulnerable to fire from the opposite bank of the river.

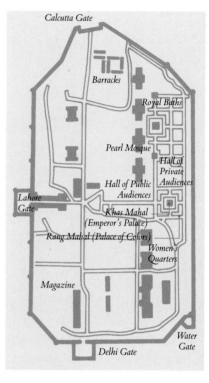

The Indian Rebellion

Delhi was captured during the Indian Rebellion in May 1857, the British garrison being much too small to defend Lal Qila. The city walls had previously been strengthened by the British to withstand artillery, which meant that it took several months for the Indian forces to recapture the city. It was only with the arrival of heavy artillery in September, which was subsequently concentrated on the Kashmir Gate to the north, that the walls were breached and the city retaken.

Lahore Gate
The wall of Lal Qila had two main gates, Delhi Gate to the south and Lahore Gate to the west. Delhi Gate was defended by a barbican and tall octagonal towers on either side of the entrance passage. Lahore Gate originally had no barbican, but one was added in 1670, featuring thick walls and heavy doors made of teak 7½ in (19 cm) thick, reinforced with steel straps.

Shah Jahan's city
Stretching in a half-moon shape beyond Lal Qila to the west is the city of Shahjahanabad, which itself had a curtain wall of brick with nine gates and several bastions and fortified towers. The Jami Mosque in the foreground outside the fortress held out for several days against the British assault to recapture Delhi during the Indian Rebellion.

THEN & NOW
The Red Fort

Agra, Uttar Pradesh

The city of Agra rose to prominence as the imperial capital of the Mughal emperors from the 16th century, though it has been a place of settlement for more than 2,500 years. Akbar the Great (1556–1605) was responsible for the Lal Qila or Red Fort, which was begun in 1564 and completed by the end of Akbar's reign.

The fort was constructed on the site of an earlier brick fort that had fallen into disrepair, and the walls were built using a thick core of rubble dressed with red sandstone blocks, which give the fort its name. An outer curtain wall is separated from the much higher inner wall by a distance of about 30 feet (10 meters), and a moat about 35 feet (11 meters) deep runs round three sides of the semicircular fort. The walls are punctuated at intervals by semicircular bastions, which are concentric in both their outer and inner walls, and there are two heavily fortified gates as well as a third that gives access from the River Jumna. On the river side the distance between the inner and outer walls is extended to create a terrace, the south part of which was kept as a recreation area for the ladies of the palace.

The Red Fort depicted in the *Akbarnama*
This painting from the *Akbarnama* shows the Red Fort not long before its completion. The *Akbarnama* was the official chronicle of Akbar's reign, commissioned by him and written in Persian by his court historian, Abu'l Fazl, around 1590. Scenes from Akbar's reign, including his restraining of a runaway elephant, were portrayed in beautiful illuminations, many of them having the striking red sandstone of the imperial city as a backdrop.

The walls surround an area of about 94 acres (38 hectares), and within them are palaces and reception halls built by Akbar and his successors, notably his grandson Shah Jahan, who was also responsible for the white marble Taj Mahal, built about a mile down the river for his wife Mumtaz Mahal. Many of the buildings are in a fine state of preservation, and the fort is a UNESCO World Heritage Site.

Present-day Red Fort

The Red Fort retains the imposing grandeur of its heyday. The Amar Singh Gate at the southwest corner is protected by two barbicans, one an extension of the outer curtain wall, the other a rectangular enclosure with a tower on either side. The outer gate is accessed via a drawbridge over the ditch that surrounds the fort, and the battlemented walls on either side have loopholes for defensive fire. After this gate there is a right turn to the gate that leads into the second barbican, an arrangement designed to slow the progress of attackers. The walls here have two rows of loopholes as well as machicolations to permit the dropping of missiles onto attackers attempting to undermine the walls below.

GALLERY OF
Eastern Medieval & Early Modern Castles

If castles in the Holy Land and Asia appear different from those of Western Europe, the distinction is less than clear cut. Byzantine, Muslim, and other styles of architecture converge in the castles of the Levant; Russian kremlins used Italian architects; while India's forts bear hallmarks of contact with a wider world.

Kumbhalgarh Fort, India
With perimeter walls that extend almost 24 mi (36 km), the 15th-century fort in Rajasthan is the world's third longest fortification. The compound encloses over 360 temples.

Sidon, Lebanon
This island fortress, built in 1228, was slighted after the fall of Acre to deny Crusaders the chance of re-establishing defenses along the coast.

Solovki monastery, Solovetsky Islands, Russia
A 15th-century frontier fortress founded by Russian monks to repel attacks by neighboring Swedes on Russia's western border.

Ivangorod Fortress, Russia
Established in 1492, Ivangorod on the River Narva displays the typical high-walled architecture of a Russian medieval fortress.

Paphos, Cyprus
Originally a Byzantine fort guarding the harbor, Paphos castle was destroyed in an earthquake in 1222. It was restored during the Ottoman occupation of Cyprus.

Byblos, Lebanon
A 12th-century Crusader castle, once moated. It was dismantled by Saladin in 1188 but the Crusaders recaptured and rebuilt it in 1197.

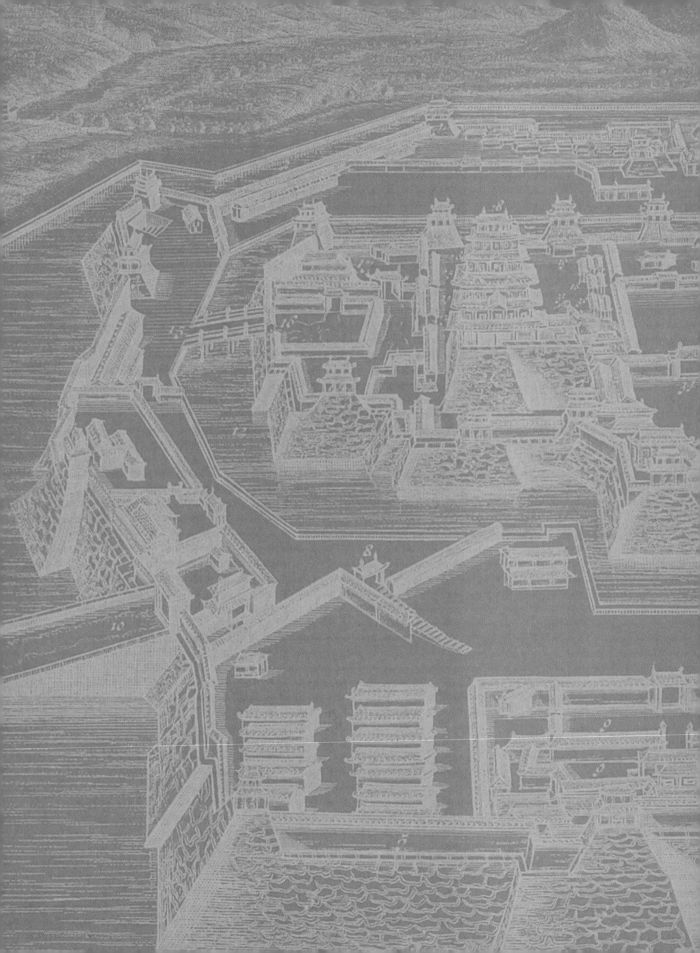

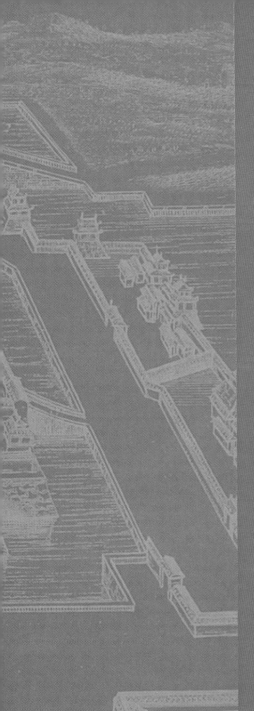

Castles
of
East Asia

Introduction

In common with Western Europe, many centuries of war in the Far East brought about the region's own traditions of fortification, and here the emphasis must be on the plural, as the evolution of a distinctive East Asian style of castle or walled town produced different results in China, Japan, and Korea. The most striking difference lay in the location. In China the tradition was that of the walled city or town, with individual castles—if such they could be called—being restricted to tiny isolated watchtowers. In Japan, by contrast, the starting point was not the desire to enclose a settlement but the establishment of a military position usually by a powerful local landlord. These castles, which could be quite modest in size, tended to be hilltop locations—so providing the frequently encountered expression yamashiro or "mountain castle." When certain lords prospered at the expense of others during the 16th century these individual castles grew greatly in size, and together with extensive urban development resulted in the first Japanese castle towns. Yet even at this stage very few of these towns were themselves fortified or enclosed.

One aspect common to East Asia's fortified places is that they all made the best use of local building materials, and all witnessed discernible development as new threats required new responses. The most basic material of all was loess, the sandy deposit that is the dust of China, which was compacted and rammed between wooden molds to produce sturdy walls. These are to be found in early Japan and Korea too. The other material used in conjunction with loess was timber, the predominant feature found in the stockade-like fortresses of the Japanese frontier between the eighth and twelfth centuries. Stone then makes an appearance in all three civilizations. In Japan, large dressed stones and rammed smaller ones combine to produce the characteristic sloping bases of Japan's classic developed fortresses such as Himeji or Matsumoto. In Korea the snakelike stone walls reach their point of perfection in Suwon's defenses, while the finest of all is the Ming dynasty's achievement of the "long dragon"—the Great Wall of China.

Timeline

ca. 1520 BCE–1030 BCE	771 BCE	221 CE	215		297
Shang dynasty walls with foundations of rammed earth begun in China	Zhou build Luoyang in west China	Unification of China under the Qin emperor	Meng Tian ordered to build defenses—the Qin "Great Wall"		Japanese fortifications are described in the *Wei Zhi*, a Chinese history book

618	634	710	794		1153
Tang dynasty founded	New palace complex added to Chang'a	Nara becomes Japan's first permanent capital	Japan's capital is moved to Heian (Kyoto)	*Great Wall*	Jin set up capital at Zhongdu (Beijing)

1180	1181	1207	1215	1366	
Gempei War begins	Nara receives temporary fortifications but is burned down	Sieges of Xiangyang and De'an	Zhongdu (Beijing) falls to Mongols	Ming walls of Nanjing begun	*Pingyao*

1359	1372	1372	1382	
Siege of Shaoxing	Ming defeated by Mongol army at Karakorum	First military structure built at Jiayuguan	Great Wall section built at Shanhaiguan	

1407	1467	1496	1543	1570	1575
Ming walls of Zhongdu (Beijing) started; The Kingdom of Ryukyu (Okinawa) is formed after unification	Ditches and palisades used during the Onin War	Rennyo founds Ishiyama Honganji	Arrival of Europeans in Japan	Oda Nobunaga's first attack on Ishiyama Honganji	Siege and battle of Nagashino

1576	1581		1586
Building of Azuchi Castle	Siege of Tottori by starvation		Building of Osaka Castle

1587	1591		1592
Invasion of Kyushu	Siege of Kunoe—unification of Japan completed	*Osaka*	First invasion of Korea

	1597	1598	1600	1603	1614
Defending Osaka	Second invasion of Korea	Death of Toyotomi Hideyoshi	Battle of Sekigahara	Tokugawa Ieyasu becomes shogun	Winter campaign of Osaka

	1615	1616	1626	1644
	Summer campaign of Osaka	Death of Tokugawa Ieyasu	The Great Wall is depicted on John Speed's map of China	Manchus enter Beijing

East Asia

The Korean peninsula provides an interesting mix of the Chinese walled fortification and the Japanese mountain castle. The *yamashiro* has its exact equivalent in Korean as the "*sanseong*," an expression written using identical Chinese characters to *yamashiro*. Yet the *sanseong* look very different. Instead of the Japanese style, whereby an existing mountainside was shaped and sculpted and then clad in massive stone blocks to give the characteristic curved wall, the Korean model resembled more the Great Wall of China in miniature. Long, curved walls ran up and down the mountain's contours to enclose a defensible space that was pierced by gates through which tunnel-like entrances ran, again on the Chinese model. Korea also had a separate tradition of the *eupseong*, which was a fortified town or village. Here comparatively low walls with offset gates followed a broadly quadrilateral course to defend a settlement.

As for the islands lying between Japan and southern China, Taiwan was not settled until the 17th century CE, so the models of fortification seen there are Spanish or Dutch colonial outposts. The Kingdom of Ryukyu, however, the collection of islands that make up the modern Japanese prefecture of Okinawa, maintained a considerable armed independence from both its large neighbors throughout the medieval period and developed the unique fortress tradition of the *gusuku*. Here we encounter stone walls not unlike those of a Korean *sanseong*, but arranged around a hill or small mountain in broadly concentric baileys after the Japanese style.

Great Wall, China
See pages 205–6

Pingyao, China
See pages 206–7

Katsuren, Japan
See pages 216–17

Katsuren, Japan
See pages 216–17

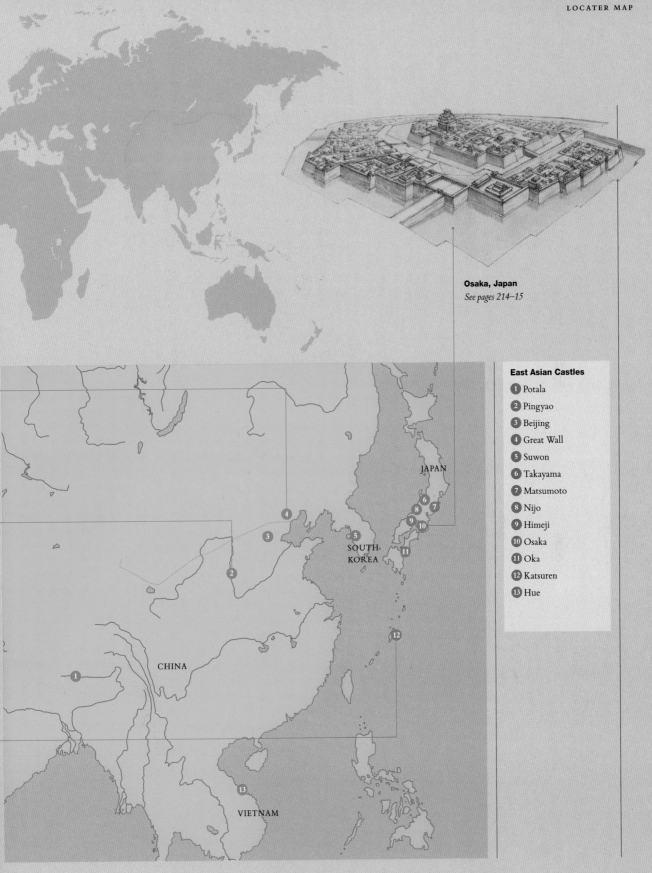

Osaka, Japan
See pages 214–15

East Asian Castles

1 Potala
2 Pingyao
3 Beijing
4 Great Wall
5 Suwon
6 Takayama
7 Matsumoto
8 Nijo
9 Himeji
10 Osaka
11 Oka
12 Katsuren
13 Hue

JAPAN

SOUTH
KOREA

CHINA

VIETNAM

CHINA POSSESSES the world's oldest tradition of fortifications. Great cities, towns, and even villages were enclosed within walls, and it was said that a Chinese city without a wall was as unbelievable as a house without a roof. The supreme achievement of the Chinese fortification tradition is, of course, the Great Wall. Here the practice of enclosing a city was extended to enclose the vulnerable northern borders of the entire nation.

CHAPTER 9

Chinese Walls

The great enclosing tradition extended even to the design of the walls, whatever their composition. In the fortified city walls of successive dynasties there existed a certain similarity in design. This is because the grand scheme of city planning—including the size of walls, the number of gates, and the street layout—was determined by set rules that were adhered to right through to the Ming and Qing dynasties. A Chinese walled city, therefore, tended to present a uniform appearance. The principle of "five gates and three royal courts" on a central axis leading to the imperial palace complex was the accepted layout for the capital according to the accepted wisdom of what could be defended—and from the Sui dynasty onward this layout evolved into a threefold system in order to guard from rebellion within as well as external threats. A favorable geographical position was also of utmost importance in selecting any site.

The most ancient form of walling in China was *hangtu* (rammed or tamped earth), in which successive layers of loess (a windblown deposit found in great abundance in China) were compacted within removable wooden shuttering, much like that used to confine concrete today while it sets. With the Tang dynasty we find fired bricks being used to encase city walls, and at Kaifeng examples exist where brick is used for the outer surface of the wall, while the inner face is buttressed with a wide angle of rammed earth. With the Ming dynasty we begin to see the extensive use of fired brick walls around a rammed rubble core—this was to be the keynote of the Great Wall of China.

The Great Wall of China

A view of the most dramatic sections of China's supreme achievement. In some places the ascent is so steep that one may question why it was thought necessary to join the various peaks together using a wall that followed the contours. In fact, although the towers provide the main means of defense, linking them by means of what was effectively a fortified, all-weather footpath added greatly to their military value and provided a powerful symbol of absolute control.

Defending a Nation's Border

The Great Wall

The Great Wall of China is the world's most famous and most impressive defensive structure. Most of what we see today owes its existence to the Ming dynasty, and runs from the "Old Dragon's Head," a tower that protrudes into the sea at its eastern extremity, to a fortress on the edge of a parched desert landscape in the west. In most cases the lowest few feet of the Great Wall, or even more, consisted of dressed stone blocks cemented together around a hammered rubble core, which was filled as the height increased. At a certain level bricks take over, sometimes as an inner layer followed by an outer layer of bricks laid up to 14 courses high. This gives the wall its final appearance featuring crenelations, gates, and walkways. Running along the length of the Great Wall are numerous towers, gateways, water gates, and forts, overlooked by hundreds of detached beacon towers. Spurs, some quite extensive, protrude from the wall at certain points and run along neighboring ridges.

Each tower along the wall was a miniature castle in its own right and provided observational, signaling, and defensive functions. There's no doubting the wall's practical function in repelling an invasion of nomads, who would have also been intimidated by its mere existence. Yet despite its impressive structure, the Ming Great Wall was as much a political statement as a military one. It provided work, prestige, and a reassurance of security to the Chinese population that disjointed and isolated sections or fortresses could not have provided.

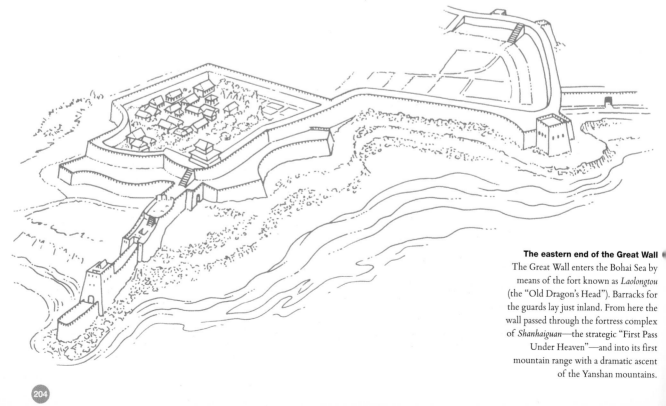

The eastern end of the Great Wall
The Great Wall enters the Bohai Sea by means of the fort known as *Laolongtou* (the "Old Dragon's Head"). Barracks for the guards lay just inland. From here the wall passed through the fortress complex of *Shanhaiguan*—the strategic "First Pass Under Heaven"—and into its first mountain range with a dramatic ascent of the Yanshan mountains.

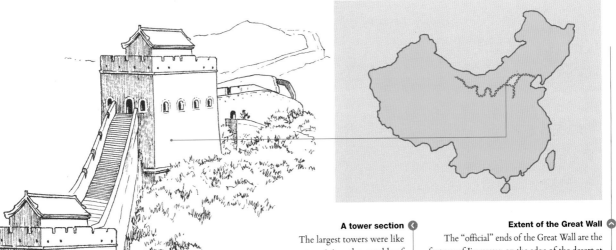

A tower section
The largest towers were like mini-castles, capable of withstanding a siege. Some even had access only by means of retractable ladders, and were well-stocked with weapons, ammunition, provisions, and signaling materials. Other towers were used primarily for storage. This one is the so-called Store Tower at Jinshanling, which was actually the commander's headquarters for the sector.

Extent of the Great Wall
The "official" ends of the Great Wall are the fortress of Jiayuguan on the edge of the desert at the west and the Old Dragon's Head tower at the east, but traces of fortification have been found that indicate that it stretched farther in each direction. In its first phase of construction, during the rule of Qin Shinghuandi, the first Emperor of China, the wall extended for about 3,100 mi (5,000 km), extending four existing fortification walls that are believed to date from 700 BCE. The Chinese name for the wall, *Wan-Li Qang-Qeng*, means "10,000- Li Long Wall"—a li being a linear measurement of about 1,650 ft (500 m).

Mount Badaling
The Great Wall is one of the world's greatest fortifications. It provided a first line of defense against the Hsiung Nu—the Huns—and other nomadic tribes who threatened China's northern territories. Most of what remains today dates from the Ming dynasty (1338–1684). Over a 200-year period the wall was extended to 6,400 mi (4,000 km) and much-renovated. Mount Badaling is shown in this engraving. This section of the wall lies just to the north of Juyongguan. Its construction took place between 1539 and 1582.

ANATOMY OF
A Fortified City

Pingyao, Shanxi Province

The wall of Pingyao, the finest surviving example of a Ming city wall, is almost square. Every 130 or 330 feet (40 or 100 meters) along the wall is a protruding tower called a *mamian* (Horse-Face), which provided flanking fire. The wall has six gates in all. Each has a forbidding narrow courtyard, and is entered by a dark archway. On top of each gate is a gate tower, superbly restored. The 3,000 battlements and 72 towers are said to represent the saints of Confucius and his 3,000 disciples, while the overall shape is supposed to represent a tortoise, the symbol of longevity. The four gates at the east and west represent the tortoise's legs, while the southern gate is its head, and the northern gate the tail.

Gate tower
The mid-point of Pingyao's walls contain very strong gateways with offset entrances, steep walls, and ornate towers above them.

Moat
Pingyao's defenses make use of a moat for much of the enclosing wall's length, which is connected to the river on the southern side. Here the wall follows the course of the river and is undulating in its design, whereas on the other three sides the water channel is straight.

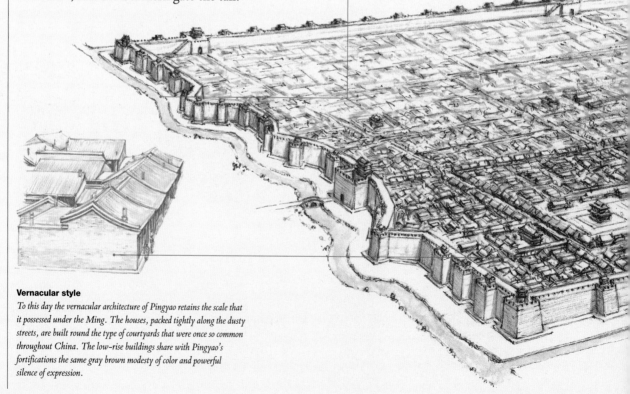

Vernacular style
To this day the vernacular architecture of Pingyao retains the scale that it possessed under the Ming. The houses, packed tightly along the dusty streets, are built round the type of courtyards that were once so common throughout China. The low-rise buildings share with Pingyao's fortifications the same gray brown modesty of color and powerful silence of expression.

Intermediate towers

The length of Pingyao's walls is broken by numerous towers. Detailed here are some of the intermediate towers along the wall that projected outward to allow flanking fire. Each has a small guard post on top of it in the form of a small tower.

Corner tower

The surviving and restored towers and gates of Pingyao are excellent examples of Chinese defensive architecture at its most graceful. This delicately ornate tower is an example of those that are found at the corners of Pingyao's walls.

Street plan

Pingyao is built according to a grid pattern with all the streets intersecting at right angles. The town is an almost perfectly preserved example of a walled town of the Ming dynasty.

Central tower

At Pingyao's heart lies an ornate multistory tower, visible from the cardinal points along the main streets.

THEN & NOW
The Walls of Beijing

Beijing City, Northern China

Very little now remains of the mighty walls that once enclosed Beijing, a city that was to provide the site for the capitals of several dynasties in or around the modern metropolis. There are remnants of a majestic complex gate structure at the south end called Qianmen or *Zhengyangmen* ("the gate that faces directly to the sun") flanked by two great towers. These towers were solidly built from brick and stone around a rammed earth core. It was from *Zhengyangmen* that the Ghongzhen emperor bade farewell to the army against the rebel leader Li Zicheng. Two months later Li Zicheng conquered Beijing and the mighty walls were rendered redundant.

The inner gate of Qianmen today
A view from inside the archway of the outer gate toward the inner gate tower. Beyond that lies the Chairman Mao Mausoleum and the bleak Tian'anmen Square, which together have spoiled the original concept of a grand avenue stretching right up to the Forbidden City.

Beijing City, southern walls, 17th century
This engraving is a brave if fanciful attempt to reproduce the complex fortified structure of the *Zhengyangmen* (Qianmen) in Beijing as it was at the time of the fall of the Ming dynasty in the 17th century. Nowadays it presents the appearance of two unconnected towers, but once a semicircular wall joined the two together. The central entrance was used only by the emperor, but there were also two side entrances each defended by a barbican. Here fairs and markets were held in time of peace. The outer tower, substantially rebuilt in recent times, was known as the Gate Tower, while the inner tower was called the Arrow Tower.

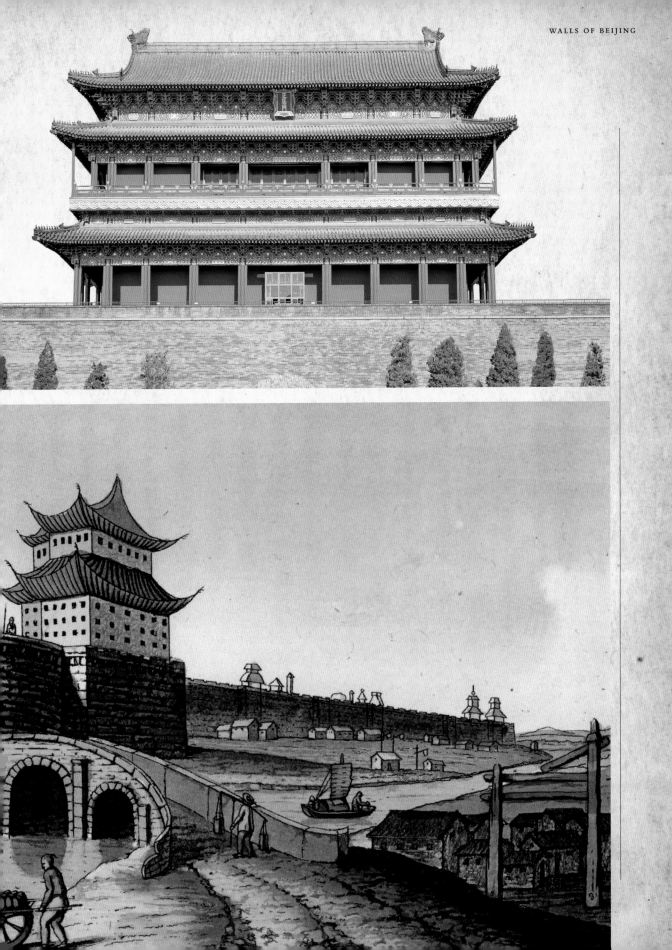

MEDIEVAL AND EARLY MODERN Japan was the land of the samurai, the aristocratic warriors who fought for their *daimyo* (lords) in a series of complex civil wars during the 16th century. The *daimyo* ruled their territories from hilltop castles. The first of these castles were rudimentary affairs made from timber and earth, but as the domains grew these fortresses developed into a unique Japanese defensive structure.

CHAPTER 10

Japanese Castles

Japan's castles were built on massive solid stone bases. Although usually referred to as "walls," this is a somewhat misleading term for the bases, as they were produced less by building "up" than by building "on." The process involved thousands of workmen following a precise geometric pattern to clad in stone the slopes of existing hillsides from which the vegetation had been removed. The bare surfaces were precisely smoothed to produce a prearranged slope that would combat erosion, add strength, and provide a secure base for building. The downward thrust resulting from the weight of the superstructures was safely directed outward.

The solidity and strength of such bases was well illustrated in 1945, when the atomic bomb dropped on Hiroshima obliterated the city's castle keep in an instant but left the stone base virtually untouched. On top of these bases lay strong and complex defensive areas of interlocking walls, towers, gatehouses, and living quarters, typically overlooked by a graceful and striking keep that would act both as a lookout tower and a final refuge in times of war.

Matsumoto Castle, Nagano, Honshu
Matsumoto is one of Japan's most beautiful fortresses. In style it is a hirajiro—*a castle on a plain—even though it is surrounded by some of the highest mountains in Japan. Its keep, encircled by a wet moat, is one of the oldest surviving tower keeps. It was built in 1597 and is complemented by a smaller secondary tower that completes the defensive and artistic ensemble.*

The *Yamashiro* Castle

Takayama, Gifu Prefecture

Takayama is an excellent example of the *yamashiro* or mountain-top Japanese castle with other notable examples at Himeji and Hikone. Its stone bases are created from the slopes of a mountain nearly 2,250 feet (687 meters) high, and the elaborate superstructures, of which nothing survives, would have formed an interlocking complex of gates, towers, and walls. Three successive baileys are identifiable within the castle's general area.

Takayama was started in 1588 by the local lord Kanamori Nagachika on the orders of the *daimyo* Toyotomi Hideyoshi who unified Japan's political factions. However, by 1603 when the third and final tower, the main keep, was added, Japan was effectively at peace, and Takayama's role was more symbolic rather than defensive. In 1692 the Kanamori family were transferred to Dewa province, and after a short period of time under the control of the Maeda, the castle passed under the direct control of the shogun in 1695. Today all that remains of the castle are its stone bases, which comprise an attractive hilltop park known as Shiroyama.

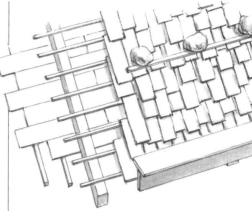

Protective rocks
The roofs of a castle such as Takayama would have been covered with wooden shingles above a framework. In many cases, heavy rocks were laid along the sections as a protection against high winds.

Roof styles
The four illustrations detail the variation in roof shapes encountered in Japanese castles. These are shown with earthenware tiles although other designs used wooden boards, plant materials, or metal.

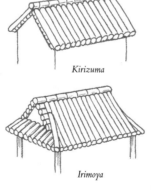
Kirizuma

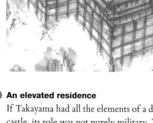
Irimoya

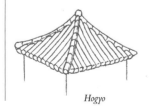
Hogyo

Yosemune

An elevated residence
If Takayama had all the elements of a defensive castle, its role was not purely military. The intention was to impress rivals, not only with the elaborate layout but with lavishly appointed residences. As with Western late medieval castles, Japanese castle architecture evolved from fortress to palatial residence.

Japanese versus Chinese

Takayama castle illustrates very well the difference between the Chinese and Japanese style of fortification. In Japan very little use is made of walls or any enclosure that follow the natural contours of the hill. Instead towers and gateways are built on leveled areas that are in themselves complete defensive systems. There is much use made of stone cladding on the exposed surfaces, and in certain places buildings are raised above stout wooden frameworks, so they projected out over the hillside.

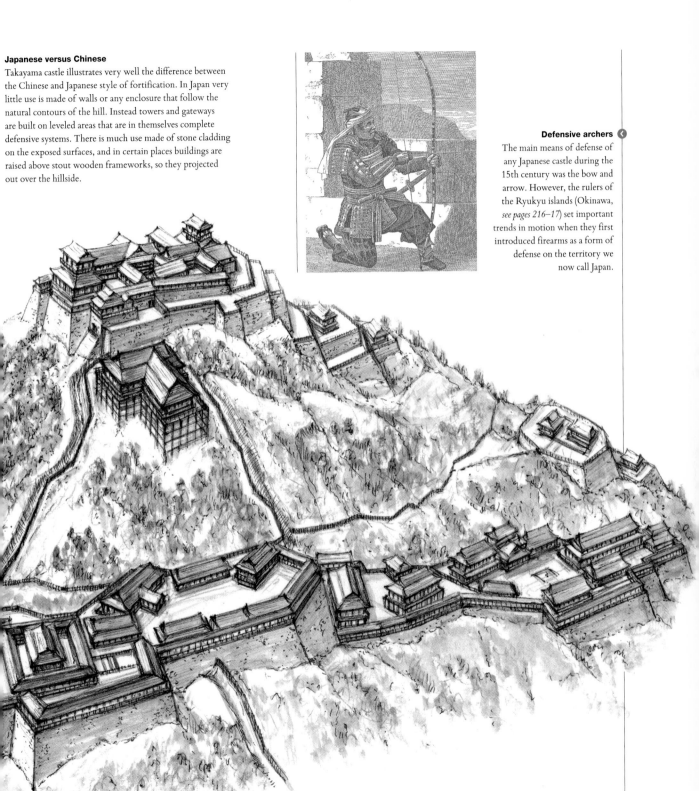

Defensive archers

The main means of defense of any Japanese castle during the 15th century was the bow and arrow. However, the rulers of the Ryukyu islands (Okinawa, *see pages 216–17*) set important trends in motion when they first introduced firearms as a form of defense on the territory we now call Japan.

ANATOMY OF
A Samurai Stronghold

Key elements of Japanese defense

The castle at Osaka on Honshu island owed its foundation to Rennyo Shonin (1415–99), the great patriarch of the "True Pure Land" sect of Buddhist monks, from whom were drawn the Ikko-ikki armies. Their strongest outpost was a fortified temple called Ishiyama Honganji, which was built on a great slope ("*o-saka*"). When the temple was conquered by the samurai lord Oda Nobunaga, his successor built the first castle at Osaka. The heart of Osaka's defenses was the complex of keep, palace, and inner walls with moats that were constructed on the site of the Ishiyama Honganji temple—and in spite of the passage of centuries the overall layout is still largely preserved.

Outer bailey
Most of the area of the Ni no maru, or "second bailey" of the castle, particularly the western side or Nishi no maru (western bailey), was a flat expanse of ground, with various buildings, each defended by low walls, around the edges. Their functions included residences for samurai, the stables, and rice storehouses.

Inner bailey
Between the Ni no maru and the castle's innermost area —the Hon maru (main or inner bailey) —was another wet moat. It was horseshoe shaped with its open side to the south. The Hon maru housed the palatial living quarters of Osaka castle and its keep.

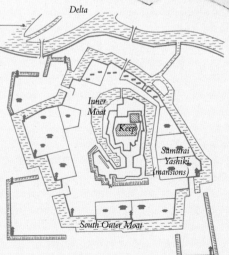

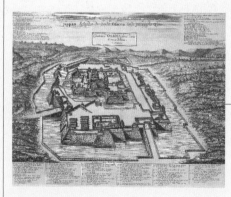

Natural defenses
The Tenma river was just one branch of a complex delta that provided a set of natural moats for Osaka on its northern side. Beyond was a maze of islands and creeks, crossed by bridges. The main area of the jokamachi (castle town) of Osaka lay to the west of the castle, where a canal had been cut between the river and the sea.

Delta

Inner
Moat

Keep

Samurai
Yashiki
(mansions)

South Outer Moat

Outer fortifications and ramps
The first wet outer moat is set with massive stone walls on its inner sides. It was split up by four fortified ramps that allowed access to the inner castle. They were known as the Kyobashi guchi, the Aoya guchi, the Tamatsukuri guchi, and the Ote guchi (or Ikutama guchi). Each had a massive gatehouse on the inner side.

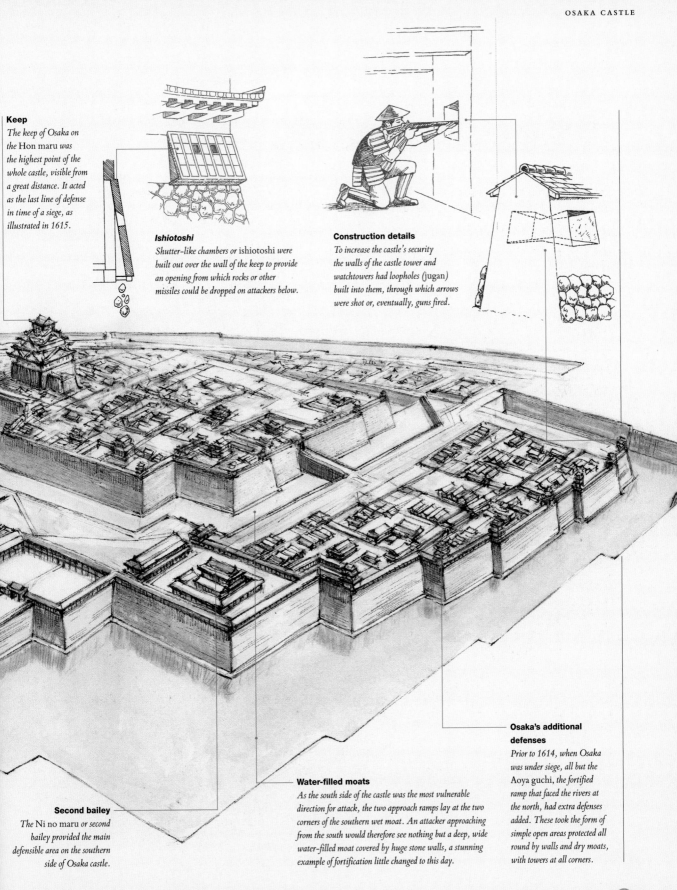

Keep
The keep of Osaka on the Hon maru *was the highest point of the whole castle, visible from a great distance. It acted as the last line of defense in time of a siege, as illustrated in 1615.*

Ishiotoshi
Shutter-like chambers or ishiotoshi *were built out over the wall of the keep to provide an opening from which rocks or other missiles could be dropped on attackers below.*

Construction details
*To increase the castle's security the walls of the castle tower and watchtowers had loopholes (*jugan*) built into them, through which arrows were shot or, eventually, guns fired.*

Osaka's additional defenses
Prior to 1614, when Osaka was under siege, all but the Aoya guchi, the fortified ramp that faced the rivers at the north, had extra defenses added. These took the form of simple open areas protected all round by walls and dry moats, with towers at all corners.

Water-filled moats
As the south side of the castle was the most vulnerable direction for attack, the two approach ramps lay at the two corners of the southern wet moat. An attacker approaching from the south would therefore see nothing but a deep, wide water-filled moat covered by huge stone walls, a stunning example of fortification little changed to this day.

Second bailey
The Ni no maru or second bailey provided the main defensible area on the southern side of Osaka castle.

215

The *Gusuku* Castle

Katsuren, Ryuku Islands (Okinawa)

Katsuren is one of the finest surviving castles on Okinawa, a group of islands stretching from Japan to Taiwan. In the local dialect they are called *gusuku*. The description refers to their positions—overlooking the sea and covering the approach to harbors. In their design the *gusuku* were nothing like Japanese castles. Their walls were not solid bases carved out of a mountain and enclosed in stone, but castle walls that would have been more recognizable to a European visitor. Although resembling Korean and Chinese walls in many respects, they did not always follow the contours of a hill in the manner of the Great Wall of China. Instead they enclosed successive baileys on a hillside in which were administrative wooden buildings.

Katsuren became the center of a vigorous trade during the 14th and early 15th centuries when it was taken over by a Ryukyu lord, Amawari, known for his ambitions for the throne of the Ryukyu Kingdom. Amawari proceeded to make Katsuren rich through agriculture and trade but both he and his castle were ruined in 1458 in a war against the Ryukyu King Shotaikyu.

Pacific Ocean

Palace

Lower Bailey

Walled Enclosures

Administrative Buildings

An ocean *gusuku*

The ruins of the *gusuku* of Katsuren present an impressive image, with the Pacific lying on both sides of the promontory. Within the *gusuku* archaeology has revealed the importance of trade in Ryukyuan history, with expensive tiles and precious Ming Chinese porcelain found among the ruins. Chinese involvement with the Ryukyus began in 1372 when emissaries visited the three Ryukyuan principalities, establishing formal diplomatic links through tribute.

Administrative buildings

Towers made of wood were raised above the graceful curving walls of the *gusuku*. They were pierced by tunnel-like gateways that were very reminiscent of Chinese and Korean models. The administrative buildings of Katsuren lay well within the defensive complex. The rebuilt palace at Shuri, the capital city of the kings of Ryukyu, gives an indication of how these ornate wooden structures would have appeared.

Island palace ⌄
Katsuren Castle consisted of several walled enclosures constructed on a high limestone ridge. The second enclosure from the top contained a large palace structure. Katsuren was the residence of Amawari, a powerful *aji* (local ruler) who held out against central control, and at one time even defeated the king's brother.

Curving walls ‹
A typical *gusuku* used curving low stone walls on the Chinese model to enclose successive baileys more reminiscent of Japanese castles.

THEN & NOW
Oka Castle

Stronghold of the Shiga family

Oka castle, which sprawls along a wooded and mountainous ridge overlooking the town of Bungo-Takeda in Oita prefecture on the island of Kyushu, is one of Japan's most impressive castle sites. The location was first fortified in 1185, although its history properly begins with Shiga Sadatomo in 1332.

Anonymous 19th-century scroll painting

Although nowadays a ruin, the sheer scale of the area occupied by Oka Castle gives an indication of its former greatness and its key strategic location. The natural shape of Mount Gagyu on which it lies was utilized to provide defense in depth, with the mountain's slopes being shaped, sculpted, and then clad in stone to produce a fortress that seems to grow out of the ground from which it springs. This 19th-century painting depicts Oka's former complex. Numerous turrets, towers, and gates were added in an almost unparalleled example of military might. During the Edo period Oka was the seat of government of the Oka Clan.

The Shiga family ruled Oka until 1586, by which time they had become close allies of the Otomo, the most powerful family in Bungo province. Like many of the Otomo, Shiga Taro Chikatsugu was a baptized Christian and had the name of Paul, and unlike many of his neighbors stood firm when the Shimazu clan invaded their territory. Oka Castle proved to be ideal as a base from which to mount guerrilla attacks against the Shimazu.

In 1594 Oka Castle was given to Nakagawa Hidenari (1570–1612), who was responsible for rebuilding the edifice in the form it was to retain. In 1663 the castle was greatly expanded by the construction of the *Nishi no maru* (western bailey). Its towers included the *Suzumi Yagura,* or "cooling tower," for the comfort of the ladies in the castle, and the *Tsukimi Yagura* ("moon-viewing tower").

The keep was destroyed by an earthquake during the Edo period, while the remaining superstructure was demolished during the Meiji period as one of many similar examples whereby local communities demonstrated their abandonment of the feudal past and their association with the new Japan.

Oka today

The present site of Oka Castle lies on one side of the town of Bungo-Takeda and extends up into the mountain that dominates the town. None of the buildings on top of the stone bases has been reconstructed, but it is nonetheless impressive as an example of the Japanese style of fortification that used the natural shape of a mountain. Oka Castle was designated a national historic site in 1936, and has today been attractively landscaped.

GALLERY OF
East Asian Castles

Iconic and distinctive, the fortifications of East Asia have evolved a style that incorporates the great traditions of oriental art and architecture with graceful, upcurving towers, a strong emphasis on wood for detailing, and a desire to incorporate the advantages of the natural surroundings into the designs.

Himeji Castle, Japan
This classic hilltop castle complex is one of the finest examples of 17th-century Japanese defensive architecture in existence. The original 14th-century fort was dismantled then remodeled as a castle and considerably extended. The complex today contains 83 buildings.

Nijo Castle, Japan
An example of a flatland castle in Kyoto set within a double concentric wall. Completed in 1626 it became the Tokugawa Shoguns' residence.

Palace at Hue City, Vietnam
The entrance to the citadel of the fortified palace inside Hue City. Three circles of brick-clad earth ramparts enclose the complex.

Palace of Potala, Tibet
First constructed in 637 by the Tibetan king Songtsen Gampo, Potala was fortified and raised in height by Tibetan monks working with craftsmen and artists from all of Asia.

Matsumoto Castle, Japan
Matsumoto's defenses included interconnecting walls, moats, and gatehouses. Its late 16th-century keep still has its original stonework.

Hwaseong Fortress, Suwon, South Korea
The 18th-century wall in central Suwon was built to enclose the royal palace when King Jeongjo planned to move his capital from Seoul to Suwon.

SECTION

5

*Modern
Fortresses*

Introduction

A long transitional period in military technology began in the middle of the 15th century. This was prompted by improvements in the art of cannon-founding, which was rapidly developed. The transition was gradual, but slowly the vulnerability of the medieval walls and towers became evident. As Edward Gibbon put it: "the proportion of the attack and defense was suspended; and this thundering artillery was pointed against the walls and towers which had been erected only to resist the less potent engines of antiquity."

Perhaps Gibbon exaggerated somewhat, inasmuch as artillery was in service for some time before it began to have any effect on the design of fortifications. Indeed, the earliest cannon threw so light a projectile that their effect on masonry walls and towers was insignificant. This began to change however, and the fall of Constantinople in 1453 was, at least partially, attributed to the Ottoman use of cannon. One of these is supposed to have been 26 feet (8 meters) long, and able to hurl a 13 hundredweight (600 kilogram) ball around a mile (2 kilometers). Such heavy weaponry was, given the technology of the time, somewhat impractical; it purportedly took 60 oxen to move it and took three hours to reload.

In western Europe Charles VII of France appointed Jean and Gaspard Bureau as Treasurer and Master of Artillery of France respectively in 1440. The Gaspard brothers are credited with so improving both the design of guns and their tactical deployment that ten years later the French king was able to take all the Normandy castles from the English within a 12-month period.

That artillery was changing the nature of warfare forever was, perhaps, only made undeniable following the invasion of the Italian peninsula by Charles VIII of France in 1494. With him was an artillery train claimed to have consisted of 300 mobile guns, including 70 siege cannon. Using these weapons the Castello di Monte San Giovanni, a work that had been credited with previously resisting a seven-year siege, fell after about eight hours of bombardment breached the walls. With the existing system of defenses becoming obsolete new ideas were required.

Timeline

1440

Charles VII of France appoints Jean and Gaspard Bureau as Treasurer and Master of Artillery of France respectively.

1456

Mehmed II invades the Balkans and advances northward, unsuccessfully besieging Belgrade.

1480

The Ottoman Empire besieges Rhodes city 23 May–17 August. The siege fails.

Rhodes city harbor before 1522

1494

Charles VIII of France invades the Italian peninsula with 25,000 men and about 70 mobile siege guns and takes the castle at Monte San Giovanni.

1521

An Ottoman force under Suleiman I marches on Belgrade and takes it before moving on into Central Europe.

1522

The Ottoman Empire conducts a second siege of Rhodes. The city surrenders after besiegers gain entry through mines and underground tunnels.

1540-1545

Henry VIII builds a series of "device forts," mainly along England's south coast.

1595

Upgrades to Portsmouth's defenses inaugurated. Town is encircled with a bastioned *trace italienne*.

1598

Upgrades to Pendennis Castle, one of Henry VIII's forts, begin under the auspices of Elizabeth I's engineer Paul Ive.

Pendennis Castle

1633

Birth of the military architect Vauban.

Seigneur de Vauban

1672

Construction of Castillo de San Marcos, Florida, begun by Spain

1688

Following the Ottoman defeat at Vienna, Belgrade is taken by the forces of the Holy League. Two years later it is re-conquered by the Ottoman Empire after a six-day siege.

1703

Peter the Great of Russia takes Kotlin Island from Sweden and begins construction of the naval base of Kronstadt.

1739

The Treaty of Belgrade returns Belgrade to the Ottomans.

1751

Construction of Fort Beauséjour by the French begun. Decision taken to construct a fortress near to Figueres taken during the reign of Fernando VI of Spain.

1754

Construction of Fort Duquesne begun by the French. Four years later, it is attacked by a British force and abandoned.

1755

The British lay siege to, and take, Fort Beauséjour.

1787-1791

The Austro-Turkish War. In 1789 the Ottoman Empire once again takes possession of Belgrade.

1794

The U.S. Congress authorizes funds for the creation of 16 (later 20) fortifications at designated sites for the purposes of coastal defense.

1802

A fortified masonry breakwater begun at Cherbourg, France.

1816

Following the 1812 British attacks on Washington (DC) and Baltimore (MD), the U.S. inaugurates the "Third System" of coastal fortifications to defend the eastern seaboard.

1846

Fort Pulaski completed on Cockspur Island in the Savannah River estuary.

Fort Pulaski

Port Arthur

1860

The Royal Commission on the Defence of the United Kingdom recommends the construction of a number of fortifications to defend Britain and her colonies.

1894

Japan defeats China in the First Sino-Japanese War, during the course of which Major General Nogi Maresuke's command takes Port Arthur in one day of combat. The following year Japan is forced to relinquish the port.

1898

China signs a treaty ceding the Liaodong Peninsula, including Port Arthur, to Russia for 25 years. Russia begins a program of fortifying the strategic port.

Modern Fortresses

The introduction of gunpowder caused a process of change that led to the end of the European medieval stone castle; the great keeps, towers, and walls proved increasingly vulnerable to gunpowder cannon. Builders of fortifications began to protect them by sinking them into the ground, which also served to increase their indirect protection by concealment. As the European powers spread their influence across the globe they also exported their technologies and their style of fortifications. The growth of navies further led to the construction of naval fortresses designed to protect fleets and provide them with secure bases from which to operate, and in which to seek shelter. Accordingly, as this map shows, nations that aspired to a maritime policy increasingly built naval fortresses.

Fort Cumberland, 1778
See pages 240–1

Mercer's Fort, Pennsylvania
See page 245

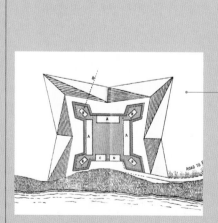

North American & Caribbean Forts

1. Fort Beauséjour/ Cumberland
2. New Amsterdam
3. Fort Duquesne/Pitt
4. Fort Norfolk
5. Fort Pulaski
6. Castillo de San Marcos
7. Fort Jefferson
8. Fort George

European & Asian Forts

9. Fort George
10. Fort Charles
11. Pendennis
12. Portsmouth
13. No Man's Land, *Solent, Hampshire*
14. Cherbourg
15. Coevorden
16. Kronborg
17. Spandau
18. Konigstein
19. Lérida
20. San Fernando de Figueres
21. Kalemegdan
22. Fort Mosta
23. Rhodes City
24. Suomenlinna
25. Kronstadt
26. Port Arthur

CHINA

SCOTLAND

FINLAND

RUSSIA

IRELAND

DENMARK

ENGLAND

HOLLAND

GERMANY

FRANCE

SERBIA

SPAIN

GREECE

MALTA

Coervorden, Holland
See page 249

THE VULNERABILITY OF MEDIEVAL DEFENSES to cannon-fire gradually became apparent during the early modern period. Prompted by rapidly developing improvements in the art of gun-founding new defensive ideas were required, and so from around the middle of the 15th century a long transitional period in military technology began.

CHAPTER II

Responses to Gunpowder

From this time on, existing defenses were augmented with detached works, called bulwarks or boulevards, which were positioned in front. These works formed a shield for the high walls and towers, and created advanced flanking positions for the defender's guns. New fortifications protected walls by sinking them in ditches, the spoil from which were used for sloping banks—the argin or glacis—which gave further protection and allowed a clear field of fire. The ditch became the main obstacle and so came into being the typical profile of a fortification constructed in response to gunpowder weapons.

Modifications to allow mutually supporting flanking fire were even more radical. The main element, developed around the beginning of the 16th century, was the bastion. Bastions project the defense forward, and thus allow defenders to subject attackers to crossfire. Before mechanical warfare there was, essentially, only one method of getting into a fortress—by climbing over the defenses (a process known as escalade) or, if a portion of them had been pulled down, by storming through a breach. The fundamental requirement of all fortification systems, no matter how apparently complex, revolved around preventing attackers from getting over the top or breaching the defenses—mining was of course a different and distinct problem. In the bastioned fortress there is no "dead" ground where attackers can avoid fire, therefore the idea, with many refinements, held the field until near the end of the 18th century.

Pendennis Castle, Cornwall, England
A view of Pendennis Castle, Falmouth, showing the original work as built in 1539. Comprising a round tower and gate enclosed by a circular wall upon which were mounted cannon, Pendennis was one of a pair designed to protect the mouth of the River Fal. It is said that Henry VIII, under whose auspices the program of fort building was undertaken, had a hand in the design of the works. Typically, they were situated to deny any enemy access to harbors or landing places.

The Fortification of Rhodes

Rhodes City, Greece

On 5 September 1307, Pope Clement V confirmed that the island of Rhodes was to become the home of the Knights of St. John of Jerusalem (also known as the Knights Hospitaller). Although they were to remain there until 1522, their occupation was not peaceful, and great efforts were made to update the Byzantine defenses they inherited— particularly those of Rhodes City— against attacks from the mighty Ottoman Empire. The threat of a large scale and sustained campaign increased greatly following the fall of Constantinople to Sultan Mehmed II in 1453, who made great use of the huge cannon constructed by Urbanus of Transylvania (also known as Urban or Orban), the use of which "sealed the fate" of the city. Accordingly, the walls of Rhodes, constructed "only to resist the less potent engines of antiquity," as Gibbon put it, were strengthened and several new towers were constructed. The old towers were protected with bulwarks and the ditch was widened. The expected Ottoman attack occurred in 1480, and the city endured a siege lasting from 23 May to 17 August before the attackers gave up— temporarily. They returned in June 1522 to find greatly strengthened defenses.

Islamic forces move to attack Rhodes, 1482
Although Rhodes' defenses had been improved and upgraded in order to deal with the expected Ottoman artillery from about 1421, the high walls and tall towers typical of a medieval fortification were still much in evidence in 1482. The commercial harbor was protected from seaborne penetration by a chain strung between the Tower of the Windmills and the Naillac Tower.

The "greatest of all the towers of Rhodes"

The Naillac Tower, constructed ca. 1400, viewed from the harbor. This distinctive structure, dubbed "the greatest of all the towers of Rhodes" by Sir Harry Luke in 1913, was some 150 ft (46 m) tall and named for Grand Master Philibert de Naillac. The lower portion housed the winding mechanism for the harbor's protective chain. The tower was damaged by an earthquake in 1863 and subsequently demolished.

View of the harbor as it appeared before 1522

The two fortifications in the foreground either side of the Naillac Tower are the Tower of St. Nicholas on the right and the Tower of the Windmills to the left. These towers were cut down and converted into forts, as were the defenses on the landward side. These measures, however, proved of little use—in 1522 the Ottomans utilized long forgotten Hellenic tunnels under the fortifications and effectively outflanked the Knights Hospitallers from below.

Civitates Orbis Terrarum

Between 1572 and 1617 Braun and Hogenberg (1535–90) published *Civitates Orbis Terrarum*; six volumes of maps depicting, mainly, European cities. They relied on existing maps, confirmed by this view of Rhodes. This representation shows the city as circular in plan surrounded by a triple wall. It must, therefore, date from before the 1420s when the medieval defenses were strengthened. Indeed the distinctive Naillac Tower (ca. 1400) is absent, though several features that remained are identifiable, such as the Tower of St. Nicholas.

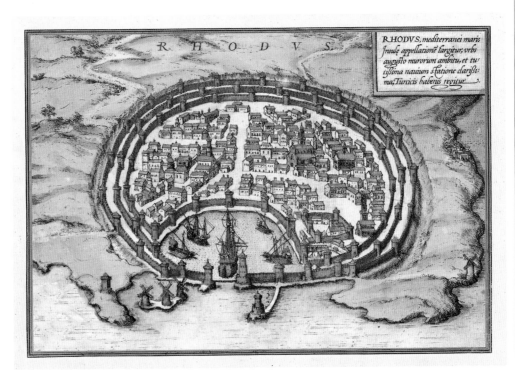

A Henrician Castle

Pendennis Castle, Cornwall

The original Pendennis Castle was constructed between 1540 and 1545. It was just one of a series of defensive forts running, in the main, along the south coast of England. One of Henry VIII's "device forts," it stands on a headland at the mouth of the River Fal, and has a counterpart at St. Mawes across the estuary. These "Henrician castles" were constructed to protect the major English ports and adjacent sea lanes from incursions by the Catholic powers of Europe, which it was assumed were imminent following Henry's schism with Rome: "Thus," wrote Brian Hugh St. John O'Neil, "it came about that the one scheme of comprehensive coastal defense ever attempted in England before modern times was undertaken during this reign."

The potential threat came from the sea power of France and Spain, both Catholic powers that might well harbor designs against Protestant England. The demise of Henry in 1547 and the eventual accession of his staunchly Protestant daughter Elizabeth I in 1558 did not ameliorate the situation, nor, except in the short term, did the destruction of the Spanish Armada in 1588. The latter did, however, grant a breathing space that was to last some six years before Spanish naval strength could once again be reassembled on a scale sufficiently large enough to threaten England.

Pendennis Castle, 1804
A somewhat stylized engraving of Pendennis from the east, showing the original work surrounded by military architect Paul Ive's bastioned defenses. The object of the exercise in constructing the new defenses being; to "impeach the riding of any ships" in the roads. Ive, described as a "military engineer of skill and reputation," was appointed "Chief Engineer or Work Master" on 15 shillings per day. Pendennis might be regarded as a step away from the Italian style of fortification and one toward the French. Indeed, despite Ive's 1589 book *The Practise of Fortification* (the earliest known treatise on fortification written in English) promoting the *trace italienne* exclusively, the orilloned bastions that exemplify it are omitted at Pendennis.

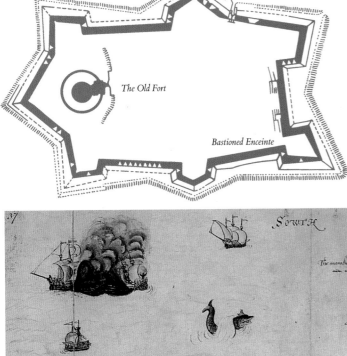

The Old Fort

Bastioned Enceinte

Plan of Pendennis

Taken from a *plat* dated ca. 1597–98 by Paul Ive, this shows the new bastioned *enceinte* around the earlier artillery fort. Ive probably produced this following a visit to the site accompanied by Sir Walter Raleigh, the Lord-Lieutenant of Cornwall and Vice-Admiral of the West, a colonial entrepreneur Ferdinando Gorges, and Sir Nicholas Parker (the Colonel-General of Cornwall and future Governor of Pendennis Castle).

Map of Falmouth Haven and Pendennis, ca. 1600

A colored chart of Falmouth Haven and the River Fal up to Truro, dating from ca. 1600, though obviously drawn prior to the creation of the bastioned *enceinte* around Pendennis. Raleigh had been informed that he should take "the advice of Paul Ive in making choice of some fit plot of ground where some bulwark may be raised to plant ordnance."

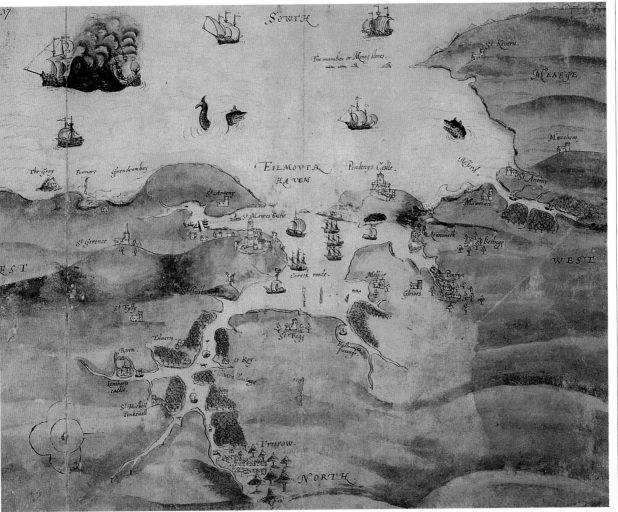

Master of Siegecraft

Seigneur de Vauban, 1633–1707

Sébastien Le Prestre Vauban, later Marquis de Vauban, was a unique and pivotal figure in the history of warfare. He served under Louis XIV of France, the "Sun King," who reigned from 1643–1715, a period of over 72 years. During this time France was at peace for only 17 years—under Louis France was an expansionist state.

Vauban thought strategically, and his schemes were designed to protect France's national borders, particularly with the Spanish Netherlands (roughly today's Benelux countries). There he constructed two lines of fortresses "in imitation of an army's order of battle." Conversely, Vauban's chief talent could be said to lie in his mastery of siegecraft. He devised a systematic and successful method, characterized by an approach using three parallel lines. Under Vauban's method the capture of a fortress by a besieging force was usually only a matter of time. Incredibly, the Japanese successfully used exactly this method during 1914 in Tsingtao, China. He is said to have personally supervised 48 sieges, all of which were successful.

Sébastien Le Prestre de Vauban
Vauban, who was created a Marshal of France in 1703, is depicted here toward the end of his career. His defensive strategy was termed *pré carré*, which, translated literally, means a "square field," though he meant it as a zone in which the king's sovereignty was undisputed, and in which no enemy fortresses could be constructed. Vauban became so famous that it was said that, "A city built by Vauban is a saved city, a city attacked by Vauban is a lost city."

The three parallels
Vauban's method of siegecraft utilizing three parallels as set out in his 1704 book *Le Triomphe de la Méthode*. He attempted to bring scientific rigor to the practice, enabling timely victory at a minimum cost in blood and treasure. He demonstrated that this was possible at the "perfect siege" of Ath (Aat, now Belgium) in 1697, which he completed in a single day.

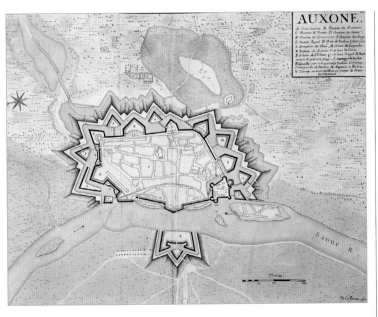

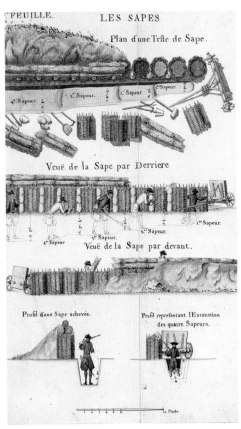

The defense of Auxonne

Situated on the River Saône, Auxonne holds a strategic position, and had been strongly fortified prior to it becoming a French possession in 1477. In accordance with the latest precepts, the defenses were improved and construction of a bastioned *enceinte* began in 1673.

"Metz defends the state"

Vauban was responsible, in whole or part, for fortifying 160 sites. The vital city of Metz was part of the "iron ring" he created around France. Retrospectively categorized into systems, his works show no adhesion to such rigidity; rather he pushed out the defenses as far as possible with a multiplicity of outerworks.

Saps and trenches

Another diagram from *Le Triomphe de la Méthode,* showing the correct method of constructing what he termed a *sape* (sap). The *sapeurs* (sappers) began the sap at an angle, and at a suitable distance from the object of attack. After advancing a specified distance they would then move laterally to construct the first parallel. From there further saps would be advanced toward the enemy and a second parallel constructed. Saps and trenches would be constructed so as to be well protected against enfilade fire by following a zigzag pattern, and usually have overhead cover. A third parallel would then be constructed, at which time the attackers would be hard up against the defender's main positions and at a point where an attempt at storming a breach of the defenses, effected by bombardment or mining, could be made.

T<small>HE DISCOVERY OF THE NEW WORLD</small>, beginning with the arrival of Christopher Columbus in 1492, led to large-scale colonization efforts by the major European maritime powers—England, France, the Netherlands, Portugal, and Spain. The rivalry between these powers was replicated on the western side of the Atlantic, and led to conflict that lasted over a period of centuries.

CHAPTER 12

North American Colonial Forts

In addition to their enmities, the Europeans brought their technologies to the New World. Spain, which at one time claimed most of the eastern and southern seaboard of what is now the United States, was among the first, and established several outposts. These Spanish possessions were repeatedly attacked by Britain, the latter also engaging in many struggles with France for control of North American territory. Of course, as well as fighting one another, the Europeans also had to contend with the Native American peoples, who often objected violently to the newcomers and their ways.

This repeated warfare led to the construction of fortifications, the more important of which, not surprisingly, tended in the main to be modeled on existing European patterns—although generally less complex and far smaller in scale. Constructed of locally available materials and frequently formed from earthen banks reinforced with timber, these structures with their bastioned traces mirroring European ideas sprang up at sites that were deemed strategically important.

Castillo de San Marcos, St. Augustine, Florida

Castillo de San Marcos saw significant action, during the 1740 Siege of St. Augustine. It was one of a number of operations in the curiously, and retrospectively, named War of Jenkins' Ear; a British attempt to relieve Spain of her American colonial possessions. From June 24 the British forces bombarded St. Augustine for 27 days, while some 2,000 Spanish colonists took refuge in the castillo. The siege was lifted following the running of the blockade by Spanish ships, and the British, abandoning their artillery, withdrew.

America's Oldest Stone Fortress

Castillo de San Marcos, Florida

According to the historian Hugh Morrison, the Castillo de San Marcos is the best-surviving example in the United States of the European-type fortress; remarkably, it is also the oldest, with its origins dating from 1672, though the present form was basically attained in 1756. It was constructed as a permanent replacement for several wooden structures that proved insufficient to protect the town of St. Augustine; the oldest continuously occupied European-established city and port in the United States.

Founded by Admiral Pedro Menéndez de Avilés in 1565, St. Augustine was the object of many attacks over the years, being burned to the ground by an expedition under Sir Francis Drake in 1586. However, it was not until 1668 that a decision was made to upgrade the defenses with a stone fort. This followed a raid by English privateer Robert Searle on May 9 of that year, which resulted in the death of some 60 people and the looting of the town.

St. Augustine under attack

This 1589 map by Baptista Boazio, an Italian cartographer who worked in England, depicts Drake's attack on St. Augustine on May 28–29, 1586. It was commissioned for a book about Drake's voyage. Note the pentagonal structure, Fort San Juan de Pinos, that predated the construction of the castillo. This map is the earliest view of any city in the territory of the present United States.

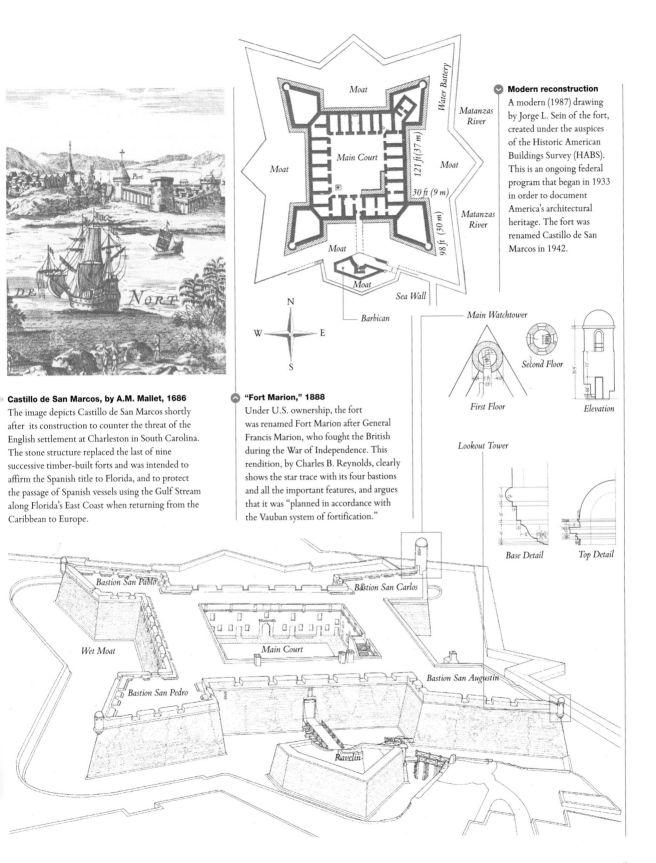

Castillo de San Marcos, by A.M. Mallet, 1686
The image depicts Castillo de San Marcos shortly after its construction to counter the threat of the English settlement at Charleston in South Carolina. The stone structure replaced the last of nine successive timber-built forts and was intended to affirm the Spanish title to Florida, and to protect the passage of Spanish vessels using the Gulf Stream along Florida's East Coast when returning from the Caribbean to Europe.

Modern reconstruction
A modern (1987) drawing by Jorge L. Sein of the fort, created under the auspices of the Historic American Buildings Survey (HABS). This is an ongoing federal program that began in 1933 in order to document America's architectural heritage. The fort was renamed Castillo de San Marcos in 1942.

"Fort Marion," 1888
Under U.S. ownership, the fort was renamed Fort Marion after General Francis Marion, who fought the British during the War of Independence. This rendition, by Charles B. Reynolds, clearly shows the star trace with its four bastions and all the important features, and argues that it was "planned in accordance with the Vauban system of fortification."

Moat
Matanzas River
Water Battery
Main Court
121 ft (37 m)
30 ft (9 m)
98 ft (30 m)
Matanzas River
Sea Wall
Barbican
N W E S

Main Watchtower
First Floor
Second Floor
Elevation

Lookout Tower
Base Detail
Top Detail

Bastion San Pablo
Bastion San Carlos
Wet Moat
Main Court
Bastion San Pedro
Bastion San Augustin
Ravelin

Defending New France

Fort Beauséjour/Fort Cumberland, Nova Scotia

New France (Nouvelle-France) was the colonial territory carved out by the French in North America. Its origins lie in the explorations of Jacques Cartier in the 1530s, who believed that the Saint Lawrence River formed the eastern entrance to the fabled Northwest Passage. By 1712 the territories claimed by France in North America were vast, and had been divided into five separate colonies. In English these were named Canada (modern-day Quebec), Acadia (modern-day New Brunswick, Nova Scotia, and Prince Edward Island), Hudson Bay, Newfoundland, and Louisiana. French possession was hotly disputed by England, but the two countries came to terms and signed the Treaty of Utrecht in 1713, whereby France, among many other transactions, ceded its claims to Acadia.

However, exactly what territory Acadia encompassed was disputed with both claiming the isthmus of Chignecto. Hostilities erupted again in 1754 leading to what is variously known as the *Seven Years War*, *La Guerre de la Conquête*, or the *French and Indian War*. In this final struggle for what was to become modern Canada, the British resolved to attack the strongest fortification in Acadia: Fort Beauséjour.

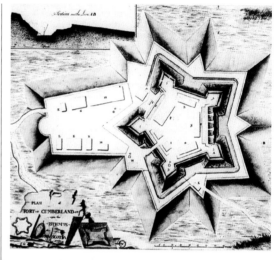

Plan of Fort Cumberland by William Spry, 1778
The British renamed Beauséjour "Fort Cumberland," and improved it with the addition of new barracks. Following the 1763 Treaty of Paris the area lost its strategic significance, though the fort remained manned until 1768. It was reoccupied in 1776 during the War of Independence by about 275 loyalist soldiers from Nova Scotia, and besieged in 1777 by some 180 men under the command of Jonathan Eddy, a colonel in the Continental Army. Eddy's forces—American militiamen, Native Americans, and disaffected Nova Scotians—made three unsuccessful attempts to storm the fort in November 1776, before being driven off by British reinforcements.

The earliest scheme, 1752

Construction of Fort Beauséjour began in 1751 atop a hill between two marshes. The ramparts were formed from earth braced with heavy timber and, according to some sources, armament consisted of 24 guns and one mortar. This 1752 drawing shows the plan, or trace, of the work and its profile. Fortifying with earth had been found most effective during the course of "The Dutch Revolt" or "The Eighty Years War" in the 1580s, and, according to Paul Ive, the technique proved "much more durable against a forcible battery" than fortifications faced with masonry.

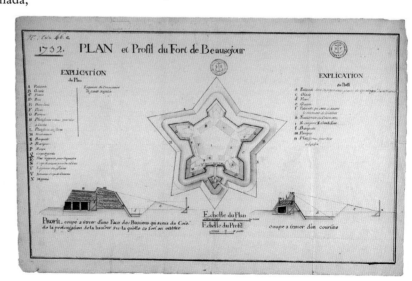

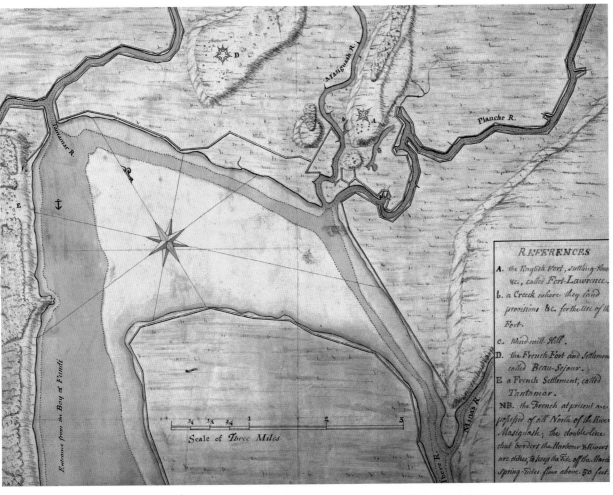

REFERENCES

A. the English Fort, Suttling-house &c., called Fort-Lawrence.

b. a Creek where they land provisions &c. for the use of the Fort.

c. Wind-mill Hill.

D. the French-Fort and Settlement called Beau-Sejour.

E. a French Settlement, called Tantamar.

NB. the French at present are possessed of all North of the River Masiquash; the double-line that borders the Harbour & Rivers are dikes, to keep the Tide off the Marsh. Spring-Tides flow above 50 feet.

Scale of Three Miles

Determining the frontier

Drawn in 1754 by Ensign Charles Husband Collins of the 45th Regiment of Foot, this map shows the relative positions of Fort Beauséjour and the British Fort Lawrence. These were only about 2 mi (3 km) apart and the *de facto* frontier between France and British territory lay between them. Fort Lawrence was constructed in 1750 and named after the British commander responsible. The garrison consisted of about 600 men.

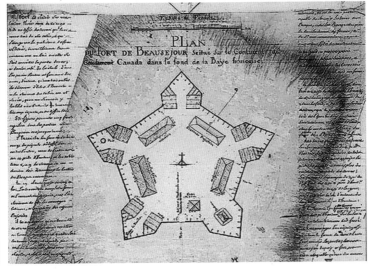

Fort Beauséjour, 1864

The British moved on Fort Beauséjour on June 3, 1755 and took 10 days to move up their ordnance. When this was ready the fort was subjected to a three-day bombardment, including fire from a 13-in (320-mm) mortar, resulting in a breach of the ramparts on June 16, whereupon the garrison surrendered. This *Plan du Fort de Beauséjour* shows the trace and profile of the work as identified by Auguste Béchard who visited the site in 1864.

241

New Amsterdam

From Fort Amsterdam to New York City
New Amsterdam (Nieuw Amsterdam) was the Dutch name for the settlement established on the southern tip of Manhattan Island, famously purchased from the Native Americans on May 24, 1626 by Pierre Minuyt, the Director General of the Netherlands colonies (New Netherland), for a nominal sum. Originally founded in 1614 as a base for the Dutch West India Company this outpost relied mainly on fur trading, but efforts were made following the purchase to establish farming settlements there and to construct the town of New Amsterdam.

A military engineer, Krijn Frederiks, was commissioned to construct a defensive fortress to protect the town. He selected a site on the shore so that the work could interdict any enemy approaching by water, and designed it with a wet ditch to protect it on the landward side. The fort was to be pentagonal in plan and constructed of stone, while within its *enceinte* was planned accommodation for company officials. Fort Amsterdam, as it was to be called, did not materialize as planned by Frederiks, and indeed was not completed for two decades, by which time the design had been simplified to a square structure.

t' Fort nieuw Amsterdam op de Manhatans

Manhattan Island, 1614
According to one eye witness, "Fort Amsterdam [. . .] has four regular bastions, mounted with several pieces of artillery. All these bastions and the curtains were, in 1643, but mounds, most of which had crumbled away, so that one entered the fort on all sides. There were no ditches. For the garrison of the said fort, and another [. , .] there were sixty soldiers. They were beginning to face the gates and bastions with stone."

Manhattan's modern skyline
New Amsterdam became New York after it surrendered to the British in 1664. It grew hugely in importance under British rule, becoming a major trading port. In 1785 the city became the national capital of the newly independent United States. Today the Alexander Hamilton U.S. Custom House is seated on the site of Fort Amsterdam.

Control of the Ohio

Fort Duquesne, Pennsylvania

On November 25, 1758 an officer unfurled the British flag over "the still smoking ruins of that formidable fortress" Fort Duquesne. That officer was George Washington, and during the campaign he had learned lessons and skills that were to become much in evidence. The fort was built at a vital strategic point— at the Forks of the Ohio, where the Monongahela and Allegheny rivers join to form the Ohio River. The French called the Ohio "La Belle Rivière," and control of it was a major objective in the struggle for control of North America. The first attempt at fortification came in February 1754, when the Ohio Company began building a work. However, in April French forces, including their Native American allies, seized

this and a much stronger structure. It was named Fort Du Quesne after the Governor-General of New France, Michel-Ange Du Quesne de Menneville, though became known later simply as Duquesne.

Despite two abortive efforts a third attempt to capture it commenced in the summer of 1758 under General John Forbes. He advanced with a force of 6–7,000 men from western Maryland but progress was slow and on September 15 a counterattack from the fort led to a setback. However, the advance continued and it was discovered the fort was weakly held. On the night of November 24, the French withdrew by boat after setting the fort alight. Washington, commanding 2,000 militiamen, took possession and personally raised the flag.

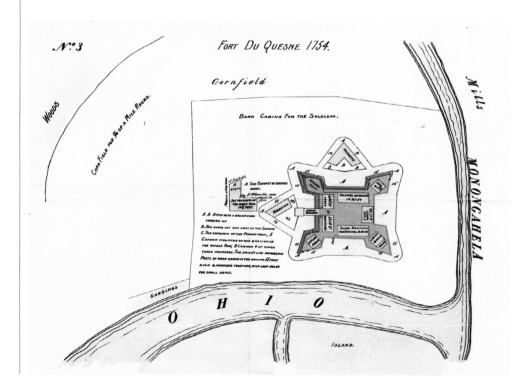

Plan of Fort Duquesne ca. 1754
According to the military history writer René Chartrand, this plan was probably drawn by a French artillery officer, Captain François Le Mercier, and is the only reliable source detailing the purpose of the various buildings in the fort.

The British made three attempts to take the fort, including one by George Washington in 1754 and another larger venture under General Edward Braddock in 1755, which ended in disaster.

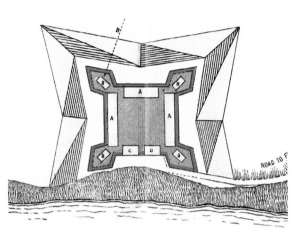

Temporary fortification

With Fort Duquesne in ruins it was necessary to construct a new fort on the site of the Forks of the Ohio. This was to become Fort Pitt, for William Pitt (the Elder) the British Secretary of State for the Southern Department (including the American Colonies). However, while the permanent fort was under construction a temporary fortification was needed. This plan shows Mercer's Fort, a temporary work constructed under the auspices of Colonel Hugh Mercer who was left in command of the site. It was gradually superseded as the permanent structure was built.

Fort Pitt Redoubt, 1795

Fort Duquesne was largely constructed of logs with the gaps between them filled with earth. The British replacements, Forts Mercer and Pitt, were raised in a similar manner. Accordingly little archaeological evidence has survived over the years and what remained was removed. The sole exception, forming the oldest structure in Western Pennsylvania, is known as the Fort Pitt Blockhouse or redoubt. It was built outside the main work by Colonel Henry Bouquet in 1764, and survives today as an attraction at Pittsburgh's Point Park

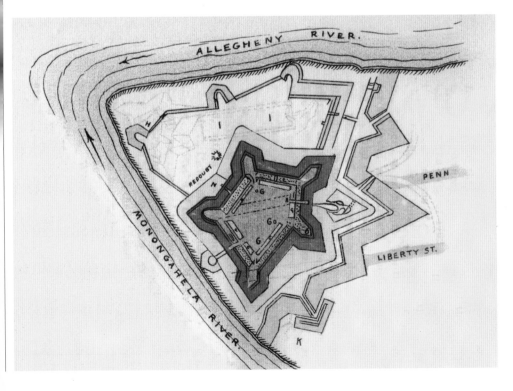

The New Fort

A view of Fort Pitt in 1761 in which the sites of the former forts Duquesne and Mercer are just visible, marked by the letters H and R. The much larger size of new fort becomes readily apparent when compared with the earlier works, while Mercer's Fort is referred to as the "First Fort Pitt." Fort Pitt was to become the nucleus around which Pittsburgh grew and two streets of the nascent city are marked.

I T HAS BEEN ARGUED that the art of fortification stagnated somewhat following the death of the master military engineer Vauban (*see pages 234–5*) in 1707, with few valuable additions until near the end of the 18th century. It is undoubtedly the case that several military engineers and theorists began to devise, and in some cases construct, overly elaborate fortifications. Some were successful, others less so.

CHAPTER 13

Eighteenth–century Artillery Fortresses

The designs of Louis de Cormontaigne (1696–1752), "the successor of Vauban," were undoubtedly complex though ultimately practical. At the other end of the spectrum those of Professor of Mathematics Charles-André Rhana have been described as "novel and singular," while others spoke of their absurdity, and reckoned them, correctly, of no practical importance.

Thanks largely to the influence of Vauban, the French "style" of fortification had become dominant, but controversy and bitter dispute arose over theory or system. Charles-René Fourcroy de Ramecourt (1715–91), a man who never directed a siege or large-scale construction, denigrated Cormontaigne and his rise to command the Corps of Engineers in 1776 heralded "the triumph of engineering conservatism in France" according to military historian Christopher Duffy. There were, however, innovators such as Marc Montalembert (1714–1800) who advocated something akin to the later polygonal system and who seemingly influenced Stefano de Tousard, the designer of Fort Tigne at Malta (1792–94). This work has authoritatively been described as "probably the most revolutionary and influential of all the fortifications built by the Knights."

Whatever French theoreticians said, and their arguments continued until the revolution of 1789, there were still practical problems to be dealt with. There is no doubt that the methodology utilized by engineers such as Nicolas Doxat de Demoret or Martín Zermeño owed more than a little to Vauban, but, in the New World, which had undergone its own revolution with the Declaration of Independence in 1776, John Jacob Ulrich Rivardi was constrained less by theory than by resources.

Fort George, near Inverness, Scotland
Fort George was built as part of the program of English occupation and pacification of the Scottish Highlands following the defeat of the 1745 Jacobite Rising. Situated on a spit of land some 12 mi (20 km) east of Inverness, it is a massive work. The landward defenses are most powerful, the main components comprising two large arrow-head bastions and a huge ravelin. The sea-facing ramparts comprise smaller bastions and a redan, and the whole enceinte encloses an area of about 17 acres (7 ha). The great size and strength of the fort, and its location at the narrowest part of the Moray Firth, probably had less to do with a fear of further Scottish risings against English rule, but rather the worry of French naval intervention and assistance in any such event.

ANATOMY OF
A Star Fort

Design for an integrated defense

This diagram of an imaginary fort shows how complex the plan of bastioned fortifications could become when enhanced with outworks. The basic building block was the bastion, which has two flanks and two faces, although the configuration and shape vary. Bastions or demibastions—a half bastion with one face and one flank—might form parts of larger works such as crownworks.

The ditch was the main obstacle in a bastioned fortress, usually revetted or strengthened on its inner side, the scarp, and outer side, the counterscarp. Above and forward of the counterscarp was the glacis—an earthen bank usually formed from material excavated from the ditch. Sloping away from the ditch it protected the fortress from artillery fire and provided a clear field of fire to defenders. Atop the counterscarp sat a covered way (covertway) to allow for the movement of troops under cover.

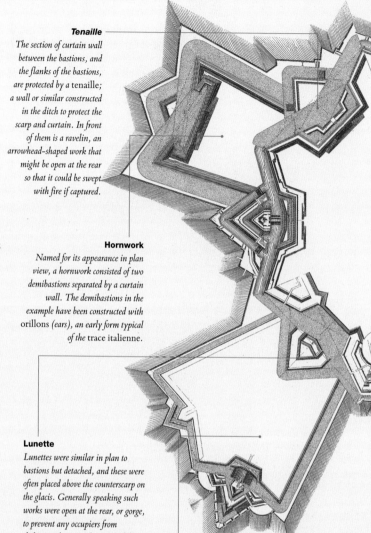

Tenaille
The section of curtain wall between the bastions, and the flanks of the bastions, are protected by a tenaille; a wall or similar constructed in the ditch to protect the scarp and curtain. In front of them is a ravelin, an arrowhead-shaped work that might be open at the rear so that it could be swept with fire if captured.

Hornwork
Named for its appearance in plan view, a hornwork consisted of two demibastions separated by a curtain wall. The demibastions in the example have been constructed with orillons (ears), an early form typical of the trace italienne.

Lunette
Lunettes were similar in plan to bastions but detached, and these were often placed above the counterscarp on the glacis. Generally speaking such works were open at the rear, or gorge, to prevent any occupiers from sheltering there. In the event of their being taken their interior could be swept by fire from the enceinte.

Composite work
A composite theoretical outwork, the lower right-hand half of which depicts a hornwork fronted by a tenaille. This is joined by a caponier to a ravelin, itself flanked by two lunettes, with a counterguard in front. The other half depicts a rampart arranged as per the tenaille trace—a line of alternating salients and re-entrants forming a zig-zag and not to be confused with a tenaille as mentioned above—with a small bastion at the re-entrant angle.

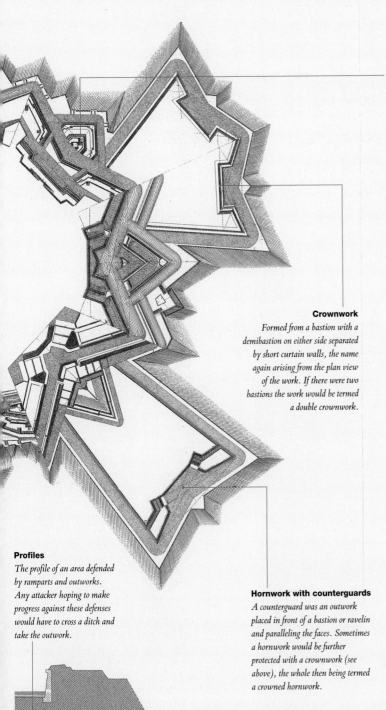

Demilune

A section of works including two bastions and a section of curtain, protected by a tenaille and a demilune. Demilunes, as the name suggests, were originally crescent-shaped and were located above the counterscarp on the glacis. Such works helped defend the covertway. An area where this was enlarged to allow them to concentrate was termed a "place of arms."

Raised artillery platforms

Situated behind the curtain wall, or in the bastions, raised artillery platforms called cavaliers might be constructed. The whole would provide for an integrated defense with interlocking fields of fire; there was no dead ground in which attackers might shelter.

Crownwork

Formed from a bastion with a demibastion on either side separated by short curtain walls, the name again arising from the plan view of the work. If there were two bastions the work would be termed a double crownwork.

Coervorden, Holland

Coevorden stood on the northeastern frontier of the Netherlands and was strategically sited in a gap between "two vast morasses." Maurice of Nassau completed the reconstruction of the city's defenses in 1605, giving it seven bastions. The *enceinte* was augmented with a *fausse-braye*—an outer rampart below the main rampart in height but paralleling it—and a wet ditch some 180 ft (55 m) wide. On the far side of this ditch were seven demilunes and seven ravelins, each with a 30-ft (9-m) ditch in front. The whole was screened by a glacis that was itself fronted by another wet ditch and marshes. Constructed of earthworks it was a position of immense strength, and many scholars considered that Dutch engineers had surpassed the Italians by 1587. It also gives an indication of why bastioned works were also christened "star forts."

Profiles

The profile of an area defended by ramparts and outworks. Any attacker hoping to make progress against these defenses would have to cross a ditch and take the outwork.

Hornwork with counterguards

A counterguard was an outwork placed in front of a bastion or ravelin and paralleling the faces. Sometimes a hornwork would be further protected with a crownwork (see above), the whole then being termed a crowned hornwork.

Defending the Eastern Seaboard

Fort Norfolk, Virginia

On March 20, 1794 the United States Congress authorized funds for the creation of 16 (later 20) fortifications at designated sites for the purposes of coastal defense. This decision was made because of tense, and deteriorating, relations between the newly independent United States of America and the principal European powers. The United States Army, such as it then was, had no engineers with the requisite knowledge and skills. President George Washington therefore directed that a number of temporary appointments be made for foreign engineers to design and direct the construction of the coastal installations.

Readily available were several military engineers that had fled France following the Revolution and subsequent founding of the Republic. Among these was John Jacob Ulrich Rivardi, also described as a Swiss engineer, who had served in the Russian army. He was appointed by Henry Knox, Secretary of War, to construct works to protect Norfolk, Virginia, and Baltimore, Maryland—with the greatest priority being Norfolk as it was deemed to be under the most immediate threat. Despite this, Fort Norfolk remained "a bastion that never blazed away at an enemy." It does though remain as the last of the coastal defense forts authorized during the tenure of George Washington.

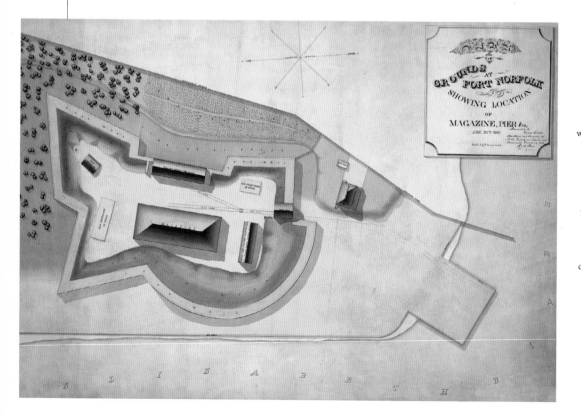

Plan of the grounds at Fort Norfolk, 1860
As originally built, the fort's ramparts would have been constructed of sloped earth with timber reinforcement. The slopes would have been covered with "knot grass" to prevent erosion, but nevertheless they did erode, "turning," as one authority has it, "mostly into piles of dirt." Accordingly, between 1808–12, Fort Norfolk was converted into a masonry structure mounting 30 cannon in its unusual curved battery. This battery is well illustrated in the "Plan of the grounds at Fort Norfolk" dated June 30, 1860.

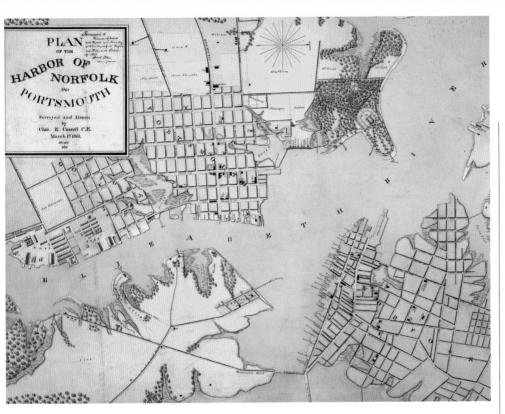

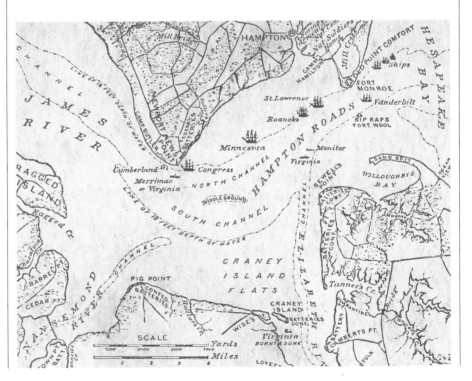

Roads, 1862

If Craney Island has faded
into insignificance, the Battle
of Hampton Roads remains
one of the most pivotal in
naval history. Virginia was of
course a Confederate state
during the Civil War, and its
coast was subject to a U.S.
naval blockade. Out-
numbered and outgunned
the C.S. Navy constructed
an armored ship to defeat its
wooden-hulled enemy. Built
at Gosport, with its magazine
filled with ammunition from
Fort Norfolk, C.S.S. *Virginia*
steamed past the fort to
engage the blockaders on
March 8. She despatched
the U.S.S. *Cumberland* by
ramming and forced the
surrender of U.S.S. *Congress*
before retiring with some
damage. Upon returning the
next morning she found a
U.S. armored ship, U.S.S.
Monitor, waiting to engage.

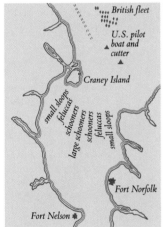

Plan of the Harbor of Norfolk and Portsmouth, Chas. E. Cassell, 1861
Fort Norfolk was constructed about a mile and a half below the town of the
same name on the eastern shore of the Elizabeth River at a place called the
"Narrows." Enemy shipping could, in conjunction with another fort on the
west shore, thus be interdicted at this point. A more or less ruined earthwork
had existed at that location and Rivaldi resolved to replace it with a new structure
fashioned from the same material.

The Battle of Craney Island, 1813
The War of 1812 between Britain and
the United States saw the powerful
Royal Navy blockade the American east
coast and mount several large-scale raids.
The British attempted to attack the
Gosport shipyard by landing a party
some 700 strong to the west of Craney
Island, passage up the Elizabeth River
being interdicted by the forts. The
American defenders only numbered
about 150 but were entrenched; the
British could not prevail and retreated,
losing some of their landing barges and
about 91 men. Although in itself a
minor affair, the battle was a defensive
victory against a much larger force.

A Byzantine Base

Fortress Kalemegdan, Belgrade, Serbia

Situated at the confluence of the Sava and Danube rivers, Belgrade occupies a position of great strategic importance and its defenses can be traced back to a Roman *castrum*. This was reconstructed as a Byzantine castle in the 12th century, but the origins of the modern fortress are rooted in the expansionist tendencies of the Ottoman Empire. In 1453, after conquering Constantinople, Mehmed II advanced north, unsuccessfully besieging Belgrade in 1456. In 1521, a force under Sultan Suleiman I marched on the city and succeeded in taking it before advancing into Central Europe. Following the 1688 Ottoman defeat at Vienna Belgrade again became a focus of battle, being conquered by the forces of the Holy League toward the end of that year. The Ottomans retook the place again in 1690 after a six-day siege. Prince Eugène of Savoy though, in a brilliant action, retook it in 1717. However, by the Treaty of Belgrade in 1739, Austria returned the fortress to the Ottomans and accepted the Danube–Sava River as delineating the common frontier.

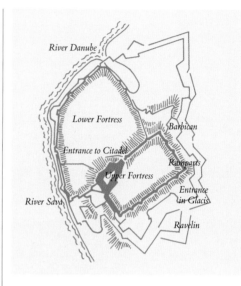

Plan of Kalemegdan

The Austrian Field Marshal Ernst Gideon Freiherr von Laudon took Belgrade again in 1789 following a three-week campaign, though it was handed back to the Ottoman Empire in 1791. Derived from a 1794 drawing by Captain von Mitesser, made during the Austrian occupation, this plan shows the defenses as reconstructed from 1740, which is more or less the form in which Kalemegdan has survived.

Map of Fortress Kalemegdan, 1718

By July 1717, Eugene was investing in Belgrade, which had the effect of drawing toward him the main Ottoman field army, double the size of the Austrian force. It arrived at the beginning of August, potentially at least trapping Eugene between two fires. He extricated himself by surprising the larger force on August 16 with an audacious attack, and putting them to flight. A week later Belgrade surrendered to him, marking the crowning point of his military career and confirming his as a "great captain." Upon retaking the position he began the process of upgrading the defenses, and this 1718 depiction, if accurate, shows the work well advanced.

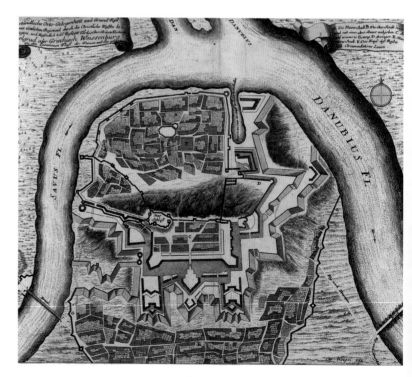

◀ **Prospect of Belgrade, ca. 1789**

Following their reacquisition of Belgrade, the Ottomans attempted to reconstruct the razed fortifications constructed by Swiss engineer Nicolas Doxat de Demoret in about 1730. They largely succeeded, but the rebuilt defenses were less complex than the originals. This view is purportedly from Sajmište (Samelin) on the left bank of the Sava toward Belgrade, with what appear to be elements of fortification in the foreground. What is well brought out is the elevated position of the main fortress.

Prospect of Belgrade city, 1736 ▼

An 18th-century view of the city of Belgrade and Kalemegdan fortress depicting both the thin walls and slender towers, both of which were obsolete and would have been vulnerable to artillery, and the addition of bastioned works forward of them. When the Austrians agreed to return the fortress to the Ottomans as part of the 1739 Treaty they destroyed the new fortifications.

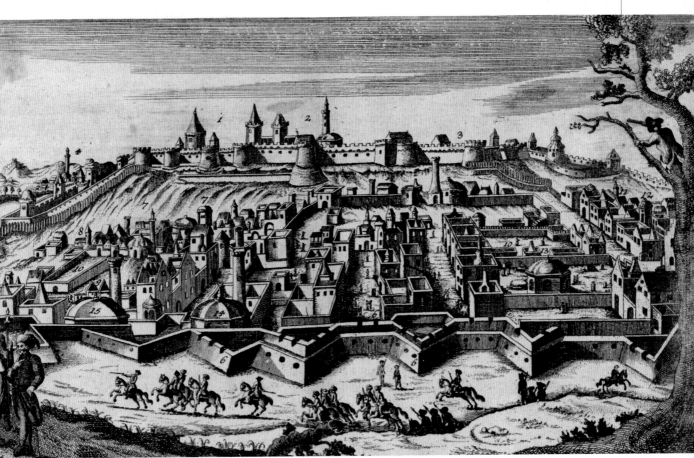

Control of the Pyrenean Passes

San Fernando de Figueres & Lérida, Catalonia, Spain

Lieutenant-General the Marquess of Londonderry wrote in his *Narrative of the Peninsular War* that the "four great passes of the Pyrenees" were commanded by four cities; San Sebastián, Pamplona, San Fernando de Figueres (Sant Ferrán de Figueres in Catalan), and Barcelona. And so, he explained, "to obtain the command of them at any cost and by any means, was the last and most urgent order given by their chief to the French generals." The "chief" was of course Napoleon I, Emperor of France since December 2, 1804, and the date was February 1808 when France turned on its Spanish ally. Except in the case of Pamplona the "any means" meant subterfuge, and it succeeded at minimal cost. Indeed, despite being a fortress of immense strength San Fernando de

Figueres had a rather poor record in resisting attack. During the War of Roussillon (War of the Convention, War of the Pyrenees) that took place between March 1793 and July 1795, the fortress was surrendered to the invading French army on November 28, 1794. The Commandant, named variously as Andrés Torres and José Andrés Valdes, seems to have been bluffed into capitulating without a shot being fired. He was later sentenced to death for his action, with the sentence being commuted to banishment for life.

The decision to construct the fortress near Figueres was taken in 1751 during the reign of Fernando VI. Designed by Martín Zermeño (Cermeño), building started in 1753 under his direction but was not completed until 1807, by which time some 25 different engineers had headed the project, the final one being Guillermo Minali. Older works were also upgraded, including the former Templar fortress of Gardeny that dated from the second half of the 12th century. Near to the town of Lérida (Lleida) it was described by Sir William Napier in 1839 as "covered by a large hornwork with ditches above twenty feet deep," all "in good condition, and armed with more than one hundred pieces of artillery."

Hornwork

Ravelin   Ravelin

Bastion   Bastion

Santa Barbara
Bastion

Hornwork   Hornwork

Bastion   Bastion

Main
Entrance

Encircling
Dry Ditch

Europe's largest fortress
The fortress of San Fernando has an irregular pentagonal *enceinte* enclosing an area of some 80 acres (32.5 ha). North–south it measured some 1,000 yd (941 m) and 645 yd (590 m) east-west, while the perimeter is reckoned to be about 1.4 mi (2.3 km). There are six large bastions, and the curtain walls between them, clockwise from the Santa Barbara bastion, are respectively, 159 yd (146 m), 128 yd (117 m), 116 yd (106 m), 116 yd (106 m), 128 yd (117 m), and 160 yd (146 m) long.

San Fernando de Figueres, 1811

The French regained the fortress in 1811, again without the necessity of a formal siege, eventually handing it back to Spain in 1814. However, on April 18, 1823 the French 4th Army Corps invaded Catalunya to restore Ferdinand VII as king. Figueres and its surrounding area were among the last places to fall to Franco's Nationalist forces; Barcelona fell on January 26, 1939 and the conquest of Catalunya was complete by February 10.

View and map of Gardeny Fort, Lérida, 1810

Originally built by the Order of the Knights Templar in the 12th century, Gardeny fortress was constructed on a hill near the city of Lérida. That the site was of great strategic importance had been evident in antiquity and Caesar had defeated the forces of Gnaeus Pompeius Magnus nearby in 49 BCE. Gardeny was a headquarters of the Templar order and the last Grand-Master, Jacques de Molay, is said to have stayed there in 1294 prior to the destruction of the Knights Templar in 1314. The fortification was upgraded during the 17th and 18th centuries in accordance with the advances made in artillery.

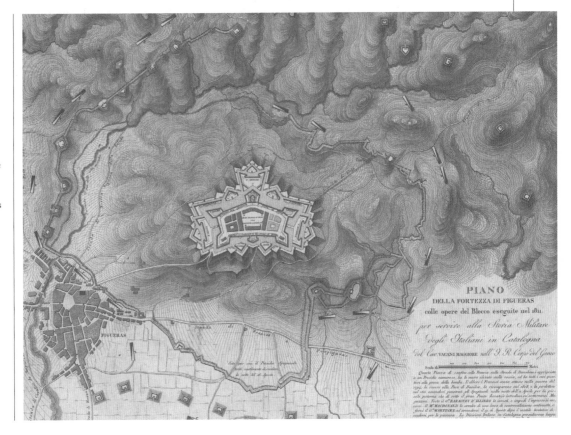

NATIONS THAT POSSESS FLEETS need secure bases from which they can operate, and in which they can shelter. Accordingly, those states that aspired to a maritime policy constructed naval fortresses, it being an exceedingly risky operation to attack stone fortifications in wooden ships— "the business of laying wood before walls," as Lord Nelson put it in 1794.

CHAPTER 14

Modern Naval Fortresses

The danger for fleets lay mainly in the use of incendiary projectiles. The concept dates back to antiquity with Greek Fire and suchlike, but the first successful use of incendiary shot fired from muzzle-loading artillery against ships is believed to have occurred in 1577 during the Siege of Danzig. The technique was used to great effect by the British during their defense of Gibraltar in 1779–83. It was comparatively rare for such vessels to be sunk in engagements where solid shot was the only ordnance, but fire on a wooden ship meant almost certain destruction.

The development of the rifled gun ensured that such missiles, particularly explosive shells, could be delivered with greater accuracy over longer ranges than had been previously possible. A detonating shell caused a primary fire at the site of the explosion, and secondary conflagrations where the red-hot splinters landed. Only ships that were armored with, or constructed from, iron dared approach properly equipped naval fortresses. Floating armored batteries had been developed for such purposes but they were not without their problems. As a popular newspaper put it in 1856: "With their depth in the water, and ominous heavy roll at the least swell, they seem inclined to be anything but floating, and loath would we be to encounter a Baltic gale or a Black Sea hurricane in one of these gaunt wrought-iron shells."

Indeed, the difficulties of attacking shore-based works from the sea were not totally resolved even when steel had replaced wood. One authority, writing in 1892, noted, "Warships are not built to attack defenses on shore, and can rarely be spared for the purpose, while the progress of military science has turned the balance heavily against them."

No Man's Land Fort, The Solent, England
The first stone of this work was laid in 1865 on a solid foundation secured some 20 ft (6 m) into the seabed. The lower gun floor contained emplacements for 24 heavy guns, while the upper floor could accommodate 25. The specification of this armament constantly changed due to the rapid advance in artillery technology both at that period and later.

Defending the Baltic Sea

Kronstadt, Kotlin Island, Russia

On March 28, 1854 Britain declared war on Russia and the resultant conflict, waged by Britain, France, the Ottoman Empire, and Piedmont-Sardinia on Russia, became known as the Crimean War, after the location of its main theater of operations.

The Crimea was far from being the only theater, however; the Baltic Sea was considered as a potentially fruitful area from which to apply pressure on the Russians. A fleet under Vice-Admiral Sir Charles Napier's command was charged with the mission to prevent the Russian fleet from leaving the Gulf of Finland and to report on the possibilities of offensive action. The supreme prize was the Russian Baltic fleet, which had withdrawn to the naval fortress of Kronstadt. Situated on the island of Kotlin, guarding the approaches to St. Petersburg, the Russian capital, it was a position of immense strength. Napier concluded that the position was impregnable with the forces at his disposal; accordingly the Allied fleet left the waters around Kronstadt on July 4, 1854. The naval fortress had proved its worth without a single shot being fired.

Plan of Kronstadt, 1808
Peter the Great had taken Kotlin from Sweden in 1703 and work on fortifying it began shortly afterward. This work had continued, and by the time of the Crimean War the island in general, and the approaches to the harbor in particular, were well protected. This plan shows that any naval attack would have been fraught with danger. Many of the forts were situated on artificial islands, and were able to utilize their interlocking fields of fire to command the approaches.

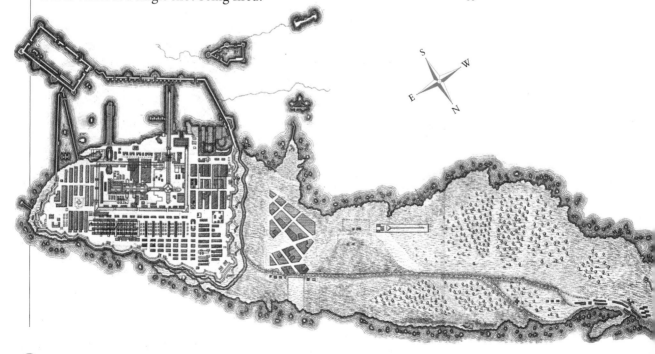

The insulated fortifications of Kronstadt, 1854

A somewhat fanciful image of a fleet sailing among the insulated fortifications. Napier's decision not to risk his wooden fleet against the stone forts and incendiary projectiles was undoubtedly correct. The Kronstadt forts were well equipped with shell and incendiary missiles and against them the Allied vessels would have been at a severe disadvantage, for although the French navy had adopted shell in 1837, with the Royal navy following suit in 1839, neither had evolved any protective measures for their wooden ships. Had the (wooden) Russian fleet given battle the outcome may have been uncertain, but against the mainly stone forts guarding Kronstadt the Allied fleet would likely have been committing suicide.

Panoramic view of Kronstadt and St. Petersburg, 1854

Kronstadt not only provided a base and haven for the Russian Baltic Fleet, but also guarded the approaches to St. Petersburg. The channel north of Kotlin island was closed to shipping by the expedient of driving piles into the shallow seabed. Therefore all vessels wishing to proceed easterly beyond Kronstadt were obliged to pass through the fortifications. Kronstadt was then, in the naval sense, the key to St. Petersburg.

Chemical warfare by "stink ships"

A British navel officer, the 10th Earl of Dundonald, proposed using vessels filled with burning sulfur, the choking fumes of which would repel any attackers within a mile downwind. He reckoned that the works at Kronstadt were particularly exposed to this mode of chemical warfare—being partly isolated and partly situated on a long sea wall running in the usual course of the prevailing wind—and he undertook to subdue every insular fortification at Kronstadt within four hours from commencement of the attack.

The Royal Navy Base

Portsmouth, The Solent, England

An important trading port since Roman times, Henry VIII oversaw the construction of defenses at Portsmouth to protect the town and harbor. The first was the Round Tower constructed in 1418 on a spit of land known as "The Point." Perhaps the most significant fortification from that period was Southsea Castle, built in 1544 as one of Henry's "device forts."

Under Elizabeth I Portsmouth was encircled with a bastioned *trace italienne*. Several military engineers, including Richard Popinjay and Paul Ive, were involved in the design and construction, which resulted in an *enceinte* consisting of five bastions and one demibastion connected by curtain walls. This remained essentially unaltered until the 1660s and the advent of the Anglo-Dutch wars. Charles II then engaged the services of the Dutch engineer Sir Bernard de Gomme to upgrade the defenses. Gomme's works were remodeled by John Peter Desmaretz in the 1750s. Desmaretz strengthened the defenses according to contemporary practice, but made no significant alterations to the trace, other than to delete de Gomme's outer ditch and add large ravelins.

Further upgrades were undertaken in the 1860s upon the recommendations of the Royal Commission on the Defence of the United Kingdom. These works resulted in a vast spread of forts around Portsmouth, mostly land based but four were built as circular, insular, works on artificial islands in the Solent.

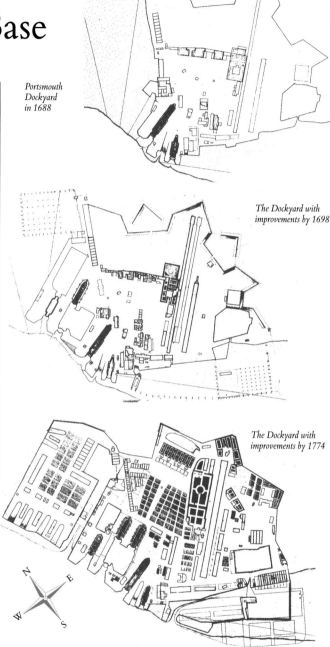

Portsmouth Dockyard in 1688

The Dockyard with improvements by 1698

The Dockyard with improvements by 1774

Plans of Portsmouth Dockyard, 1688, 1698, and 1774
As the home of the Royal Navy, and Britain's most important naval base and dockyard, Portsmouth was of considerable interest to potential enemies. Accordingly it had been equipped with powerful defenses since its inception, including a large chain boom or blockade fitted between the Round Tower and Fort Blockhouse at Gosport, which could be raised to prevent ships entering the harbor. These drawings detail the evolution of the defenses during the 17th and 18th centuries.

De Gomme's defenses of Gosport, 1678–79
This map shows the design for defending Gosport in 1678-79 as reported by Admiral George Legge, appointed Governor of Portsmouth in 1673, the most prominent feature of which being the west-facing crownwork. During the Civil War Gosport had sided with Parliament, and artillery sited there had bombarded Royalist Portsmouth in 1642 during the siege of the town. This section of the plan of Portsmouth town and dockyard, Gosport, and Southsea Castle, shows the proposed fortifications, with eight ships at anchor in the main channel of the harbor.

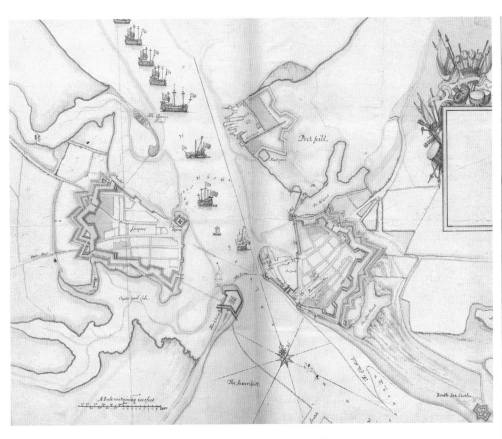

The Saluting Platform
The Saluting Platform, so named because it housed the guns used to salute naval vessels entering the harbor, was constructed in ca. 1522. It was rebuilt in stone in the 1560s. An 1830 account declared, "The correctness of this view will be immediately recognized by every person in the least acquainted with Portsmouth."

Spitbank Fort, 1881
Four sea forts, named *Horse Sands, No Man's Land, St. Helens,* and *Spitbank* (*Spitsand*) were constructed following the 1860 report. The former two were some 200 ft (60 m) in diameter and fully armor-plated, while the latter pair are slightly smaller at 160 ft (50 m) in diameter with iron plating on the front only. They were to be heavily armed with 12.5-in (310-mm) rifled muzzle loading (RML) guns, but were controversial. One critic opined in 1868 that while they would prove admirable marks to guide an enemy into the harbor, they would not be able to keep iron-clad ships out.

A Fortified Seaport

Cherbourg, Normandy, France

Cherbourg, a naval station, fortified town, and seaport is situated at the mouth of the Divette River. It is located in the extreme west of Normandy between the Cap de la Hague and the Pointe de Barfleur on the north shore of the Cotentin Peninsula.

Cherbourg's major drawback as a harbor was the lack of any natural shelter to the north, thus rendering it exposed to the prevalent severe weather and, because it was open to the sea, to potential seaborne attack. In an attempt to counter these problems, in 1750 Louis XIV first conceived of constructing a fortified breakwater, though the technical problems remained unresolved. In 1783 an engineer, Alexandre de Cessart, hit on the idea of constructing such a device from 90 truncated cone-shaped timber structures (*caissons*), but the arrangement proved unsuccessful. Work was anyway halted during the French Revolution and did not resume until 1802 when the design was changed to employ a masonry parapet, constructed on a berm foundation of stone. The structure was completed in 1850 but the conclusion of the project was not celebrated until 1858 when Emperor Napoleon III visited the site.

Cherbourg, 1863
This map of Cherbourg shows the detached breakwater, the *grand digue*, completed. Three forts were incorporated into it and a road ran along the along the crest. A French fleet could then be based at Cherbourg and be assured that any conventional attack from the sea would face formidable opposition. Indeed, its imminent completion in 1846 had led Lord Dundonald, the famous British admiral, to propose an extremely unconventional attack utilizing his "Secret War Plan," an early, though workable, version of chemical warfare.

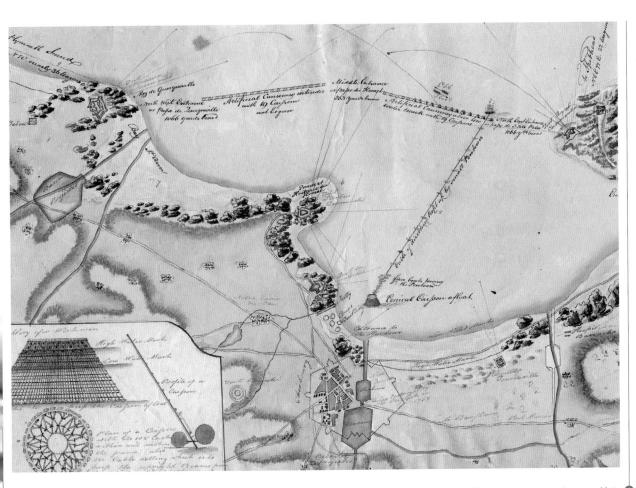

Plan of Cherbourg, ca. 1787/8

A hand-drawn plan drawn up to accompany "A Description of the Port of Cherbourg with the New Works now constructing to cover and defend that Road, particularly of the Truncated Cones or Conical Caissons, invented by M. De Cessart, Inspecteur General des Ponts et Chaussées." Approximately 64 ft (19.5 m) tall and 150 ft (45.5 m) in diameter at the base tapering to 64 ft (19.5) m at the top, each cone would be filled with stone after being sunk in place and then capped with a 6-ft (2-m) layer of concrete. By 1789 some 2½ mi (4 km) of breakwater had been completed, but with only 18 cones which were between 64 and 426 yd (59 and 390 m) apart.

***Caisson* being towed into position, ca. 1785**

This view shows a *caisson* (cone) before and after being sunk into position. At high water the top was only just clear of the sea, which would have made any gun platform sited there difficult to work in any sort of bad weather.

In any event, these large and extremely expensive structures were unable to withstand the effects of the sea and weather, and began to disintegrate almost immediately after being put in place. Attempts to fill the gaps between the cones with stone were also unsuccessful, though by 1790 over 95 million cu ft (2.7 million m^3) of stone had been deposited in the attempt.

THE ADVENT OF efficient rifled artillery and ammunition in about the mid-19th century gave explosive shells great range and penetrative power. To counter this increase in offensive power, fortification builders began to increase protection by sinking their works farther into the ground. At least part of the answer came from the polygonal system, developed by the military engineer Montalembert in the 18th century and particularly favored by Prussia and Austria.

CHAPTER 15
Polygonal Forts

The vastly increased range of rifled artillery over its smoothbore predecessor also forced the adoption of the detached fort system, which comprised an outer screen of individual mutually supporting fortifications. These were placed with the object of keeping enemy artillery out of range of the place being defended, this being the rationale behind the concept of the fortification of the Great Fault—Malta's harbor area. Such detached works were essentially defended batteries with their guns mounted *en barbette* or in purpose-built emplacements, as in Fort Mosta. A narrow perimeter ditch, configured so that oblique incoming fire would be less likely to destroy the scarp, protected polygonal forts. Cut out of rock by choice, and with vertical scarps and counterscarps, the defenses of the ditch consisted of either *caponiers* or galleries built into the counterscarp, or both.

From the 1880s onward, masonry began to give way to concrete as the material of choice. The development of reinforced concrete, the adoption of usable and efficient machine guns (ca. 1895–1900), and the deployment of barbed wire (invented in 1874 but first used in warfare ca. 1900) transformed the science of fortification, and all of these materials and devices were in evidence during the siege of Port Arthur 1904–05. The ring of detached forts constructed by the Russians around Port Arthur (1898–1904) had galleries and caponiers constructed of thick reinforced concrete, and was supported and flanked by trenches. These positions were fronted with belts of barbed wire, and machine guns were deployed in large numbers.

Caponier and rampart, Fort George, Brimstone Hill, St. Kitts
Fort George forms the citadel of the Brimstone Hill fortress complex atop the eponymous hill on the island of St. Kitts. Construction of these fortifications began in 1690 and continued for two centuries, the hill becoming known as the "Gibraltar of the West Indies." Having fallen to a French siege in 1782, St. Kitts was restored to British rule in 1783, whereupon Fort George was constructed. One of the earliest examples of a polygonal work the fort is magnificently situated at some 750 feet (228 m) above sea level. The whole site, which was built by African slave labor, was awarded UNESCO World Heritage Status in 1999.

ANATOMY OF
A Polygonal Fort

Fort Pulaski, Georgia

Although a polygonal structure, Fort Pulaski owed very little to European techniques and methods. This was despite it being designed by Simon Bernard, a French engineer and former aide to Napoleon I. Cockspur Island, upon which the fort was constructed, was about 1 mile (1.5 kilometers) long and $^6/_{10}$ mile (1 kilometer) wide.

The fort's defensive strength lay in the fact that it was immune to all but the heaviest guns, which did not—at least at the time it was designed—have the range to reach it. The fort was named after Casimir (Kazimierz) Pułaski from Warsaw, Poland, who had "saved Washington's life" on September 11, 1777 during the Battle of Brandywine Creek. Among the engineers involved in its construction was a young Robert E. Lee.

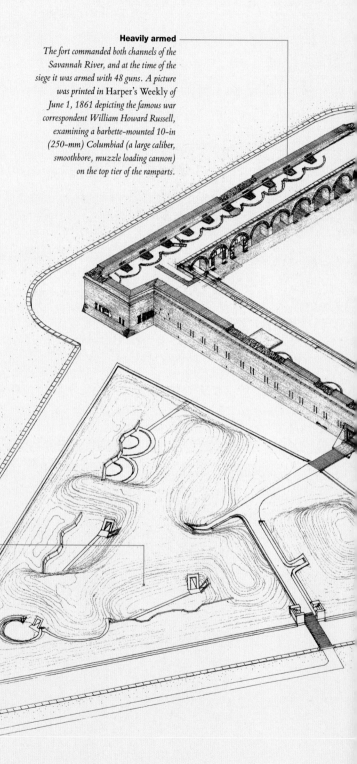

Heavily armed

The fort commanded both channels of the Savannah River, and at the time of the siege it was armed with 48 guns. A picture was printed in Harper's Weekly *of June 1, 1861 depicting the famous war correspondent William Howard Russell, examining a barbette-mounted 10-in (250-mm) Columbiad (a large caliber, smoothbore, muzzle loading cannon) on the top tier of the ramparts.*

The gorge

The rear, or gorge, of the fort, together with the main entrance, or sally port, was protected by an earthwork ravelin, or demilune. In order to gain access to the fort proper, any attacker would have to cross two ditches under fire from the ramparts at the rear. The second entrance was further protected by a drawbridge and was subjected to crossfire from galleries, or bastions, projecting into the ditch.

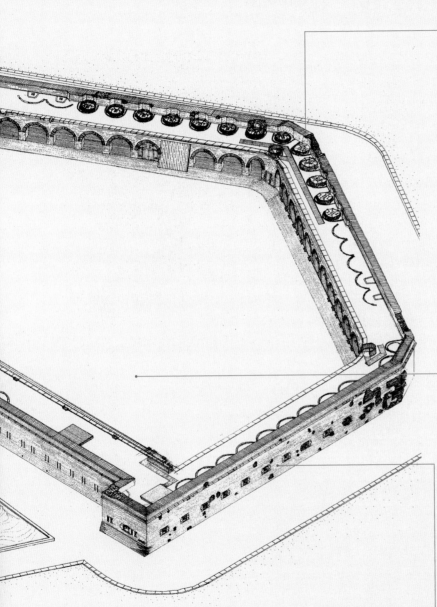

Cut corners

Fort Pulaski was constructed as a flattened pentagon with each of the forward-facing salient angles (corners) radiused to form a pan-coupé (literally "cut-corner"). The surrounding ditch was water-filled and because of this, combined with the location and nature of the ground, there were no arrangements for providing flanking fire into the ditch. European polygonal works had either caponiers or counterscarp galleries to perform this function.

Parade ground

Because of the nature of the ground, the fort was constructed on pilings driven over 65 ft (20 m) into the mud of the island. The open parade ground was surrounded by a structure, supported on 67 brick arches, containing accommodation for the garrison together with storerooms and magazines. The lower tier of artillery was housed in casemates while the upper sat on the 30-ft (9-m) wide terreplein—the top horizontal surface of the rampart.

Ramparts

Fort Pulaski also differed from most European designs inasmuch as the ramparts were unprotected by the ditch and were therefore exposed to enemy fire. As explained, this was largely due to the belief that no hostile artillery could get close enough to cause damage. It was, however, designed for a specific purpose at a certain time and only failed because its design was overtaken by the rapid march of artillery technology, itself accelerated by war.

The Demise of Masonry

Fort Pulaski, Georgia

The "Third System" of coastal fortification was built following the 1812 British attacks on Washington (DC) and Baltimore (MD). The last of these works was Fort Pulaski, constructed on Cockspur Island to command the Savannah River estuary. It was designed to withstand battering from anything but the very heaviest smoothbore artillery. With the nearest solid ground about a mile away, this meant that, at the time it was designed, it was effectively out of range of any gun that could damage it. Finally completed in 1846, it was then effectively mothballed. By the time the Civil War erupted in 1861 Fort Pulaski is recorded as having been in a state of decay, with a garrison of two. It had, however, become a place of strategic importance, and so was swiftly occupied by Confederate forces.

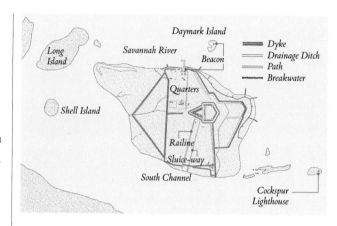

Plan of Fort Pulaski, 1862

Sited on an island in the Savannah River, Fort Pulaski was a two-tier brick structure with walls some 7.5 ft (2 m) thick. With five casemated sides or faces each able to mount two tiers of guns, one in the casemates and the other *en barbette*, it stood some 25 ft (7.5 m) above the water. A ditch, 48-ft (14.5-m) wide, protected the main work while the earthen ravelin to the rear had a 32-ft (9.75-m) ditch. Some sources say the construction required around 25 million bricks, mostly locally produced with harder bricks (for the casemate faces) being imported from farther afield.

Copy of the official plan of the siege of Fort Pulaski

Quincy A. Gillmore took command of the operation to bombard the fort, and 11 batteries of guns and mortars, totalling 36 artillery tubes, were emplaced on the shoreline of Tybee Island. On the morning of April 10, and following the rejection of an offer to surrender, the batteries began firing at about 08:15 hours. The fort returned fire with those guns that could be brought to bear, but after some five hours it became clear that the federal shell-firing guns were wreaking great damage on the brick fort.

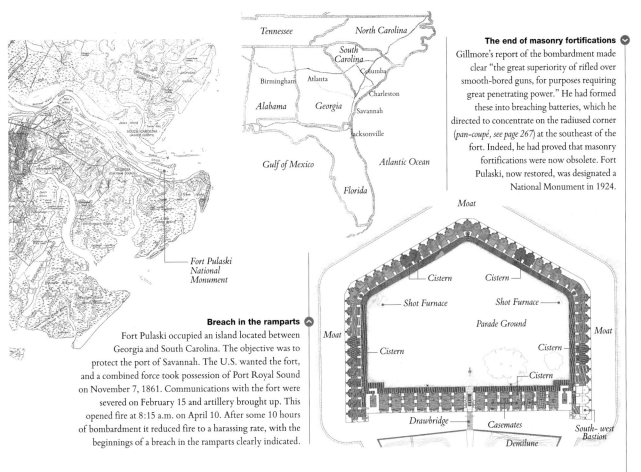

The end of masonry fortifications ⌄

Gillmore's report of the bombardment made clear "the great superiority of rifled over smooth-bored guns, for purposes requiring great penetrating power." He had formed these into breaching batteries, which he directed to concentrate on the radiused corner (*pan-coupé, see page 267*) at the southeast of the fort. Indeed, he had proved that masonry fortifications were now obsolete. Fort Pulaski, now restored, was designated a National Monument in 1924.

Moat

Cistern   *Cistern*

Shot Furnace   *Shot Furnace*

Moat   *Parade Ground*   *Moat*

Cistern   *Cistern*

Cistern

Drawbridge   *Casemates*   *South-west Bastion*

Demilune

Breach in the ramparts ⌃

Fort Pulaski occupied an island located between Georgia and South Carolina. The objective was to protect the port of Savannah. The U.S. wanted the fort, and a combined force took possession of Port Royal Sound on November 7, 1861. Communications with the fort were severed on February 15 and artillery brought up. This opened fire at 8:15 a.m. on April 10. After some 10 hours of bombardment it reduced fire to a harassing rate, with the beginnings of a breach in the ramparts clearly indicated.

Bombardment of Fort Pulaski, 1862 ‹

When the bombardment resumed it quickly created a major breach. Shellfire then swept the interior including the magazine. Faced with the destruction of the entire fort, the commanding officer gave the order to surrender. It was a famous victory for Gillmore, who had proved that rifled guns could destroy a masonry fortification at long range, a circumstance, as he put it, "altogether new in the annals of sieges."

The Great Fault Defenses

Fort Mosta, Malta

"Palmerston's Follies" constructed following the 1860 Royal Commission report were not confined to the United Kingdom, —some 10 years later Malta's defenses were similarly upgraded. Since the opening of the Suez Canal in 1869 Malta overlooked a shipping route of crucial importance to the British Empire, the control of which became a vital national interest.

One project put in hand was the reinstatement of a scheme first initiated by the Knights, the fortification of the Great Fault—a ridge that more or less bisects Malta in an east–west direction, from Fomm ir-Rhi Bay on the west coast to Bahar ic-Caghaq on the east. It forms a natural barrier of high ground, and so is difficult to approach undetected. It does however have several weak points in that there are several gaps and gently sloping portions that presented little in the way of a natural obstacle. Chief among these are the gaps at Naxxar, Falca, and Bingemma, and the eastern coastal area near Madliena.

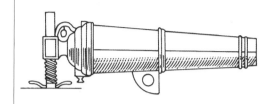

Diagram of a carronade

Fort Mosta was constructed with counterscarp galleries, which were originally equipped with carronades to sweep the ditch clear of intruders. Named for the Carron Ironworks in Scotland, where they were first built in the mid-18th century, they were effectively giant shotguns firing case, or canister, shot, an anti-personnel projectile with small iron round shot or lead musket balls in a metal can. They remained useful for fortress defense until the advent of magazine rifles and machine guns.

The Elswick mounting

Emplacements for two 6-in (100-mm) guns on hydropneumatic disappearing carriages were installed at Fort Mosta between 1880 and 1890. The picture at right shows a similar gun in the firing position. Known as the Elswick mounting they were developed and put into use between 1880 and 1890. Although undoubtedly a clever design, they were not generally considered successful due to their complexity, expense, and slow rate of fire. They were replaced by barbette-mounted weapons; emplaced in a pit with only the gun muzzle and shield visible. The increase in visibility was reckoned to be more than compensated for by the increased rate of fire.

Howitzer battery

According to the 1901 record plans the howitzer batteries were positioned behind the Victoria Lines. Visible remains are limited since the batteries were constructed mostly from mounds of earth.

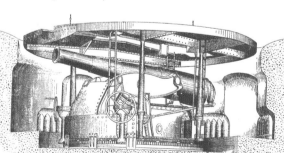

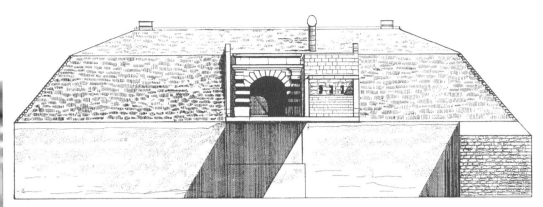

Mosta's keep

The keep, which provided accommodation for the garrison, is rock hewn. The magazines for the guns were underground. Also visible are the openings of the three casemates in the scarp of the keep and the interior portion of the gateway at the south of the terreplein.

"The Victoria Lines"

The mainstays of the Great Fault defenses were Forts Bingemma (1874) and Madliena (1878), which protected the western and eastern ends, and Mosta (1878), which commanded the center. These became known as the Victoria Lines in commemoration of Queen Victoria's Diamond Jubilee. The system was completed by a wall some 5 ft (1.5 m) in height, reinforced at intervals with gun batteries and emplacements.

Design of Fort Mosta

The main characteristics of polygonal works, or "flankless forts," were the straight ramparts. In order to allow gunfire into the length of the perimeter ditch, caponiers or counterscarp galleries were constructed, and the ditch was comparatively narrow to better protect the scarp from artillery fire. Fort Mosta was partly concentric in design, with a pentagonal keep within the main perimeter. Because of the small size of Malta, the artillery mounted in the two positions was capable of both sea and land use.

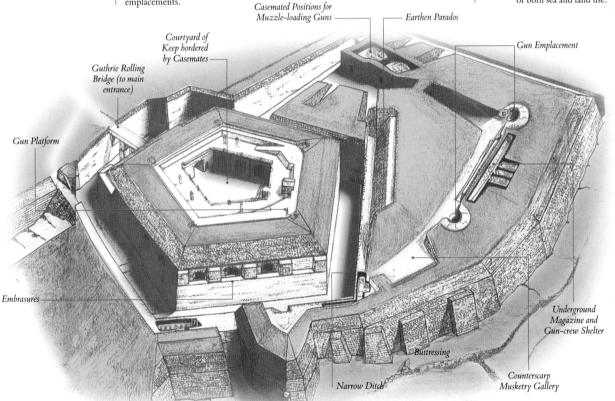

Casemated Positions for Muzzle-loading Guns

Earthen Parados

Courtyard of Keep bordered by Casemates

Gun Emplacement

Guthrie Rolling Bridge (to main entrance)

Gun Platform

Embrasures

Underground Magazine and Gun-crew Shelter

Buttressing

Counterscarp Musketry Gallery

Narrow Ditch

Control of the Yellow Sea

Port Arthur, Liaodong Peninsula, China
Japan had taken Port Arthur during the Sino-Japanese War (1 August 1894–17 April 1895) but had been forced to give up this conquest by the *Dreibund* (Russia, Germany, and France). Russia, the prime mover behind this "Triple Intervention," wanted Port Arthur for itself and in December 1897 sent warships there under the pretext of protecting China from Germany. In March 1898 the port, and the Liaodong Peninsula, were leased to Russia for 25 years.

It was clear to Japan that if she wished to compete with the European powers, then she could only do so by being equally as powerful. A program of naval and military development was thus undertaken. Russia of course understood that Japan might not acquiesce in the situation, and began a process of fortifying Port Arthur, basing its Pacific Fleet there.

On the night of February 8th 1904, the Japanese carried out a surprise naval attack and subsequently, large contingents of troops were landed in Manchuria and these drove down the Liaodong Peninsula, forcing the Russians toward Port Arthur. In late July 1904 the last of the Russian force was behind the Port Arthur fortifications, whilst facing them was General Nogi Maresuke commanding some 90,000 men of the Third Army.

Nogi had stormed and taken Port Arthur in 1894 losing only 16 men in the process. His attempts to repeat the performance in 1904 led to disaster. Port Arthur had three basic lines of defense, the first around the town itself was a ditch. Some 2 miles (3.5 kilometers) further out to the northeast was the "Chinese Wall," obsolete but strengthened with a line of modern pentagonal forts and batteries with entrenchments in between. Farther out again was a series of fortified hills and other works, including the Waterworks Redoubt to the north.

Following the failure of attempts to storm the fortifications by infantry assault during early August 1904, losing 18,000 men in the process, Nogi decided on a systematic approach reminiscent of Vauban (*see pages 234–5*). The first such operation was conducted against the Waterworks Redoubt, beginning on August 19.

› Port Arthur's line of forts and batteries
Following the taking of the Waterworks Redoubt the 9th Division moved eastward to besiege Fort Ehrlung. The ground was far rockier here and on occasions the trenches and saps were very shallow and, being reinforced with sandbags, partly above ground. The assault trenches dug by the Japanese provided the infantry with good protection whilst they remained in them. However, when assaulting from the third parallel they were shot down. At one point the infantry succeeded in getting into the 25-ft (7.5-m) deep ditch of the fort, only to be devastated by fire from the counterscarp gallery. A change of tactics was thus enforced, and the alternative was to make the final approach underground. Tunnels were dug through the rock under the fort and explosives planted. The detonation of one such mine on December 28 finally led to the fall of Fort Ehrlung.

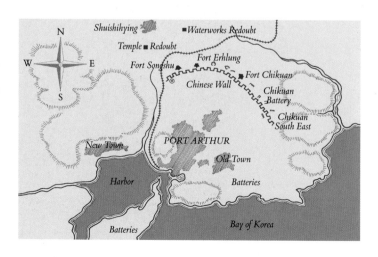

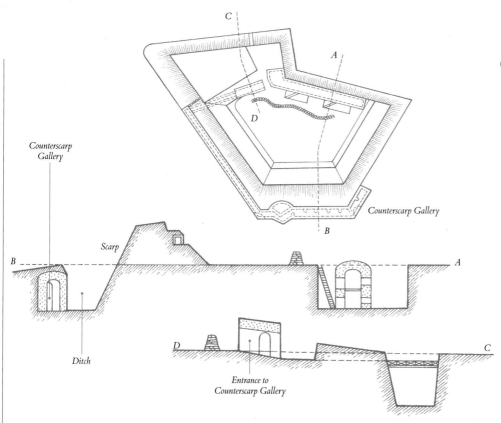

Counterscarp Gallery

Counterscarp Gallery

Scarp

B ——— A

Ditch

Entrance to Counterscarp Gallery

D ——— C

Coast defense howitzers

In an effort to reduce the forts the Japanese utilized several coast defense howitzers, based on the Krupp 1892 11-in (280-mm) howitzer. Their use in the field had not previously been considered feasible; each piece weighed in at some 36 tonnes, and their fire proved effective when it began on October 1. Nevertheless, mining was required to completely subdue the defenses, and Fort Chikuan succumbed following a massive explosion on December 18 that collapsed a large section of the ramparts into the ditch, allowing the assault force to get across and into the fort. Port Arthur was formally, and controversially, surrendered on January 5, 1905.

Fort Chikuan's counterscarp gallery

The Japanese also tunneled under Fort Chikuan, a manoeuver opposed by Russian counter-mines. They detonated a mine on October 29 1904, revealing a portion of the counterscarp gallery. Built of 7-ft (2-m) thick concrete, this was partitioned off into eight chambers communicating with each other by narrow arched doorways. The Japanese penetrated the wall and after a fierce struggle took possession of about half the chambers. They could get no farther, and the subterranean struggle went on for nearly three weeks. The attackers tried an unconventional stratagem. They sent down a man in a diving suit who pumped asphyxiating gas, derived from burning material soaked in arsenic, into the gallery. This proved unsuccessful, for while it drove out the Russians it also kept out the Japanese.

GALLERY OF
Modern Fortresses

One of the hallmarks of the modern artillery fortress is its projecting defense works. These ensure there is no dead ground unswept by the fire of the defenders. The profile of such works marks a transition toward the subterranean; if soaring stone edifices indicate archetypal medieval works, then the modern descendant is the underground bunker.

Kronborg, Zealand, Denmark
The sea-fort of Kronborg, a former castle, commands one of the few outlets of the Baltic Sea at the narrowest point of the sound between Denmark and Sweden.

Suomenlinna, Helsinki, Finland
Begun in 1748 as defense against Russian expansionism the star-fort design of Suomenlinna was adapted to the rocky islands on which it is sited.

Charles Fort, Cork, Ireland
Built on the site of a former stronghold, this 17th-century maritime star fort was designed specifically to resist attack by cannon-fire.

Spandau Citadel, Berlin, Germany
One of Europe's best-preserved bastioned fortresses, the citadel was built in 1559–94 to protect the town of Spandau. It saw service again during WWII.

Castillo de San Marcos, Florida
America's oldest masonry fort was built by the Spanish between 1672 and 1695. This star fort was renamed Fort Marion when Florida became U.S. territory in 1821.

Königstein Fortress, near Dresden, Germany
Originally a medieval mountain-top castle, Königstein's fortifications were continually updated and expanded to maintain its defenses despite advances in arms technology.

Fort Jefferson, Florida
Designed as an invincible gun platform in the early 19th century to help

Glossary

ACROPOLIS A Greek term, literally translated as "high city." In defensive architecture, an Acropolis is an elevated, fortified city or town.

ARROW LOOP A fortification in a wall, usually shaped as a vertical or splayed split, which provided protection for the archer when firing arrows. Round openings were used to accommodate larger crossbows or firearms.

ARX PALATINA Roman stronghold or, more generally used to describe a fortified palace.

ASHLAR The rectangular blocks of stone used as an inner and outer facing for castle walls, fitted with mortar in layers.

BAILEY The courtyard of an early castle overlooked by a motte (raised earthwork) and enclosed by castle walls. The bailey was normally used as a living area for craftsmen and servants.

BALLISTA A military siege device, rather like a huge crossbow, used for hurling large missiles during warfare.

BARBETTE A platform, raised or not, on which guns are mounted to fire over a parapet. Pieces so mounted are said to be *en barbette*.

BARBICAN The additional castle defense built in front of the gatehouse and used to restrict access to the main entrance of the castle.

BARTIZAN A small, overhanging mounted turret usually built on corners of a castle and used as a lookout. It could be open or enclosed with arrow loops in the walls.

BASTIDE A planned, fortified town or strong point, mainly built in medieval France.

BASTION A projection of the wall of a castle that faces outward, providing a wide-angled defensive position for the building. Also known as a bulwark. Although configuration and shape may vary greatly, all bastions have two flanks and two faces. *See also* LUNETTE.

BATTERY A unit for housing troops and artillery.

BATTLEMENTS The fighting position on the ramparts built on top of the castle walls. This comprises a crenelated wall, which allowed for arrows or other missiles to be shot or fired from the wallwalk.

BELFRIES The original name for siege towers, which were used to protect assailants when approaching to attack a castle or fortification.

BOWER A living space. In a castle this was an extension of the *solar* (q.v.), forming a private apartment for the lady of the castle.

BUTTRESSES Square projections of masonry on the outside or corner of a castle used to support and strengthen it.

CAPONIER Originally a term referring to a covered means of access to the outworks. *"Caponier"* later described a structure sunk into the bottom of the ditch from which to provide fire cover to a sweep of ditch to thwart attempts to storm a fort.

CASEMATE A chamber behind a wall in which artillery was mounted.

CAVALIER A raised work, located either on a bastion or behind the curtain wall, equipped with artillery.

CHEMISE The inner walled enclosure of a castle. Also used to describe the surrounding wall.

CITADEL A fortress or stronghold for protecting a town, normally incorporating a castle.

CORBEL Projecting blocks of stone built into a wall or corner to bear a downward weight. They were used to support parapets, hoardings, machicolations, and corner turrets.

COUNTERGUARD An outwork located in front of a bastion or ravelin parallel to the faces.

COUNTERSCARP The outer wall of the ditch. *See also* SCARP.

COVERTWAY A pathway allowing the movement of troops under cover. Also called "covered way."

CRENELS The gaps between the raised sections of stonework at the top of the castle wall, used for shooting arrows or firing guns.

CROWNWORK A bastion with a demibastion on either side separated by short curtain walls.

CURTAIN WALL A wall or set of walls between two bastions, or other works. The curtain wall surrounds and protects the interior of a castle.

DEMIBASTION Literally a half bastion with one face and one flank. *See* BASTION.

DEMILUNE Originally, a crescent (halfmoon)-shaped outwork set above the counterscarp on the glacis. The term may be used interchangeably with lunette and ravelin.

DRAWBRIDGE A bridge or roadway across a moat designed to lift in order to prevent crossing either way.

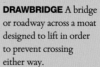

EARTHWORKS Early castles that relied on defenses of wood and earth, such as motte-and-bailey castles.

EMBRASURE A narrow opening in a battlement between the raised merlons (q.v.). Embrasures are the opening or cross in the curtain walls and towers (arrow loops), used for firing arrows.

ENCEINTE The innermost, continuous ring of fortifications surrounding a town or castle.

ESCALADE Word meaning to scale defensive walls or ramparts using ladders, while normally under fire from the castle's defending forces.

ESPLANADE The forecourt of a castle, often used for important or public events.

FOREBUILDING A subsidiary tower or extension to the castle keep, normally guarding its entrance.

FOSSE Another word for the ditch or moat that surrounds a castle.

GARDEROBE Originally used to store clothes, the garderobe became the castle latrine. A chute often provided a means of discharge into the castle moat or cesspit.

GARRISON Troops stationed at a fortified place to provide defense and protection.

GATEHOUSE A strongly fortified structure enclosing the gateway to a castle, normally housing at least one portcullis and other defenses.

GLACIS An earthen bank (originally termed an argin), usually formed from the material excavated from the ditch. Sloping away from the ditch it protects the scarp (q.v.) and provided the defenders with a clear field of fire.

HILL FORTS Defensive structures, typically on high ground, that normally followed the contours with several lines of earthworks and included enclosures, ramparts, and moats to protect the fort.

HOARDING HOLES Holes in the castle wall that were used to support the hoardings.

HOARDINGS Temporary wooden structures placed on the ramparts of a castle as a walkway for fighting. Hoardings were built as part of preparations for battle.

HORNWORK A freestanding fortification consisting of a pair of demibastions, with a separating curtain wall. A hornwork is normally placed in front of the main wall. A crowned hornwork refers to the combination of crownwork (q.v.) and hornwork.

INNER WARD Large inner courtyard contained inside a castle, usually the ward located around the keep.

KEEP A strong, fortified tower, usually built pre-13th century. It was normally the heart of the castle and may have formed the main living area. A keep was formerly known as a *donjon*.

LEGIONARIES Rigorously trained professional soldiers of the Roman army.

LUNETTE An outwork similar in plan to a bastion but detached. Usually placed above the counterscarp on the glacis and open at the rear or gorge.

MACHICOLATIONS Projecting galleries on supports outside a fortified building, through which boiling liquids and rocks were rained upon attackers below.

MANGONEL A type of catapult used to hurl low-trajectory missiles at castle walls to destroy them. It was less accurate than the later trebuchet, which hurled projectiles over a castle's walls into the bailey.

MANTLET A portable barrier or shield deployed by attacking forces to provide protection from missiles.

MEGARON Usually referring to Mycenaean palaces, the *megaron* was the Great Hall, main reception, or central room of a building.

MERLON The raised sections of a crenelated wall, sometimes pierced by embrasures.

MOAT A deep, broad ditch built around the castle walls, used as part of the castle's defenses. In suitable locations it would be filled with water, making it difficult for siege weapons to be used against a castle.

MOTTE A type of castle that used an mound as the base for a defensive structure built on the summit. Normally a ditch was dug and this material was used to build the mound, but sometimes natural hills were used.

MURDER HOLES Holes in a ceiling or floor that enabled stones, arrows, or burning substances to be shot or dropped into the floor below.

ORILLON An orillon was a rounded off, and sometimes square ended, extension of the face of a bastion designed to protect its recessed flank. The addition of orillons (Italian for ears) to bastions often gave them an "ace-of-spades" appearance in plan view.

Glossary

OUBLIETTE A form of dungeon, only accessible from a hatch set in a high ceiling. Normally it was a pit in which prisoners were incarcerated, forgotten, and left to die.

PALISADE A wooden fence built around an early fort or defensive structure, built as a deterrent against small-scale attack.

PARAPET The crenelated wall protecting the defenders of the castle on the wallwalk.

PELE TOWERS Also known as peel towers, these fortified keeps or tower houses were used as watchtowers for signaling approaching danger. The towers carried an iron basket ready to provide a smoke or fire signal.

PORTCULLIS A heavily grilled door that formed the fortified entrance to a castle. One or more of these gates was situated in the barbican and rapidly dropped using ropes or chains if the castle came under attack.

POSTERN GATE Also known as a sally port, this was a discreet exit underground from the inner to the outer works of a fortification, enabling defenders to make a sudden unexpected entrance or exit.

RAMPART Protective embankment built from earth or stone surrounding a fortified location, often surmounted by a parapet.

RAVELIN A pointed fortification surrounding the curtain walls of a castle with faces at salient angles used to split an attacking force. The ravelin may be attached or detached.

SCARP The inner, vertical surface of the ditch.

SHELL KEEP A type of fortification made up of a stone structure encircling the top of a motte, a successor to the traditional motte-and-bailey castle.

SIEGE The surrounding of a castle by an armed force to cut off its supplies of food and water and force the occupants to comply with their demands or to surrender.

SIEGE ENGINE A device designed to break city walls and other fortifications in siege warfare. They included the ballista and the trebuchet (qq.v.).

SLIGHTING The deliberate and often unopposed destruction of fortifications in such a way that renders it indefensible. The term came into use in England following the civil wars of the 17th century.

SOLAR The sleeping area and private quarters of a castle. It was normally situated in the part of the castle with the brightest aspect.

STELE A tall stone erected for commemorative purposes, usually inscribed or carved in bas-relief. Stelae were also placed at boundary points and could be used to provide information relating to the territory they defined.

STOCKADE A defensive barrier made of palisades or strong posts, used for protecting an early fort.

TENAILLE A wall constructed in the ditch to protect the scarp and curtain wall (qq.v.).

TERREPLEIN A level platform behind a rampart on which guns are mounted.

TRACE ITALIENNE The modern style (*alla moderna*) of Italianate fortification, which saw the introduction of the bastion. Early modern fortresses which contained bastions were then deemed to be utilizing the Italian trace (*trace italienne*). Many American forts display this many-sided design and the U.S. Pentagon Building also borrows ideas from it.

TREBUCHET A siege engine that utilized a catapult to fling projectiles at enemy fortifications. Originally using only manpower, the later devices relied on a huge counterweight on a short arm to swing a long arm carrying the load high over castle walls.

TURRETS Small defensive towers on a fortress. In medieval times they were used to provide a projecting defensive position allowing covering fire to the adjacent wall, but eventually became ornamental features.

UNDERCROFT Traditionally a basement used as a cellar or storage room.

UPPER WARD Sometimes known as the outer ward, this was the large courtyard outside of the inner ward but still held within the outer curtain wall, sometimes called the bailey.

WALLWALK A footpath around the castle wall, making it easy to move between the towers. They were used as a fighting platform to defend the castle against attackers.

WATCHTOWER A high tower raised over the castle walls to give a view of the surrounding countryside. Watchtowers were also built at important sites and along trading routes.

Resources

GENERAL

CLARKE, G. S., *Fortification: Its Past Achievements, Recent Developments, and Future Progress,* J. Murray, London, 1890

KELLY, COL. E. H., *'Fortification and Siegecraft,'* in The Encyclopaedia Britannica 14th Edition, London, 1929

THUCYDIDES (WARNER, R., TRANS.), *The History of the Peloponnesian War,* Penguin, Harmondsworth, 1954

TZU, S. (GILES, L., TRANS.), *The Art of War,* London, 1910

WHEELER, SIR. M., *The Indus Civilization,* University of Cambridge Press, Cambridge, 1968

ZEDONG, M., *On Protracted War,* Foreign Languages Press, Beijing, 1967

VISUAL RESOURCES

ARMITAGE, E. S., *Early Norman Castles of the British Isles,* J. Murray, London, 1912

ASHDOWN, C., *British Castles,* A&C Black, London, 1911

CLARKE, G. T., *Medieval Military Architecture in England, 2 vols,* Wyman & Sons, London, 1884

CORROYER, E., *Gothic Architecture,* Macmillan, London, 1893

REY, G., *Etude sur les Monuments de L'Architecture Militaire des Croisés en Syrie et dans l'Ile de Chypre,* Paris, 1871

THOMPSON, A. H., *Military Architecture in England During the Middle Ages,* Oxford University Press, London, 1912

TOY, S., *Castles: Their Construction and History,* Dover Books, New York, 1985

VIOLLET-LE-DUC, E. E., *Dictionnaire Raisonné de L'Architecture Française du XIe au XVIe siècle,* 10 vols, Paris: Bance, 1854–68

ANCIENT

BREWER, R. J. (ED.), *Roman Legions and their Fortresses,* Society of Antiquaries of London, Cardiff, 2000

CAMPBELL, D. B., *Roman Legionary Fortresses, 27 BC–AD 378,* Osprey Publishing, Oxford, 2006

FASS, V., *The Forts of India,* HarperCollins, London, 1986

FIELDS, N., *The Walls of Rome,* Osprey Publishing, Oxford, 2008

FORDE-JOHNSTON, J. L., *Hillforts of the Iron Age in England and Wales,* Rowman & Littlefield, Liverpool, 1976

GOLDHILL, S., *Jerusalem: City of Longing,* Harvard University Press, Cambridge, MA, 2008

GRAJETSKI, W., *The Middle Kingdom of Ancient Egypt: History, Archaeology and Society,* Gerald Duckworth & Co., London, 2006

KEMPINSKI, A., *The Architecture of Ancient Israel from the Prehistoric to the Persian Periods,* Ahva Press, Jerusalem, 1992

McNICOLL, A. W., *Hellenistic Fortifications: From the Aegean to the Euphrates,* Clarendon Press, Oxford, 1997

NOSSOV, K., *Greek Fortifications of Asia Minor 500–130 BC,* Osprey Publishing, Oxford, 2009

OATES, J., *Babylon,* Thames & Hudson, London, 1986

OPPENHEIM, A. L., *Ancient Mesopotamia: Portrait of a Dead Civilization,* University of Chicago Press, Chicago, 1964

RICHMOND, I. A., *The City Walls of Imperial Rome: An Account of its Architectural Development from Aurelian to Narses,* Oxford, 1930

SCHOFIELD, L., *The Mycenaeans,* J. Paul Getty Museum, London, 2007

TAYLOUR, W. D., *The Mycenaeans,* Thames & Hudson, London, 1983

TODD, M., *The Walls of Rome,* Osprey Publishing, London, 1978

TOY, S., *A History of Fortification from 3000 BC to AD 1700,* Pen and Sword, Barnsley, Yorks, 2006

TOY, S., *The Strongholds of India,* Heineman, London, 1957

VOGEL, C., *The Fortifications of Ancient Egypt, 3000–1780 BC,* Osprey Publishing, Oxford, 2010

MEDIEVAL

BARKER, P., AND HIGHAM, R., *Timber Castles,* University of Exeter Press, London, 1992

CRUDEN, S., *The Scottish Castle,* Spurbooks, Bourne End, Bucks, 1981

FRY, P. S., *Castles: England, Scotland, Wales,* David & Charles, Newton Abbot, Devon, 2005

GARNIER, T., *Gisors ou la Chronique Vulcaine,* M2G Editions, Gaillon, France, 2011

Resources

GRAVETT, C., *English Castles 1200–1300*, Osprey Publishing, Oxford, 2009

GRAVETT, C., *Norman Stone Castles: British Isles 1066–1216*, Osprey Publishing, Oxford, 2003

GRAVETT, C., *Norman Stone Castles: Europe 950–1204*, Osprey Publishing, Oxford 2004

GRAVETT, C., *The History of Castles: Fortifications Around the World*, The Lyons Press, Guilford, CT, 2001

HULL, L. E., *Britain's Medieval Castles*, Praeger Publishers, Westport, CT, 2006

KAUFMANN, J. E., *The Medieval Fortress: Castles, Forts and Walled Cities of the Middle Ages*, De Capo Press, Cambridge, MA, 2004

LE MERCURE DE GAILLON (*Les Archives du Serpent Rouge*, magazine historique trimestriel), M2G Editions

NOSSOV, K. S., *Medieval Russian Fortresses AD 862–1480*, Osprey Publishing, Oxford, 2007

THOMPSON, M.W., *The Decline of the Castle*, Cambridge University Press, 1997

VIOLLET-LE-DUC, E. E., *Annals of a Fortress*, Boston, 1876

WARNER, P., *The Medieval Castle: Life in a Fortress in Peace and War,* Penguin, London, 2001

CRUSADER

KENNEDY, H., *Crusader Castles*, University of Cambridge Press, Cambridge, 1994

MULLER-WIENER, W., *Castles of the Crusaders*, Thames & Hudson, London, 1966

FAR EAST

TURNBULL, S., *Chinese Walled Cities 221BC–AD 1644*, Osprey Publishing, Oxford 2009

TURNBULL, S., *The Great Wall of China 221BC–AD 1644*, Osprey Publishing, Oxford 2007

TURNBULL, S., *Strongholds of the Samurai: Japanese Castles 250-1877*, Osprey Publishing, Oxford 2009

MODERN

BECKETT, A. S., BLANTON, D. B., AND LINEBAUGH, D. W., ET AL., *A Cultural Resource Management Plan of Fort Norfolk,* Norfolk, Williamsburg, VA, 1995

CAPMANY, C. D., *El Castell de Sant Ferrán de Figueres, La Seva Historia,* Generalitat de Catalunya, Barcelona, 1982

CRICK, T., 'Fortifications from Vauban to Jervois' in *Fort 24*, FSG, 1996

DOUGHERTY, K., *Strangling the Confederacy: Coastal Operations in the American Civil War,* Casemate, Philadelphia, 2010

FISKE, J., *New France and New England,* Houghton Mifflin, Westminster, 2008

GIBBON, E., *The History of the Decline and Fall of the Roman Empire,* London, 1788

GRIFFITH, P., *The Vauban Fortifications of France,* Osprey Publishing, Oxford, 2006

HUGHES, Q., *'Cherbourg: a French Naval Base,'* in *Fort 8,* FSG, 1980

HUGHES, Q., *'Kronstadt and the Crimean War,'* in *Fort 21,* FSG, 1993

HUGHES, Q., AND MIGOS, A., *Rhodes: 'The Turkish Sieges,'* in *Fort 21,* FSG, 1993

JENKINS, S., *'Pendennis Castle, Cornwall,'* in *Fort 25,* FSG, 1997

MANDIC, S., MARJANOVIC, P., AND MILOŠEVIC, N., *Belgrade,* Belgrade, 1969

MORRISON, H., *Early American Architecture: From the First Colonial Settlements to the National Period,* Oxford University Press, New York, 1952

O'NEIL, B. H. ST. J., *Castles and Cannon: A Study of Early Artillery Fortifications in England,* Greenwood Press, Westport, CN, 1975

SPITERI, S. C., *British Military Architecture in Malta,* Malta, 1996

STEPANOV, A., *Port Arthur: A Historical Narrative,* Foreign Languages Press, Moscow, 1947

ZAMMIT, R. C. (ED.), *The Victoria Lines,* Progress Press, Malta, 1996

WEB SITES

Castle Studies Group:
www.castlestudiesgroup.org.uk
The aim of the Castle Studies Group is to to promote the study of castles in all their forms and by all possible means: documentary studies, architectural history, fieldwork, and excavation. The Group also promotes the study of castles as resources for a more widely based appreciation of medieval society, emphasizing their social and political history, their defensive and domestic evolution, their role in settlement development and their value as a source for the reconstruction of landscapes and economic environments.

Individual castles normally have their own web site but the information and detailed provided on the following sites may also prove fruitful:

www.casteland.com

www.castleuk.net

www.castlewales.com

www.castles.org

www.castles.me.uk

www.castlesandmanorhouses.com

www.castles.francethisway.com

www.castlexplorer.co.uk

www.guide-to-castles-of-europe.com

www.lemercuredegaillon.net

www.lemercure.degaillon.org

www.medieval-castle.com

www.middle-ages.org.uk

www.militaryarchitecture.com

Fortress Study Group:
The Fortress Study Group is the only international society concerned with the study of all aspects of military architecture and fortifications and their armaments, especially works constructed to mount and resist artillery. The group actively encourages the research, study and recording of fortifications and publishes its journal FORT annually and its magazine *Casemate* three times a year.

www.fsgfort.com
info@fsgfort.com
secretary@fsgfort.com

Gazetteer

Index

Index

Acknowledgments

Consultant Editor's acknowledgments

My profound thanks are due to the Fortress Study Group (FSG) both generally and in this particular instance. The FSG is an international society concerned with the study of all aspects of military architecture and fortifications and their armaments, especially those constructed to mount and resist artillery. For over 35 years the work and publications of the Fortress Study Group have added greatly to the sum of knowledge of fortifications, and its dissemination.

Publisher's acknowledgments

A number of individuals and organizations have given considerable help with the research for this book. Particular thanks go to Lydia Ballester, John Bleach, Sebastian Fattorini, Thierry Garnier, Mark Hartwell, Chris Lunn, Chris Milburn, Marc Morris, Thea Randall, and Stephen Spiteri.

Contributors

CHARLES STEPHENSON, Consultant Editor, is a historian and writer, whose recent military titles include: *Servant to the King for His Fortifications: Paul Ive and the Practise of Fortification*; *The Admiral's Secret Weapon*; *Fortifications of the Channel Islands, 1941–45: Hitler's Impregnable Fortress*; and *The Fortifications of Malta, 1530–1945*.
Charles is currently working on a history of the Italo-Ottoman War of 1911–12.
Contributions: General Introduction, pp. 6–11; Modern Fortresses, pp. 222–275

DAVID BOYLE is a former editor of *Town & Country Planning* and the author of *Building Futures* and several titles on history, economics, and politics.
Contributions: Islamic & Crusader Castles, pp. 154–77; Russian Kremlins, pp. 178–85

ANDREW KIRK was educated at Oxford and was formerly Senior Editor at Liverpool University Press in the UK. He is the author of several books, three on historical subjects, and a contributor to *The Grammar of the Ancient World*.
Contributions: The Ancient World, pp. 12–41; Indian Fortresses, pp. 186–95

JOHN MAY is a journalist whose work appears in numerous newspapers and international magazines. He is the author of *Buildings without Architects: A Global Guide to Everyday Architecture*.
Contribution: Western Castles of the Middle Ages, pp. 42–151

STEPHEN TURNBULL is an expert on many aspects of Japanese culture and has written books on the samurai, martial arts, and the military history of East Asia and Europe. He also lectures on Japanese religion at the University of Leeds, England.
Contribution: Castles of East Asia, pp. 196–221

PICTURE CREDITS

AKG Images/British Library: 81B, 108, 233B, 261BL; Historic-maps/Braun: 231B; 234B, 235B, 242; Archives CDA/Guillot: 235TR; World History Archive: 239TL.
Alamy/Iconotec: 27; The Art Archive: 38; Jethro Collins: 109; The Art Gallery Collection: 112T; ITAR-TASS Photo Agency: 185; Black Star: 243; Chris Laurens: 246; Niccodeamus: 256.
Archives Nationales d'Outre-Mer: 240B.
By Kind Permission of the Sussex Archaeological Society: 60T, 60C, 61B.
Cambridgeshire Record Office: 263T.
Cartoteca del Centre Excursionista de Catalunya: 255.
Collection M2G Editions, Le Mercure de Gaillon: 112C, 113TL, 118, 119TR, 120BL, 121TR, 125B.
Corbis/Nik Wheeler: 18; Skyscan: 28; Jon Arnold/JAI: 158; Frédéric Soltan/Sygma: 177; Atlantide Phototravel: 186; Stapleton Collection: 209B; Karen Kasmauski: 236.
Sion Prys Davies, www.sionprysphotography.co.uk: 264.
Digital National Library of Serbia: 11T, 222, 252, 253.
Dover Publications Inc./*Castles: their Construction and History* by Sidney Toy: 87B, 88B, 89TL, 97,

99TR, 100T, 101TR, 106T, 106T, 107T, 107BL, 119TL, 120BR, 137TR.
English Heritage Images: 84, 85, 92, 95T, 95B, 96.
Fotolia/Max Topchii: 2; Vladislav Gurfinkel: 26; Child of Nature: 39; Yory Frenklakh: 41TL; Steheap: 41BL; Yousaf Fayyaz: 41C; JimJag: 110; Edobric: 150B; Tupungato: 151TR; Margaret Dickson: 151BL; Wolszczak: 193; Aleksander Kaasik: 195C; Diak: 195TL; Furan: 195TR; Diak: 195BR; Michalis Palis: 195BL; Claudiozacc: 209T; MasterLu: 221TR; Badazoo: 221BR; Scanrail: 274B; Detlef: 275TR; Thomas Barrat: 275BR.
Lionel FRANCES: 149.
Getty Images/Martin Brewster: 81T; Hulton Archive: 263B.
iStockphoto/Steven Wynn: 101B, 213TR; Duncan Walker: 190B, 191B; Georgios Kollidas: 225CR, 234T; Hedda Gjerpen: 274T.
Library and Archives, Canada: 226T, 240T, 241B.
Library of Congress Images: 181T, 181B, 225BL, 239R, 239B, 239TR, 241T, 250, 251T, 259BR, 266, 267, 268, 269, 273B; Gift of Jay I. Kislak Foundation: 238.
Mary Evans Picture Library: 10, 167T.
M-Louis: 219
Chris Peen, www.oldtowns.co.uk: 105B.

Photolibrary/The Irish Image Collection: 6, 48; Peter Lewis: 82.
Picture Desk/The Art Archive/Bibliothèque des Arts Décoratifs Paris/Gianni Dagli Orti: 230.
Reproduced by Permission of the Staffordshire and Stoke on Trent Archive Service: 56, 57, 58, 59.
Fritz-Gerald Schröder: 275.
Shutterstock/Richard Bowden: 40; Pavle Marjanovic: 41BR; Panos Karapanagiotis: 41TR; Maksim Budnikov: 151BR; Max Topchii: 151TL; Euro Color Creative: 151CL; Mitrofanov Alexander: 178; Jeremy Richards: 194; Vincent 369: 202; Martin Mette: 220; Hung Chung Chih: 221C; Bluehand: 221BL; Wolfmaster 13: 221TL; Crazy 82: 275TL.
Skipton Castle: 104, 105T.
Dr. Stephen C. Spiteri: 270C, 271B, 271T.
Staffordshire Record Office, www.archives.staffordshire.gov.uk: 261T.
Charles Stephenson: 259, 262.
Thinkstock/Photos.com: 71B; iStockphoto: 150T; Getty Images: 196, 210BL, 214L; Hemera: 275C.
Topfoto/The Granger Collection: 148, 176, 231TL; Roger-Viollet: 235TL; Topham/Fotomas: 260.
Stephen Turnbull: 218.
V&A Images: 192.